SOCIAL POLICY REVIEW 16

Analysis and debate in social policy, 2004

Edited by Nick Ellison, Linda Bauld and
Martin Powell

First published in Great Britain in July 2004 by

The Policy Press
University of Bristol
Fourth Floor, Beacon House
Queen's Road
Bristol BS8 1QU

Tel +44 (0)117 331 4054
Fax +44 (0)117 331 4093
e-mail tpp-info@bristol.ac.uk
www.policypress.org.uk

British Library Cataloguing in Publication Data
A catalogue record for this book is available from the British Library

Library of Congress Cataloging-in-Publication Data
A catalog record for this book has been requested

ISBN 1 86134 581 X paperback
A hardback version of this book is also available

Nick Ellison is a Senior Lecturer in the Department of Sociology and Social Policy, University of Durham, **Linda Bauld** is a Lecturer in Social Policy in the Department of Social Policy and Social Work, University of Glasgow, and **Martin Powell** is a Reader in Social Policy in the Department of Social and Policy Sciences, University of Bath.

Cover design by Qube Design Associates, Bristol.
Front cover: photograph of Selfridges, Birmingham, supplied by kind permission of Future Systems.
Printed and bound in Great Britain by Hobbs the Printers, Southampton.

Contents

Notes on contributors

Judith Allsop is Professor of Health Policy in the Department of Health Policy, Simon de Montfort University.

Rob Baggott is Professor of Public Policy in the Department of Public Policy, Simon de Montfort University.

Fran Bennett is a Senior Research Fellow at the Department of Social Policy and Social Work, University of Oxford, and also works as a self-employed author/researcher on social policy issues.

Paul Chaney is Lecturer in Public Sector Management at Cardiff University School of Social Sciences.

Mark Drakeford is Professor of Social Policy and Applied Social Studies at Cardiff University School of Social Sciences, and the Cabinet's special adviser on health and social policy at the Welsh Assembly Government.

Howard Glennerster is Emeritus Professor of Social Policy at the London School of Economics and Political Science.

Anton Hemerijck is Director of the Netherlands Scientific Council for Government Policy.

Bill Jordan is Professor of Social Policy at Exeter and Huddersfield Universities, and Reader in Social Policy at London Metropolitan University.

Kees van Kersbergen is Professor of Political Science in the Department of Political Science, Vrije Universiteit, Amsterdam.

Hilary Land is Emeritus Professor of Family Policy in the School for Policy Studies at the University of Bristol.

Jonah D. Levy is Associate Professor in the Department of Political Science at the University of California, Berkeley, USA.

Brian Lund is Principal Lecturer in Social Policy at Manchester Metropolitan University.

David Marsland is Professor of Health Informatics and Director of Research in the Department of Health and Social Care at Brunel University.

Robert M. Page is Reader in Democratic Socialism and Social Policy at the University of Birmingham.

John Stewart is Principal Lecturer in British Political History in the Department of History at Oxford Brookes University.

Sally Tomlinson is Emeritus Professor of Educational Policy at Goldsmiths College London, and a Senior Research Associate in the Department of Educational Studies, University of Oxford.

Joseph White teaches 19th- and 20th-century British history at the University of Pittsburgh, USA.

Introduction

Nick Ellison, Linda Bauld and Martin Powell

This edition of the *Social Policy Review* marks a departure from previous *Reviews* for two reasons. First, following a decision taken by the SPA membership at the 2003 Annual Conference, this edition and all future editions will be sent directly to members, the cost being included in the (increased) membership fee. Second, and not unrelated to this change, the content of the *Review* itself has been reorganised to reflect that it is now effectively compulsory for members to have a copy! After consultation and discussion with the publishers, The Policy Press, and debate among members of the SPA Executive Committee as well as among past and present editors, it was decided that the *Review* had to fulfil at least three important functions if it was to prove useful to what is a wide and varied membership. First, it must appeal to those – social policy teachers and students – who need up-to-date information and analysis about key policy changes in the most significant areas of British welfare. Second, it is clearly important that it fulfils a 'research function' by containing chapters written by respected national and international commentators that actively address a range of social policy research agendas. Finally – bearing in mind that lead-in times for the *Review* are comparatively short – it was felt that it could also act as a forum for stimulating debate about a pressing issue or contemporary theme, or as in the current volume, for acknowledging a particularly significant 'moment'. Depending on the matter in hand, chapters here might have a more personal, less formal, character – allowing those who are involved in social policy in other than an academic capacity to make a contribution.

Taking these three elements together – and with undoubted overlaps among the sections – it was agreed that the *Review* should be organised in the following manner.

Part One will be devoted to contemporary 'developments in social policy' across the core areas of UK welfare. In practice, this is seen as being the 'big five' sectors of healthcare, education, housing, social security and social care. Wherever possible, the focus will be on events that have taken place in the year immediately preceding publication, although historical and contextual factors are likely to be important. The point is to build up a running commentary on core changes in social policy so that students, teachers and researchers alike have a simple port of call when they find themselves in need of factual information about policy developments and their impact.

Part Two is more concerned with substantive material drawn from what may broadly be characterised as the social policy research agenda. There is no imperative for this section to be themed so its contents will vary a good deal from year to year. The main objective is to provide a range of work which sheds light on ongoing debates, deals with issues not always sufficiently widely discussed in the social policy community or provides new ideas or ways of thinking about the (inter)national state of welfare.

Part Three will be devoted to themes and issues chosen by the editors of the *Review*. The fact that contributors may be invited to depart from strict academic custom and express personal views where they wish to do so is an important component of this section.

Part One: UK policy developments

As New Labour enters the middle of its second term in government, the outcomes of early reforms are becoming clearer and new priorities for future change are emerging. This section provides a review of UK policy developments in housing, health, social security, education and the personal social services. In some policy areas – such as health and social security – there have been a relatively large number of changes. In others – such as education – reform has continued but the pace has slowed. Each of the chapters in this section has a slightly different tone and focus. Some concentrate on describing relevant policies while others take a much more personal or analytical approach. Each provides a valuable overview of important reforms and poses some challenging questions about next steps.

Brian Lund opens the review of policy developments by reflecting on housing policy in 2002-03. His chapter looks in detail at changes in housing procedures and examines the implications of the Communities Plan and the recent Barker Review of housing supply. Lund argues that the publication of these two documents can be interpreted as signalling an important shift in policy direction. He describes the marked decline of state intervention to influence the supply and affordability of homes during the 1990s. Recent developments are in contrast to this previous pattern and suggest the return of a more 'purposeful' housing policy.

Lund concludes his chapter by critically assessing plans for more extensive targeted state intervention in the housing market as well as proposals to significantly reform the planning system.

Judith Allsop and Rob Baggott examine the frantic pace of recent reform in health policy. They describe how an ongoing process of structural and organisational change has accompanied the significant additional resources channelled into the NHS since 2000. They focus their attention specifically on developments aiming to improve patient choice and increase patient and public involvement. They also describe recent developments on the supply side of healthcare including foundation hospitals and an increased role for private providers. Allsop and Baggott argue that most recent policy has focused on these supply side issues and has been accompanied by strenuous efforts to manage and regulate the performance of healthcare providers in an attempt to improve quality and efficiency.

Fran Bennett provides an overview of recent social security reforms. In this diverse policy area a significant number of important changes to both the tax and benefit system were introduced in 2003. Perhaps most significant was the introduction of a new system of tax credits (including working tax credit and child tax credit). Bennett describes how these will function in practice and assesses some of the potential implications for those eligible. She also describes developments affecting children and families including the introduction of new rights for parents and changes to the child support system. A summary of the new pension credit and developments in welfare to work policies and housing benefit is also provided.

Sally Tomlinson reviews developments in education. She argues that New Labour's second term has thus far been characterised by a more gradual approach to educational reform than the flurry of education Acts and special initiatives established between 1997-2001. Tomlinson's chapter focuses on issues of selection and diversity within current reforms and describes the growing role of the private sector in education. She critically assesses the concept of meritocracy and its relevance to education and argues that current efforts to improve access and opportunity may in practice widen rather than reduce inequality.

The last chapter in this review of UK developments is provided by Bill Jordan. Jordan outlines recent changes in social services by placing them within the context of a series of longer-term policy shifts beginning in the 1970s. In particular he focuses on developments in social care since 1989 and reflects on the degree of continuity between earlier policies and New Labour's reform agenda since 1997. He critically assesses some of the implications of the 1998 White Paper *Modernising social services* and the 2001 Health and Social Care Act. Jordan's chapter provides a balanced as well as personal view of the role of the personal social services in supporting families and individuals in a changing society where inequalities persist.

Part Two: Social policy in the wider context

The aim of the second section of *Social Policy Review* is to go beyond the structure of analysing developments in the big five services to look at social policy issues in a wider context. This year's chapters focus on developments in Scotland and Wales, an historical comparison of Labour governments, and on 'new social democracy', 'progressive governance', the 'Third Way' or other assorted labels in Europe and the USA. It has been pointed out many times that 'British' social policy tends to be English social policy. We have taken the opportunity of the elections for the Scottish Parliament and Welsh Assembly to assess the Scottish and Welsh social policy in the first term of the devolved administrations. John Stewart places Scottish devolution in its historical context, before concentrating on the policy record in the areas of education and health, the two main areas of devolved social welfare powers. He goes beyond the usual example of continuing care to examine the wider field of 'policy divergence'. He makes the important point that Scotland historically had a degree of autonomy in certain welfare fields and it was primarily these that were handed over to the Edinburgh Parliament. This pre-existing autonomy had allowed for a degree of policy divergence prior to devolution, and in important respects this has increased since 1999. He rejects the simplistic argument that Scotland is a bastion of 'Old Labour', instead arguing that Scottish distinctiveness might be better viewed in terms of 'social democratic communitarianism'. Nevertheless, it might be argued that in welfare policy it has been Blair's government, not the devolved administrations, which have 'diverged' – from, that is, the 'classic' welfare state of the post-war era.

As Paul Chaney and Mark Drakeford point out, in contrast to the Scottish Parliament, the Welsh Assembly lacks both primary legislative and tax-varying powers. However, they argue that this 'social policy body' has the capacity for divergence and policy innovation. According to First Minister, Rhodri Morgan, "the actions of the Welsh Assembly clearly owe more to the traditions of Titmuss, Tawney, Beveridge and Bevan than those of Hayek and Friedman", and are based on an understanding of equality that embraces not simply issues of opportunity but "the fundamentally socialist aim of *equality of outcome*". As a practical example, Morgan praises the comprehensive school rather than the selective school but conveniently forgets that the glory years of Welsh rugby were based firmly on the grammar schools! In healthcare, the Welsh 'experiment' contrasts starkly with the national policies pursued elsewhere, its focus reflecting the work of Julian Tudor Hart in that it places emphasis on primary care and public health – or – prevention rather than cure. These chapters show that events in Scotland and Wales during the devolved administrations' first terms support the claim that as the devolution process evolves, it seems increasingly necessary to speak of the UK's *national health services* rather than of its NHS. The examples of Scotland and Wales also illustrate the tensions between equity and responsiveness/democratic accountability. As policy in Scotland and Wales becomes more responsive to their national policy agendas, equity from a UK point of view might decrease. This gives rise to social policy 'West Lothian' questions: why should older residents in West Lothian have free continuing care, and why should younger residents of (the former) West Glamorgan have free prescriptions, both of which are denied to the West Sussex resident who contributes financially to them via the 'Barnett formula'?

In a chapter commissioned to record another event – Tony Blair becoming the longest-serving Labour Prime Minister in British history – Robert M. Page compares the achievements of the Attlee government during its six years in office between 1945 and 1951 with those of Blair's New Labour administrations during their first six and a half years in power. Although such comparisons are fraught with difficulty, Page carefully examines the context, aims and achievements of the two governments. It will come as no surprise that a 'Reader in Democratic Socialism' tends to view the Attlee government more favourably. Page argues that the Attlee government can be regarded as operating at the more radical end of the reformist spectrum. In contrast, Blair's New Labour government has been criticised for operating on the less radical end of the reformist spectrum, not least because of its willingness to make an accommodation with Thatcherism. But Page makes an interesting observation: in cricketing parlance New Labour's 'occupancy of the crease' may yield better long-term gains than a shorter, albeit more entertaining innings. From this perspective it would be unfair to compare their modest achievements to date with the giant strides made under Attlee. However, Page is far from convinced that New Labour's final scorecard will break many records.

We end this section with two chapters that throw light on the UK Labour government from an international perspective. Kees van

Kersbergen and Anton Hemerijck examine the thesis of the 'Christian democratisation' of British social democracy. Much of this debate has been conducted in German and so might be new to readers whose German stretches as far as *Schwartzbier* or *Rauchbier*. They argue that the adoption of a comparative perspective may help to appreciate and understand better the communitarian switch of New Labour and its distinctiveness vis-à-vis conservatism and continental social democracy, because much of New Labour's communitarianism does seem strikingly similar to some of the central tenets of continental European Christian democracy. After indicating that continental social democracy tried unsuccessfully to break with Christian democratic policies in the second half of the 1990s, Kersbergen and Hemerijck conclude that European Third Way social democracy did not 'Christian democratise' but rather has tried to 'social democratise' the continental Christian democratic welfare state regime.

Jonah D. Levy argues that progressive policy is not necessarily an *alternative* to economic liberalisation, as this dichotomous vision rests on a narrow, impoverished conception of economic liberalisation. He advocates a progressive approach to economic and social reform that he terms 'new social liberalism'. This approach has marked the actions of European governments, particularly left-led governments, in a variety of areas including budget cutting, tax relief, and competition in public services. This chapter focuses on one strand of the new social liberalism, labour market activation, which is defined by two key features: a concern for the *quality* of employment, for improving the situation of activated workers, not just for the *quantity* of employment; and a much more extensive, positive role for public policy. This strategy is viewed as a 'thick' rather than a 'thin' approach to activation. Levy then discusses the perils of inaction (France), thin activation (USA), and thick activation in the liberal (UK) and social democratic worlds (Sweden). He concludes that neo-liberalism is a subset of liberalism, not a synonym, and *how* a country liberalises is as important as *whether* it liberalises.

The chapters in this section all illustrate the advantages of widening contexts and debates in a geographical and temporal sense. 'British' social policy needs to be seen as British rather than de facto English, and British social policy needs to be placed into wider comparative and historical contexts.

Part Three: Social policy since 1979 – the impact of Thatcherism

For Part Three of this year's *SPR*, the editors decided to mark the 25th anniversary of the Conservatives' 1979 general election victory. No one date, or moment, can ever be said to constitute the precise point from which fundamental changes can be said to have commenced. The multiple causal factors that contribute to change in social and political affairs ensure that explanations of change tend to focus on the interaction of complex processes rather than stress the role of any one particular factor or event. However, if the Conservatives' victory in May 1979 was not the sole cause of the changes subsequently made to the British welfare state – these both pre- and post-date the beginning of Mrs Thatcher's premiership as some of the contributors suggest – it is nevertheless a powerful symbolic, indeed iconic, moment from which the turn away from the state and 'collectivism' towards markets and individualism can be dated. For this reason it seemed appropriate to persuade a number of established social policy academics, who were already deeply involved in debates about the role and nature of the welfare state at the time of the 1979 election, to review what they regard as the key changes in social policy over the past 25 years and, further, to comment on how (if at all) their own perceptions of the role of welfare have shifted during this time. The contributors have obeyed the editors admirably! Each has produced a chapter that balances an account of what he or she regards as the major features of social policy change with personal observations about the necessity, advisability or otherwise of the Thatcherite welfare agenda.

What follows provides a brief introduction to these accounts. The section starts with what can still be labelled fairly accurately as a view from the 'Right', from David Marsland, and then moves progressively 'leftwards' through Howard Glennerster's piece, which acknowledges some of the positive qualities of Conservative social policies in addition to their negative features; Hilary Land's chapter, which is more critical than Glennerster about the turn to privatisation; and finally Joe White's contribution, which provides a unique 'view from the USA' grounded in a defiant endorsement of 'old-style' British welfare state collectivism.

Although he is happy enough to have his chapter titled 'a view from the right', Marsland is surely correct to question whether the left–right dichotomy continues to have much analytical purchase. Coming undeniably from an 'anti-state' position, he sees the welfare state changes made over the past quarter century as a move towards sanity in the wake of more than a century of creeping collectivism – much accelerated, of course, after 1945. Ideally, for Marsland, Margaret Thatcher's approach to social policy "will come to be seen ... as neither 'left' nor 'right' – but simply as straight ... realism, efficiency and justice properly construed". Endorsing the – now traditional – 'new right' welfare agenda which argued that the welfare state was essentially bureaucratic, coercive and dependency inducing, Marsland applauds what the Conservative governments of the 1980s and 1990s achieved, while acknowledging that they could, perhaps should, have gone further. Reducing trade union power was an important precursor to social policy reforms which not only saw far-reaching privatisation of goods and services (council housing being the most successful of all these ventures) but the introduction of a market logic into what remained of state-delivered welfare. Of particular interest in this chapter, however, is not just the account of Mrs Thatcher's social policy crusade, which after all is well known, but the fact that John Major's rather different contribution is separately discussed. Too often the Major years are subsumed within the general ambit of 'Thatcherism' but as Marsland points out it was the quieter, understated Major administration that actually implemented many of the Conservatives' most significant reforms, welding them into a "coherent national framework [which incorporated] both local competitive autonomy and central government frameworking, standard-setting and regulation". Major, too, is credited with the important rhetorical shift of 'Unemployment Benefit' into the 'Jobseeker's Allowance'. Finally Marsland considers the fortunes of the Conservative welfare legacy under New Labour – and finds echoes of Majorite instrumentalism in Tony Blair's pragmatic Third Way rhetoric. Rhetoric, however, is what Marsland believes New Labour is primarily about and he is sceptical that the government will succeed indefinitely in sustaining what on the one hand is an essentially Conservative commitment to welfare reform while on the other remaining reluctant to challenge the pro-collectivist culture with which much of the Labour Party and the public sector more widely is still imbued.

Beginning with an overview of four perspectives on Thatcherism – ranging from the 'wicked witch' theory to views that, in reality, not much changed – Glennerster's chapter argues that there have indeed been significant changes in the British welfare state, some of which, in retrospect at least, were probably necessary. If certain elements of policy, for example the sale of council housing and changes in social security, had 'malign consequences', initiatives proved beneficial. Glennerster is thinking particularly of the challenges the Conservatives posed to traditional assumptions about the role of the state, the association of universality with *uniformity* and the (benign) authority of professionals. The diversification of service delivery through privatisation, the enhancement of the role of the voluntary sector and various forms of quasi market created a greater variety of services and in some cases *better* services because competition drove up standards and because (in the case of schools, for example) public sector professionals found themselves increasingly accountable to 'consumers'. For all their faults – the misaligned priorities that competition can introduce, the two-tier services that can result – Glennerster argues that the introduction of quasi markets gave consumers more choice and curtailed the power of public sector professionals. Whether these benefits outweigh some of the 'costs' of the Thatcher era will continue to be debated. As Glennerster points out, the destruction of the UK's industrial base and the high levels of unemployment associated with it, combined with the dramatic rise in the inequality of incomes and the rise of the 'get rich quick' society may be a high price to pay for a partially reorganised welfare state.

For Land, the price has certainly been too high. Taking privatisation as the core dimension of social policy change during the Conservative years, Land endorses the view that the UK shifted from a 'Keynesian national welfare state', in Jessop's terms, to a Schumpeterian competitive state. The major risks of unemployment, sickness and old age that were collectivised in the post-war period were 'privatised' in two senses of the word. First, individuals and their families were expected to take greater responsibility for their own care and welfare; second, public sector services were broken up with elements being relocated in the private marketplace. On the first dimension, Land considers the ways in which changes to benefit arrangements have forced young people into increased dependence on their parents, while lone mothers were initially coerced into greater dependence on absent fathers through the crude actions and assumptions of the Child Support Agency. On the second, Land considers how the privatisation agenda (assisted by the growing influence of European Competition law) affected the personal social services, where developments in the residential care sector led to a private market in the care of older people and the effective collapse of direct public provision in this area. Taken in the round, Land fears that the substitution of the 'private' for the 'public' in so many areas of the welfare state has undermined social well-being. Far from increasing individual freedom, as Marsland believes, the changes of the past 25 years, by removing social protection for the most vulnerable members of the national community, have done much to reduce it.

The final chapter in this section is written by Joseph White from 'an American perspective'. White quite rightly wonders of what such a perspective might consist, commenting that a distinctly American view of the British welfare state probably does not exist. What he does manage to convey, however, is a view from 'outside' and in so doing he is able to provide an insight (American or not) into how others see us. Coming from the 'old left', White's intensely personal view of Thatcherism's influence is illuminating not least because he makes it clear how important a symbol the postwar British welfare state was for progressive Americans. Mrs Thatcher's election victory and its aftermath changed that and contributed to the growing conviction that the UK and USA were ideologically united in a campaign to roll back the state and end welfare dependency. Whether or not Thatcherism *directly* influenced US social policy is hard to say but White sees little evidence for such an assertion. In some ways, as British commentators like Alan Deacon have noted, the flow was in the opposite direction, with the Conservative Party and associated think tanks looking to free market America for inspiration. White's personal concern, however, is with whatever is left of socialism, which was of course fatally damaged in the 1980s and 1990s. Here he is pessimistic (we might nowadays say 'realistic') but not entirely without hope. The real issue underlying this chapter perhaps – and one that also preoccupies Glennerster and Land (if not Marsland for obvious reasons) – is how to preserve a sense of the 'common good' and collective well-being in what has become a highly marketised, privatised and competitive social and economic environment. For all its faults, New Labour has attempted to bridge this divide – whether to any effect remains to be seen.

Part One:
Developments in UK social policy

ONE

Housing policy: coming in from the cold?

Brian Lund

If housing policy is interpreted to mean state intervention to influence the supply and affordability of homes then, in early 2003, the answer to the question 'Did the late 1990s mark the end of a meaningful housing policy?' (Bramley, 1997; Malpass, 1999) would have been a resonant 'yes'. New Labour's housing policy consisted of implementing the 'avalanche of new procedures for every nook and cranny of the housing sector' contained in the 2000 Housing Statement (*Roof* Briefing, 2000, p 20), but the big picture of a market-dominated housing system, set by the Conservatives, remained unchanged. This chapter examines the developments in housing procedures during 2002-03 and then explores the implications of *Sustainable communities plan: Building for the future* (ODPM, 2003a) and the 'Review of housing supply: securing our future housing needs' (Barker, 2003) for the future of a 'meaningful housing policy'.

Private renting

Under New Labour, the private rented sector of the housing market remained constant at about 10%. New Labour's contentment with private landlords was reflected in its limited yet protracted reform agenda. Its 1997 manifesto promised only "protection where it is most needed for tenants in houses in multiple-occupation" by "a proper system of licensing by local authorities which will benefit tenants and responsible landlords alike" (Labour Party, 1997, p 26). Although this promise was not redeemed in England and Wales during New Labour's first term of office, the 2003 Housing Bill included a mandatory national licensing system for three-storey houses occupied by five or more persons and discretionary powers for local authorities to license other types of houses in multiple occupation. In addition, local authorities would acquire powers to license all landlords operating in 'low-demand' areas – a response to evidence that some landlords were contributing to neighbourhood decline by buying properties in such areas and renting them to unruly tenants (ODPM, 2003b).

Social housing

Stock transfer

The Office of the Deputy Prime Minister defines social housing as accommodation let at a rent below the market price. The term was coined in the late 1980s to blur the distinction between local authority and housing association-owned dwellings, thereby facilitating the transfer of housing stock from local government to registered social landlords.

Rather than allocate large-scale resources to a small number of areas as the Conservatives had done under the Estate Action Initiative, New Labour promised to upgrade all social housing dwellings to a 'decent' standard by 2010. In the Spending Review 2002 this promise was extended to a proportion of 'vulnerable households' in the private rented sector. A decent home was defined as 'one which is wind and weather tight, warm and has modern facilities' (ODPM, 2003c). 'Modern' was specified further as 'reasonably modern', having a bathroom less than 30 years old and a kitchen less than 20 years old. Four resource channels were made available to local government to help them achieve the 'decent' homes standard:

- Mainstream Housing Revenue Account resources supplemented by the 'Single Capital Pot' available for spending on all local authority capital spending initiatives.
- Housing transfer to a Registered Social Landlord providing access to private finance which, unlike public finance, was not subject to the constraints of the Public Sector Borrowing Requirement.
- The Housing Private Finance Initiative which, while retaining ownership of dwellings by the local authority, taps private finance. A private sector contractor supplies assets and services to the local authority in return for a payment related to performance (ODPM, 2003d, p 2).
- Under the Arm's-Length Management Organisations Initiative local authorities could access additional public sector resources if they delivered housing management through arm's-length companies with significant tenant involvement. Arm's-Length Management Organisations must have received a 2★ or 3★ rating from the Housing Inspectorate.

Three of these options allow local authorities to retain a degree of control over their housing stock but mainstream housing resources are restricted (Wilson, 2003, p 14). The Housing Private Finance Initiative is still in the development stage and the Arm's-Length Management Organisations Initiative disperses public funds on a highly selective basis. Given that the *English house conditions survey 2001* (ODPM, 2003e, p 4) revealed that 43% of the 2,790,000 council dwellings failed to meet the 'decent' standard, then large-scale stock transfer to landlords unfettered by the constraints of the Public Sector Borrowing Requirement will be necessary to achieve the government's target. Between 2001 and 2003, despite tenant resistance in some areas, 404,000 dwellings had either been transferred or were in the transfer process.

New Labour has also promoted stock transfer by rent restructuring. The rents of homes owned by local authorities and registered social landlords will converge over a 10-year period so that, by 2012, similar properties in similar areas will cost the same and there will be no cost advantage to tenants who stay with their local authority. The 'formula rent' is based on a combination of local property values, local earnings and property size. Rents will rise or fall each year by the Retail Price Index + 2% or –2% until the formula rent has been achieved. Given that the rents charged by registered social landlords are higher than local authority rents 'rent restructuring' means significant increases for many council tenants – an inducement to acquiesce to transfer proposals.

The Right to Buy

The Right to Buy, introduced in 1980, enabled 1.5 million tenants to become homeowners. When sitting tenants buy their houses the affordable housing stock available to new tenants is not restricted immediately but, over time, when the houses are resold, the number of affordable rented properties diminishes (Wilcox, 2003, p 55). Moreover, New Labour uncovered evidence that, in some areas, private companies use cash incentives to encourage tenants to buy their homes (Jones, 2003). In return for a payment residents agree to move out of their homes so that the company can let them at market rents. Tenants then sell the homes to the company after three years so they can keep their discounts. To maintain the affordable housing pool and curtail the abuse of the system the maximum discount on right to buy sales was reduced from £38,000 to £16,000 in 41 local authority areas where affordable housing was scarce. In addition, the 2003 Housing Bill proposed the extension of both the initial qualification period for the Right to Buy and the time after sale, when local authorities may require owners to repay some of their initial discount, to five years. Clear blue water between New Labour and the Conservatives emerged in 2002 when the Conservatives issued a consultation paper announcing their intention to reverse New Labour's changes to the right to buy and to grant a new right to buy to housing association tenants. Currently housing association tenants have restricted opportunities to purchase under the 'Right to Acquire' scheme.

Older homes

The ending of mandatory grants by the 1996 Housing Grants, Construction and Regeneration Act, produced a large reduction in state spending on the improvement of older homes (Wilcox, 2003, p 107). Nonetheless, housing booms generate private investment in renovation and the *English house condition survey 2001* revealed an improvement in the condition of the private housing stock. Unfitness in the owner-occupied sector had declined from 834,000 in 1996 to 468,000 in 2001 and from 337,000 to 238,000 in the private landlord sector. The proportion of private sector dwellings below the 'decency' standard had declined from 7.1 million to 5.3 million (ODPM, 2003d).

The 2002 Regulatory Reform Order marked the end of detailed involvement of central government in renovation policy and its replacement by a 'managerial' target. The Order abolished mandatory regulations on grant levels and a target was set to increase the proportion of people in private sector homes with decent housing from 57% in 2001 to 63% in 2005 and 70% in 2010. Target achievement would be monitored through the *English house condition survey* to be carried out annually from 2001. In future, it would be the responsibility of each local authority to integrate renovation policy into its strategy for urban renewal and to set up mechanisms to tap private finance for housing renewal.

Housing Benefit

Between 1996-97 and 2000-01 the cost of Housing Benefit declined – the outcome of increased employment, Working Families Tax Credit (taken into account in assessing Housing Benefit eligibility) and the implementation of the 'local reference rent' thresholds devised by the Conservatives. In 2003, 8 million households were in receipt of Housing Benefit, with a weekly payment of £47.90 in the local authority sector, £66.60 for registered social landlord tenants and £74.20 for private tenants – £113 in London (ONS, 2003a). Given a Housing Benefit 'taper' of 65 pence in the pound, these rent levels illustrate the contribution of rent and Housing Benefit to the 'poverty trap' and work disincentives. Walker and Bingley (2001) suggest that reducing the taper or reducing rents directly through a bricks and mortar subsidy would have a strong, positive impact on work participation.

The Audit Commission's investigation into the administration of Housing Benefit concluded that 'the service has worsened overall in the last five years' (Audit Commission, 2002) and attributed part of the blame to the increasing complexity of the regulations issued by central government. New Labour's response was to publish *Building choice and responsibility: A radical agenda for Housing Benefit* (DWP, 2002). It proposed a means-tested Housing Benefit, to be piloted in selected areas, normally paid directly to the tenant and based on a standard rent to be determined for each locality. The government claimed the reform would give 'a new deal for tenants' because:

> ... tenants who rent a property at below the standard allowance or who move to cheaper property in their local area, or who negotiate to keep the rent below the standard allowance, will be able to keep the difference – putting the decision in their hands. (DWP, 2002, p 4)

Initially the scheme was to be confined to the private landlord sector but, in his 2003 Budget statement, the Chancellor of the Exchequer announced that the scheme would be extended to the social sector and become nationwide. The new scheme has the potential to simplify the Housing Benefit system thereby making it easier and quicker to claim. It also gives all tenants personal responsibility for rent payment and mimics the market by making rent increases more transparent. However, it does nothing to alleviate the poverty trap; the experience of 'pre-tenancy determinations' indicates that few tenants will be able to shop around for lower rents and rent arrears are likely to become a bigger problem.

Homelessness

The Office of the Deputy Prime Minister divides homelessness into two categories – rough sleeping and statutory homelessness. In so doing it omits a large number of people not covered by the homelessness legislation and not sleeping rough. Crisis, a homelessness charity, has estimated that there are about 106,000 'hidden' single, homeless people living in bed and breakfast accommodation, hostels and squats or sleeping on friends' floors (Crisis, 2002).

Rough sleeping featured strongly in New Labour's 1997 manifesto and the Rough Sleeping Initiative, introduced by Michael Heseltine in the early 1990s, was extended to selected areas outside London. Despite the misgivings expressed about the validity of the counts, New Labour claimed that the number of people sleeping rough on one night in England dropped from 1,850 in June 1998 to fewer than 600 in 2003 (ODPM, 2003f, p 19). The 2002 Priority Need Order, which extended the groups of people who have a priority need for housing to include young people leaving care, people fleeing from domestic violence and people vulnerable as a result of having been a member of Her Majesty's forces or having served a custodial sentence, will help to sustain this apparent reduction in rough sleeping.

Statutory homelessness, that is the homeless households covered by the specific provisions of the homelessness legislation, increased rapidly under New Labour. In June 1997 there were 54,930 households in temporary accommodation compared to 81,170 in June 2002. The number of households placed in bed and breakfast hotels by local authorities increased from 4,100 in 1997 to 13,240 in 2002. New Labour reacted to these figures by concentrating on the households in bed and breakfast accommodation. A Bed and Breakfast Unit was established in the Office of the Deputy Prime Minister, which was later amalgamated with the Rough Sleeping Unit to form the Homelessness Directorate. This Directorate was charged with ensuring that, by March 2004, no homeless families with children were living in bed and breakfast hotels except in an emergency and even then for no more than six weeks. The government allocated extra resources to local authorities to help them meet this target and the 2003 Homelessness (Suitability of Accommodation) (England) Order prohibited the use of private sector bed and breakfast accommodation to lodge children for more than six weeks. The Homelessness Directorate also attempted to shift dominant notions of the causes of homelessness from the 'political' to the 'personal'. It promised a new approach to statutory homelessness with a focus "as much on the personal problems that homeless people face – such as family or relationship breakdown, domestic violence, debt, alcohol and drug misuse, and poor physical or mental health – as on the places they live" (Homelessness Directorate, 2003, p 7).

Between June 2002 and June 2003 the number of households with children in bed and breakfast hotels declined by 44% to 3,730 but the total number of households in temporary accommodation increased to

90,680 (ODPM, 2003f). Part of this growth can be attributed to the more liberal rules for acceptance as homeless contained in the 2002 Homelessness Act but a growing shortage of affordable accommodation in parts of England has also contributed to the increase (Barker, 2003). In Scotland, under the 2001 Housing (Scotland) Act, local authorities are required to house homeless people, whether they are considered in priority need or not, while a homelessness claim is investigated. Moreover, if assessed as non-priority homeless, local authorities have to provide accommodation for a reasonable period. The 2003 Homelessness (Scotland) Act extended local authority duties to the homeless. Under the Act the distinction between priority and non-priority need will be phased out and, by 2012, all unintentionally homeless people will be entitled to a permanent home. The prospects of a similar commitment in England will depend on the success of local authority homelessness strategies - mandatory under the 2002 Homelessness Act – and the increase in the supply of dwellings promised in *Sustainable communities plan: Building for the future* (ODPM, 2003a).

Supporting People

The development of supported housing schemes in the 1980s and 1990s was erratic. A range of funding streams – the Audit Commission (1998, p 22) identified 25 different mechanisms – were used by social services departments, health authorities, the probation service and housing associations to meet the growing demand for 'accommodation with support'. However, concern was expressed at the motives underlying some of the projects (the shunting of long-term costs to other authorities and onto Housing Benefit) and whether the pattern of provision was in line with need. In 1998, the government announced that in 2003 funding streams for housing-linked support would be united in a single pot to be administered by local government working in partnership with other agencies (DSS, 1998). Supporting People became 'live' in April 2003. Despite concerns about the integration of new capital projects with the process of revenue support, some cost shunting of mainstream social services responsibilities to the new scheme and the robustness of the need-mapping mechanisms (Carter, 2003), it appears to be operating reasonably well. A virtue of the new scheme is its ability to promote 'floating support' (support detached from a specific housing project).

'Unpopular housing'

One of the first investigations by the Social Exclusion Unit was into 'unpopular housing'. The report *Bringing Britain together:A national strategy for neighbourhood renewal* (1998) identified 'several thousand' poor neighbourhoods in England characterised by multiple problems co-existing in the same area. The overall failure of earlier programmes was attributed to a lack of joined-up thinking and action, too many initiatives, a dearth of resident participation and a concentration on 'bricks and mortar' rather than 'human' and 'social' capital. New Labour's response to 'unpopular housing' was to introduce the New Deal for Communities. This promised funding over 10 years to 39 local authorities to tackle high levels of crime, educational under-achievement, poor health, inadequate housing and a poor physical environment in an intensive and coordinated way. Later, New Deal for Communities resources were augmented by the Neighbourhood Renewal Fund set up to facilitate joint action at neighbourhood level. This fund was available to the most deprived local authorities to help them to prepare and implement neighbourhood renewal schemes, involving the appointment of neighbourhood managers and the coordination of mainstream services.

There is a dearth of robust information on the outcomes of New Deal for Communities and the Neighbourhood Renewal Fund. The official evaluation of New Deal for Communities, published by the Office of the Deputy Prime Minister in October 2003, identified a number of concerns about its operation. These included the cost of community engagement in terms of "burn-out of key local community players; intra-community tensions; the demands placed on the time and resources of NDC employees and agencies' and a scarcity of links between 'needs and aspirations' and 'appropriate projects and outcomes"(ODPM, 2003g, p 1). Nonetheless, the evaluation argued that the lasting benefits of community engagement and agency partnerships may be worth the initial cost of promoting joined-up working and community involvement. Some imaginative schemes have been promoted but the extensive public involvement at the heart of the initiative (believed to promote human and social capital) seems to have promoted delay and disillusionment in many areas. An unofficial review of New Deal for Communities claimed that:

> Ten of the 39 New Deal partnerships have run into trouble, with residents, staff and communities feeling exhausted, disaffected and betrayed.... Many NDC partnerships entering their fourth year are only just embarking on their housing strategy or recruiting registered

social landlords, and have not committed any spending to 'live projects'.
(Knutt, 2003, p 3)

Belatedly, the government has partially recognised the need for funds to improve the physical appearance of areas containing 'unpopular' housing. In 2001 it identified the problem of low demand (an economic term for 'unpopular housing'), concentrated in the North and to a lesser extent in the Midlands. The government estimated that 550,000 privately-owned dwellings and 360,000 held by 'social' housing landlords were in 'low demand'. A Market Renewal Fund was set up to tackle the problem to which nine 'pathfinder' agencies would have access. The pathfinders covered about 50% of the identified low-demand stock and were charged with creating successful and sustainable communities. The funds were available for detailed, local studies on the nature of the problem. Selective demolition, physical improvements and schemes such as home exchanges – allowing residents to transfer their mortgage from a house with negative equity to a nearby dwelling whose value reflects the mortgage – are other potential uses of the fund. The pathfinder initiative was accompanied by an announcement from the Office of the Deputy Prime Minister that the amount of urban greenfield housing planned for the North West and the North East would be reduced (ODPM, 2003h, p 12). This will limit new supply in low-demand areas and, according to Lupton and Power (2002), reduce the social segregation caused by people with choice leaving inner cities.

Housing policy returns?

By May 2002, after five years of New Labour governance, it had become clear that the housing situation in England had deteriorated when compared to the last year of John Major's government. New social housing completions had fallen from 32,463 in 1996-97 to 22,347 in 2001-02 and, in London, social housing lettings declined by 6%. Overcrowding was on the increase (New Policy Institute, 2003) and the number of households in temporary accommodation had almost doubled in the five years. There were no signs that sustained housing demand had promoted extra supply: the completion of new dwellings – 175, 499 in 2001-02 – was the lowest since 1945 and had remained steady for the five years. The annual rate of house price inflation, fuelled by a fourfold increase in buy to let mortgages, was 18.5%.

New Labour's initial response to rising house prices was to introduce the Starter Home Initiative. This targeted key workers, particularly nurses, teachers and police officers, to help them buy where high prices would otherwise prevent them from living in or near to the communities they serve. The Starter Home Initiative promised a cash injection of £250 million to assist 10,000 key workers between 2001 and 2004 but, by August 2003, only 3,300 workers had been helped (Press Association, 2003).

The Communities Plan

New Labour's interest in housing supply was revitalised on John Prescott's return to the housing portfolio. In May 2002 the Department of Transport, Local Government and the Regions was abolished and its housing responsibilities transferred to the Office of the Deputy Prime Minister. Publication of the detail of the housing dimension of the Chancellor's 2002 Comprehensive Spending Review was postponed until Prescott had re-examined housing policy. The result was the publication of *Sustainable communities plan: Building for the future* (ODPM, 2003a), hereafter referred to as the Communities Plan, which promoted targeted intervention in the housing market to influence supply. It identified a housing shortage in the South East where housing construction was well below the target set by the government. This shortfall was to be met by growth in four areas: the Thames Gateway, Ashford, Milton Keynes/South Midlands and the London-Stansted-Cambridge corridor, supported by £610 million, over three years, for site assembly and infrastructure work. Extra resources for affordable housing were promised and two thirds of the total national resources for affordable housing were earmarked for the South East.

Planning reform

In addition to a modest resource injection to promote housing supply the Communities Plan included proposals to reform the planning system. The government promised to introduce a new, more clearly-defined power for planning authorities to acquire land for carrying out development, redevelopment or improvement. The local development plan process would be accelerated and £350 million, over three years, was to be injected into the planning system to quicken the decision-making process and improve planning decisions. Moreover, in a move calculated to abate the influence of rural pressure groups, County Structure Plans would be abolished and strategic planning decisions would be made by regional authorities charged with linking transport, housing, economic and environmental issues. The initiatives requiring legislative support were included in the 2003 Planning and Compulsory Purchase Bill.

The Barker Review of housing supply

Although promoted as a 'step change' in New Labour's housing policy the Communities Plan was a small step. Just how small was demonstrated by the *Review of housing supply: Securing our future housing needs, Interim Report - Analysis* (Barker, 2003). The Barker Review of housing supply was set up following the Chancellor's statement on UK membership of the single European currency. Here, Brown identified the operations of the UK's housing market as the major obstacle to membership of the European Monetary Union. He claimed that "Britain has experienced difficulty in balancing housing supply and demand", stating:

> ... most stop-go problems that Britain has suffered in the last fifty years have been led or influenced by the housing market. The volatility of the housing market and potential for higher inflation is a problem for stability that we are determined to do more to address to produce greater stability and reduce the risks of inflation irrespective of the decision on the euro. (Chancellor of the Exchequer, 2003, p 8)

Housing, consumption and EMU, one of the background papers accompanying the Chancellor's speech, noted the "relatively weak response of UK housing supply to the long-term rise in house prices" (HM Treasury, 2003, para 4.21). The Barker Review was set up to examine the impact of limited supply and the long-term upward trend in house prices on the economy and social inequality, and to explore the reasons for the weak relationship between supply and demand. It identified a range of estimates of the potential housing shortfall (Barker, 2003, pp 9-10):

- 90,000 homes to compensate for the failure of rates of house building to meet Regional Planning Guidance targets over the last six years.
- 39,000 homes per annum to meet the current shortfall between the number of planned homes and projections of household formation.
- 430,000 homes to meet the backlog of households without self-contained accommodation.
- Between 93,000 and 146,000 homes per annum to keep affordability for new households in line with that of the 1980s.
- 240,000 dwellings to reduce the long-term trend in house prices to zero.

Barker noted that reduced housing supply damaged the flexibility and performance of the economy by its negative impact on business location and labour mobility and through its contribution to macroeconomic volatility. High house prices created affordability problems, with only 37% of new households able to afford to buy a property in 2002 compared to 46% in the late 1980s. In addition, rising house prices produced transfers of resources: the gainers being homeowners trading down, property speculators, outward migrants and landowners; with the losers including homeowners trading up, inward migrants, non-homeowners and first-time buyers. Barker estimated that "first-time buyers in 2001 paid £27 billion more than if house prices had remained at 1975 levels in real terms. This is equivalent to each first-time buyer paying an extra £48,000" (Barker, 2003, p 8).

The government's initial response to the Barker Review was to extend the Starter Home Initiative, insert a clause into the 2003 Housing Bill to allow private developers to claim Social Housing Grant and announced a consultation exercise on the provision of incentives to encourage Real Estate Investment Trusts to boost the supply of private rented accommodation. However, the Barker Review identified the planning process as a major reason, perhaps *the* major reason, for the failure to supply houses at a socially optimum level. Although limitations in the house-building industry were a cause of poor responsiveness to demand, Barker "found little evidence, at least across the country as a whole, to substantiate concerns that ... the practice of landbanking allows house builders to erect barriers to entry into the market" (Barker, 2003, p 13). Moreover, some of the limitations of house builders were linked to the operations of the planning system. The planning system itself was a major factor in limiting supply because all the decision makers in the planning process – from regional to local level – had more to gain by restricting, rather than promoting, residential development (Barker, 2003, p 12). This analysis suggests that reform of the planning system, over and above the measures in the Communities Plan, is necessary if a socially optimal level of housing supply is to be delivered.

Housing and social justice

New Labour fulfilled its 2001 manifesto commitment to examine ways of helping tenants gain an equity stake in the value of their homes. The examination concluded that equity shares in council housing would be potentially expensive – up to £7 billion over 30 years – and therefore no scheme would be introduced (ODPM, 2003i).

Ownership of residential dwellings is an important component of personal wealth in Britain. This wealth can be realised through inheritance, borrowing with housing assets used as security and moving down market. In 1997, homeownership formed 27% of total personal wealth – a percentage likely to have increased since 1997 because of the rise in house prices and the decline in share values. Inland Revenue statistics on the distribution of wealth are out of date but the latest available figures show that between 1996 and 2000 the share of the wealth owned by the wealthiest 10% of the population increased from 52% to 54% (Inland Revenue, 2003). As the Barker Review notes, house price increases above inflation – undeserved income – have contributed to this increasing inequality in the distribution of wealth. In 2002 CACI Limited identified the most affluent and the poorest postal code areas in Britain (CACI Limited, 2002). Between 1997 and 2003 the average house in the most affluent areas had increased by £170,000 whereas the increase in the poorest areas was £22,000 (Upmystreet, 2003).

The contribution of housing to inequalities in the distribution of income can be assessed by examining the series *Households below average incomes*. In 2001-02, 2.7 million children were living below 60% of median income before housing costs. This increased to 3.8 million after housing costs (DWP, 2003, pp 53-5). In 1996-97 the gap between the percentage of children below 60% of median income before and after housing costs was 8%. This increased to 10% in 2001-02 (ONS, 2003b) indicating the growing contribution that the absence of state financial assistance for homeowners makes to the persistence of child poverty.

Conclusion

In the 1990s housing policy was 'low' politics: the supremacy of the market, promoted by the Conservatives and endorsed by New Labour, determined the supply and distribution of dwellings. This market operated with the constraints of the planning system, which by restricting the availability of land for new building, served to push up prices to the advantage of existing owners of housing assets. The Communities Plan and the Barker Review mark a revival of a specific, economically driven policy promoted by the Treasury. After years in the wilderness, the supply and hence the affordability of housing are back on the agenda as 'high' politics.

References

Audit Commission (1998) *Home alone: The role of housing in community care*, London: Audit Commission.

Audit Commission (2002) *Housing benefit: The national perspective*, London: Audit Commission.

Barker, K. (2003) 'Review of housing supply: securing our future housing needs, Interim Report – Analysis' (www.hm_treasury.gov.uk/consultations_and_legislation/barker/consult_barker_index.cfm).

Bramley, G. (1997) 'Housing policy: a case of terminal decline?', *Policy & Politics*, vol 25, no 4, pp 387-408.

CACI Limited (2002) 'Wealth of the nation 2002' (http://216.239.41.104 search?q=cache:1kY_Vh2rfn4J:www.casa.ucl.ac.uk/2003 wealthofthenation.pdf+wealth+of+the+nation+2002&hl=en&ie=UTF-8).

Carter, A. (2003) 'Part of the equation', *Inside Housing*, June, p 29.

Chancellor of the Exchequer (2003) 'Statement by the Chancellor of the Exchequer on UK membership of the single currency', 9 June (www.hmtreasury.gov.uk/documents/the_euro/assessment/euro_assess03_speech.cfm).

Crisis (2002) 'Hidden homeless campaign' (www.crisis.org.uk/about/crisis_hidden_homeless.php).

DSS (Department of Social Security) (1998) *Supporting people: A new policy and funding framework for support services*, London: DSS.

DWP (Department for Work and Pensions) (2002) *Building choice and responsibility: A radical agenda for Housing Benefit*, London: The Stationery Office.

DWP (2003) *Households below average incomes, 1994/5-2001/2*, London: The Stationery Office.

HM Treasury (2003) 'Housing, consumption and EMU' (www.hm-treasury.gov.uk/documents/the_euro/euro_index_index.cfm).

Homelessness Directorate (2003) *Achieving positive outcomes on homelessness*, ODPM, London: The Stationery Office.

Inland Revenue (2003) 'Personal wealth' (www.inlandrevenue.gov.uk/stats/personal_wealth/dopw_t05_1.htm).

Jones, C. (2003) *Exploitation of the right to buy scheme by companies*, Housing Research Summary 177, London: ODPM.

Knutt, E. (2003) 'It was never meant to be like this', *Housing Today*, 13 June.

Labour Party (1997) *New Labour because Britain deserves better*, London: The Labour Party.

Lupton, R. and Power, A. (2002) 'Social exclusion and neighbourhoods', in J. Hills, J. Le Grand and D. Piachaud (eds) *Understanding social exclusion*, Oxford: Oxford University Press.

Malpass, P. (1999) 'Housing policy: does it have a future?', *Policy & Politics*, vol 27, no 2, pp 217-28.

New Policy Institute (2003) 'Monitoring poverty and social exclusion' (www.poverty.org.uk/intro/index.htm).

ODPM (Office of the Deputy Prime Minister) (2003a) *Sustainable communities plan: Building for the future*, London: The Stationery Office.

ODPM (2003b) Research summary 177, 'Exploitation of the right to buy scheme by private companies' (www.odpm.gov.uk/stellent/groups/odpm_housing/documents/page/odpm_house_609025.hcsp).

ODPM (2003c) 'A decent home: the revised definition and guidance for implementation' (www.housing.odpm.gov.uk/information/dhg/definition/index.htm).

ODPM (2003d) 'Private Finance Initiative (PFI) for housing revenue account: early lessons from the Pathfinder programme', Housing Research Summary No 193 (www.housing.odpm.gov.uk/hrs/hrs193/index.htm).

ODPM (2003e) *English house condition survey 2001: Building the picture*, London: Queen's Printer and Controller of HMSO.

ODPM (2003f) 'Homeless statistics March 2003 and prevention of homelessness', Policy briefing 4 (www.homelessness.odpm.gov.uk/policybriefing/pdf/briefing04.pdf).

ODPM (2003g) Research summary 7 'New Deal for Communities: the national evaluation 2002/3, key findings' (www.neighbourhood.gov.uk/formatteddoc.asp?id=549).

ODPM (2003h) *Annual report 2003*, London: The Stationery Office.

ODPM (2003i) 'Equity shares for social housing' (www.odpm.gov.uk).

ONS (Office for National Statistics) (2003a) 'Housing benefit and council tax benefit, quarterly statistics' (www.statistics.gov.uk/StatBase/Product.asp?vlnk=64&Pos=1&ColRank=1&Rank=272).

ONS (2003b) 'Proportion of children living in households below 60 per cent of median income, 1979-2000/01' (www.statistics.gov.uk/STATBASE/Expodata/Spreadsheets/D6268.xls).

Press Association (2003) 'Apply now for starter homes says Prescott', *The Guardian*, 5 August.

Roof Briefing (2000) No 39, April.

Social Exclusion Unit (1998) *Bringing Britain together: A national strategy for neighbourhood renewal*, London: The Stationery Office.

Upmystreet (2003) www.upmystreet.com/

Walker, I. and Bingley, P. (2001) 'Rents and work: the implications of housing costs and housing benefit for work incentives in the UK', *Economic Journal*, May.

Wilcox, S. (2003) *UK housing review 2003/2004*, York: Joseph Rowntree Foundation.

Wilson, W. (2003) *Delivering the decent homes standard: Social landlords' options and progress*, London: House of Commons.

TWO

The NHS in England: from modernisation to marketisation?

Judith Allsop and Rob Baggott

Introduction

Two years ago, a review of health policy by the King's Fund described the Blair government's reform programme as 'relentless, almost hyperactive intervention' (Appleby and Coote, 2002, p 5). If anything, the pace of change has since increased. Despite the decentralisation agenda set out in the aftermath of the NHS Plan, the deluge of policy documents from the Department of Health has continued. So is this 'more of the same', or can significant changes in the direction of policy be detected?

It is possible to interpret the policies that have developed as having elements of both modernisation and marketisation. 'Modernisation' can be seen as an attempt to shift the political economy of the National Health Service from a centralised command and control model, with its associated corporate politics, towards the delivery of health services through a series of separate local, independently managed, components. The efficient and effective use of resources in this devolved NHS is to be achieved by, on the one hand, centralised controls that hold local providers accountable for achieving particular outcomes, and on the other, by the manipulation of both demand and supply side factors to alter the behaviour of those who consume and those who provide health care.

Underlying Labour's policies is therefore a recognition of the power of 'market' forces. Politically, 'modernisation' is driven through enhancing and harnessing the powers of healthcare users as individuals wishing to access good quality health care, while at the same time curbing the potential monopoly powers of those who provide that healthcare through new employment contracts and changes in the division of healthcare tasks (DoH, 2000). Whether this more devolved arrangement can also achieve a delivery system that is equitable in terms of the distribution of resources and healthcare outcomes is more open to question and a matter of concern for many.

Within this general framework, this paper explores areas where significant changes have taken place. Given the breadth and depth of the health policy agenda, it would be foolish indeed to attempt to cover all issues (for further analysis see Baggott, 2004). Instead we shall focus on two aspects where the Blair government's health policy seems to have shifted significantly compared with its early years in office. First, there have been attempts to influence the demand side factors. As the Wanless Report (2002) acknowledged, this implies activity at two levels: the individual and the collective. First, there is emphasis on both increasing opportunities for patient choice and on introducing new mechanisms for patient and public involvement. Second, a variety of methods have been used to influence supply side factors such as the introduction of foundation trusts; an enhanced role for the independent sector and the reinvigoration of the internal market. However, these policy shifts have taken place within the context of increasing central control. There is greater accountability to government for performance through regimes of regulation such as target setting, audit, performance review and inspection, as well as a range of new regulatory bodies to oversee standards.

In Labour's second term of office, policies have been developed against a background of significant additional resources being channelled into the health service. During the 1980s and 1990s, governments were often criticised for underfunding the NHS. By the end of the 1990s, the UK spent less on health care than comparable countries. Initially, New Labour adhered closely to its predecessor's spending plans and consequently the rate of increase in NHS expenditure in its first term was not that generous. However, at 4.7% per annum in real terms it was considerably higher than in the early 1990s. Following the NHS Plan, and a commitment to raise spending levels towards the European average, the NHS budget was increased substantially. In the 2002 budget a 7.5% increase per annum over a five-year period was announced. It was estimated that this would bring UK health expenditure to 9.4% of GDP by 2007-08. Although these amounts are impressive, the UK still lags behind other European countries such as France and Germany who spend around 10% of GDP on health. Furthermore, the lower levels of resource inputs in the past will continue to affect the health infrastructure for a considerable time, particularly in terms of manpower supply and health facilities. For example, the ratio of practising doctors to population in the UK is much lower than in all but five other OECD countries (OECD, 2003).

Consumerism and patient choice

In the early years, the approach of the Blair government was highly paternalistic. It attempted to disassociate itself from the pseudo-consumerism of the *Patients' Charter* (DoH, 1991), introduced by the Conservatives, by focusing on both individual rights and responsibilities. However, many of the standards set out in the Charter continued to provide benchmarks for assessing the performance of the NHS. Under Labour, these evolved into new and tougher targets to reduce waiting times, culminating in the NHS Plan (DoH, 2000). These included a commitment to: reduce the maximum wait for outpatient appointments to three months, and for inpatients to six months, by the end of 2005; reduce the maximum wait in Accident and Emergency to four hours by 2004; and guaranteed access to a primary care professional within 24 hours and to a GP within 48 hours, also by 2004.

Despite criticism of the commercialisation of the NHS under its predecessor, the Blair government began to conceptualise the patient as a consumer. In some respects, this can be seen as a response to external forces. First, a change in patients' attitudes to the NHS was identified. Researchers claimed that patients were becoming more assertive. They wanted to participate more in deciding on their own care, required better quality and more timely information, and expected a quicker and more convenient service (Kendall, 2001). A greater assertiveness was reflected in the increasing numbers of complaints and negligence claims (Allsop and Mulcahy, 2001). Second, there has been an explosion of information on the performance of health providers in the form of 'league tables', performance indicators and reviews by the Commission for Health Improvement and other bodies. These showed wide variations in performance, but were often difficult to interpret (see Parry et al, 1998; Jacobson et al, 2003). Similarly, evidence-based information on the effectiveness, or not, of particular health care interventions gave a promise of more rational decisions but raised questions of who was to decide and how. Finally, stung into action by the Bristol Royal Infirmary Inquiry (2001) and other high-profile service failures, the Blair government began to explore ways of protecting patients' interests through systems of quality assurance and regulation. It also sought ways to improve access to information; strengthen complaints procedures; widen the scope for patients to exercise choice and introduce mechanisms for public involvement.

The government continued to emphasise the importance of partnership between patients and health professionals, and between stakeholders in healthcare within local communities and at the national level. These ideas were reflected in the NHS Plan, which emerged from a review process that involved people from a range of backgrounds, including patients, the voluntary sector, NHS managers and professionals. More recently, the policy has shifted strongly towards choice and competition. A key policy document published in 2003, *Building on the best: Choice, responsiveness and equity in the NHS* (DoH, 2003), argued that services in future should be more closely geared to people's needs and convenience. However, what is apparent is that those who use health services are to be given both greater opportunity and greater responsibility for articulating their needs and their choices.

This policy built on earlier developments. Decisions made by the European Court had increased the scope for cross-border flows of patients between member states. The government responded with a commitment to give patients in certain specialties (initially, patients needing surgery for coronary heart disease) who had been waiting for more than six months, the choice of where to have their operation, either abroad in the independent sector, or in an NHS hospital. It had already committed itself to the concept of patient self-management for those with chronic illness and had extended the options for care and treatment open to people with long-term conditions (DoH, 2001). The Expert Patients programme, developed in collaboration with health consumer groups, acknowledges the expertise of patients with long-term conditions in understanding their own needs and in planning their future care.

Building on the best, which resulted from a widespread consultation with healthcare users and health consumer groups, proposes further ways of easing access and increasing choice. For example, community pharmacists will be able to dispense repeat prescriptions in collaboration with a patient's general practitioner. It is expected that people will have greater choice in the location of their primary healthcare provider. It has also been proposed that pregnant women, if they wish, will have direct access to midwives to develop a birth plan rather than going through their general practitioner. A further proposal is for an electronic personal health record so that people can have access both to their previous treatment and also record their preferences for future treatments. It is envisaged that this could be used to outline a chosen birth plan or preferences for the end of life – areas where there may be personal preferences and where a predetermined plan could guide health professionals. Could this be seen as a modern version of a 'womb to tomb' health service that seeks to be responsive and is aided by new technologies?

Like other measures referred to in this section, the intention seems to be to empower patients as a means of promoting service improvement. However, it is salutary to recall the fate of *Changing childbirth* (DoH, 1993), which was intended to usher in an era of choice in childbirth and women-friendly services (Tew, 1998). A full history of why this promise was not fulfilled has yet to be written, but part of the explanation may lie with two factors long recognised as barriers to policy implementation. First, the health service has tended to be supply side led. There were not the midwives, the obstetricians or the local level patterns of service to meet the range of preferences for every woman. Second, knowledge as well as information is necessary for choice, and the course that bodily events will take is inherently uncertain. Preferences may change, autonomy may be difficult to maintain and people may vary in their capacity to access information and to make a choice.

As illustrated by the arguments put forward by Harry Cayton, the former Chief Executive of the Alzheimer's Society and currently Director of Patient and Public Involvement at the Department of Health, proponents of policies to empower patients have a strong belief in the ability of people to choose wisely (Carvel, 2003). There are some grounds for thinking that the political dynamics of healthcare have changed. Higher levels of education, greater access to information on health via the internet (de Lusignan, 2003), extensive media coverage of health issues and the development of voluntary groups that both support and represent the collective interests of users and carers, have contributed to producing better informed health consumers (Baggott et al, 2004).

There have also been important institutional changes that may impact on the demand side. In England, the local patient watchdogs established in the 1970s – the community health councils (CHCs) – have been replaced with patient and public involvement forums (PPIFs) in each NHS trust covering acute, community and primary care. PPIFs consist of volunteers who will listen and report upon people's concerns about local services, carry out inspections and represent the views of people to the trust concerned. The forums are supported at local level by networks of voluntary organisations and overseen at national level by the Commission for Patient and Public Involvement in Health (CPPIH), a new statutory body reporting to the Secretary of State for Health and to Parliament. The local dimension in healthcare could be strengthened by a scrutiny role given to local authorities. In addition, a statutory duty has been imposed on NHS bodies to consult with, and involve, patients and the public. Furthermore, a new independent complaints and advocacy service has been commissioned, ahead of the new complaints procedure for the NHS due to be introduced in 2004 (DoH, 2004). There are also Patient Advice and Liaison Services (PALS) in each hospital trust to advise patients, their families and independent advocacy services for those who have been dissatisfied with the services provided. It is too soon to tell whether entirely new bodies will be fit for their purpose; whether people will wish to serve on patient forums on a volunteer basis and whether they will have sufficient powers to promote and represent local interests.

Modernising the NHS: supply side changes

In attempting to improve the efficiency of the NHS while improving the supply of high-quality responsive services, the Blair government has used a combination of approaches. First, the internal market model introduced by Margaret Thatcher as part of the 1990 reforms has been revived. Second, central directives to meet particular standards and targets have been combined with quality control mechanisms. The most significant was the introduction of clinical governance systems (DoH, 1999), which provided accountability through a structured management process with clear lines of responsibility to the chief executive. However, as mechanisms for ensuring cost effective services, both approaches have flaws. There remain difficulties in obtaining accurate and up-to-date information on the relative costs, outputs and outcomes of healthcare interventions. Skilled professional manpower is still in short supply and both historic costs and the legacy of local circumstances and politics may have a negative effect on the local healthcare economy.

The internal market

Since 1997, following an initial period when the importance of the internal market was played down, the NHS has in fact been restructured in a more market-oriented manner. Primary care trusts (PCTs) in England act as commissioning bodies and contract with trusts to provide services. In line with the policy set out in the NHS Plan and subsequent documents, PCTs are to be allocated the majority of the NHS budget. Most recently, a new incentive scheme has been proposed which will link payments to providers on results, thereby rewarding providers who increase output. Eventually it is expected that trusts will be paid on the basis of the volume of work they undertake. The prices they receive will be a fixed tariff based on Healthcare Resource Groups (to reflect the costs of treating patients with similar conditions), adjusted for regional differences in costs (such as higher wage levels in the South East). Although policy is to be introduced gradually, it is nonetheless potentially quite radical as it provides a price mechanism on which commissioners and providers can base contracts.

The Blair government has denied that its approach is akin to that of its Conservative predecessor. Indeed, there are important differences with the internal market of the Conservatives, such as the fixed price tariff for providing particular services. Some believe that this will eliminate a number of the perverse incentives and anticompetitive practices that characterised the internal market of the 1990s. Nevertheless, some providers will be in a better position to benefit from the fixed price regime than others. This could lead to the usual problem of 'cherry picking' by those providers that are able to do so. For example, the new diagnostic and treatment centres (see below), which specialise in carrying out particular procedures, are likely to benefit financially from being able to treat routine, relatively unproblematic and therefore low-cost cases. The losers will probably be the larger high-cost hospitals, whose efficiency will be further undermined as they lose business to their low-cost and nimble competitors.

Foundation trusts

The establishment of foundation trusts can be seen as part of a process of creating a more pluralist supply of health services. Foundation trusts will also enable government to devolve responsibility for service provision down to local level. The ideas behind the policy are derived from two main sources. First, foundation hospitals are a form of public ownership that could strengthen links with the local community; second, a number of countries, notably Spain and some Nordic states, have devolved systems of hospital management. However, the policy has proved controversial and the government has struggled to achieve the majority needed for legislation. Concessions were given, including a promise to review the impact of the initial wave of foundation trusts.

Acute and specialist trusts (but not currently mental health trusts) in England can apply for foundation trust status. Initially the scheme will be open only to the highest-performing trusts (those awarded three stars in the annual performance ratings) but it is expected that all acute and specialist hospitals could become foundation trusts within the next four to five years. A first wave of 25 foundation trusts has been lined up, with a further 32 to follow. Mental health and other organisations may be eligible in the future.

Why has the policy for foundation trusts aroused such controversy?

One of the main concerns is that the additional freedoms promised will place other trusts at a disadvantage. These freedoms include the ability to retain surpluses and sell assets, borrow from the public or private sector and decide how to spend these funds to improve facilities and attract staff. There will also be greater flexibility in deciding on staff pay levels. Thus, it is argued, foundation trusts will have a competitive edge and, as revenues are more closely linked to workload in future, inequities between trusts may increase (see House of Commons Health Select Committee, 2003).

The government has emphasised that foundation trusts remain within the NHS and will not be able to set charges for NHS patients. They will have a duty to cooperate with partner organisations and will have limits on their borrowing powers. A new independent regulator will be created to authorise the framework for each foundation trust, including the range of services to be provided, the level of private practice and which assets will be protected from sale. The standard of care provided will also be subject to regulation by the new Healthcare Commission responsible for audit and inspection, formerly the Commission for Health Improvement.

Foundation trusts will be run as public interest companies limited by guarantee and will be accountable to local communities. Their governance structures will be required to grant membership rights to current service users and carers, local residents and staff. Although the precise details will be determined by the foundation trust itself, these members will elect the majority of a governing body that will also include purchasers. This body will oversee a board of directors responsible for running the trust. In the process of debate on the policy, doubts were expressed on whether residents and patients would join the trust, and that only people already active in local health policy would participate. As a consequence, the legislation allows foundation trusts to introduce schemes so that people opt out of membership rather than opt in. There have been concerns that the governing body is relatively weak: it cannot veto strategy or intervene in day-to-day affairs. There has also been strong criticism of the inconsistencies between the proposed arrangements for the governance structures of foundation trusts and the systems for patient and public involvement described earlier. The government subsequently agreed that all foundation trusts would have a Patient and Public Involvement Forum.

Others have been critical of the additional regulation that foundation status will bring. Recalling the promised freedoms of self-governing trusts in the Conservative reforms of the 1990s, they are cynical about the actual scope for autonomy (Robinson, 2002). Another observer noted that the scheme would result in a "cacophony of accountabilities" (Klein,

2003), with foundation trusts at the junction of conflicting pressures to conform to both national standards and local priorities. Another worry was that foundation trusts would undermine interagency relationships and thereby damage the healthcare system at the local level. Although there must be a local government representative, there is no requirement to include social services in the governance arrangements of foundation trusts. While primary care trusts are represented as purchasers, this is fairly minimal, at least one member of the governing board should be drawn from the local primary care trusts. Considering that as purchasers, primary care trusts hold most of the budget for healthcare, this level of representation may not give them sufficient leverage, particularly as foundation trusts will have legitimacy as mutual organisations. Indeed Walshe, (2003) has argued that foundation trusts may reinforce the dominance of the acute sector, detracting from the primary care focus that has been engineered since the early 1990s. However, given the flexibility built in to the final legislation, it is difficult to predict the impact of foundation hospitals on relationships between primary and secondary care, and several different scenarios have been outlined (Lewis et al, 2003).

The most fundamental problem facing governments concerned with achieving an effective use of NHS resources is the limited competition between suppliers in the local health economy and the shortage of an important ingredient of supply, namely the availability of highly trained health professionals. As part of achieving greater output from the medical professionals working within the NHS, health ministers in the second Blair administration have attempted to renegotiate the contracts of both GPs and consultants to ensure greater commitment to NHS work (Smith, 2003). Although achieved by the end of 2003, this was a long and arduous process and may create barriers to the flexible use of resources.

Increasing the supply of services

Using a number of strategies, the Blair government has attempted to establish a more pluralist supply system. One of these, already mentioned, is paying for NHS patients to be treated in centres in continental Europe. Another is the use of private hospitals in the UK independent sector. After initially distancing itself from the sector – there is no reference in the 1997 White Paper, *The new NHS: Modern, dependable* (DoH, 1997) – the government began to make overtures. This culminated in the concordat between the Department of Health and the independent sector signalling a commitment to using independent provision to meet the needs of NHS patients. The subsequent development of independent diagnostic and treatment centres took this a stage further. These will offer significant opportunities for the independent sector to provide healthcare in areas of routine operations such as hip replacements, cataracts and some cardiac surgery and may, as noted earlier, affect the viability of some NHS providers. It is envisaged that some providers may come from Europe and operate in the South East where there is a shortage of facilities. Other developments that have supported an extended role for the independent sector include franchising, where the management of an NHS body can be taken over by a new management team, including independent sector managers, and the use of private nursing homes for intermediate care, and of course public–private funding partnerships (see Robinson and Dixon, 2002).

In summary, supply side changes have increased the diversity of providers of NHS services. Responsibilities for making decisions on priorities have been developed to the local level. Both these measures have raised concerns about the consequences for equity. As indeed have the measures for increasing choice of patients. Will variety and diversity lead to differences in the quality of healthcare in different parts of the country, reinforcing the historically determined inverse care law so that poorer communities with poorer health have poorer facilities? (Appleby et al, 2003). For example, one consequence of dedicated diagnosis and treatment centres is that they could cherry pick simpler and more straightforward cases, leaving the more complex and costly ones to NHS trusts. Also, extending choices about where to be treated may disadvantage elderly people and those without resources who will have to travel further to the new diagnostic and treatment centres. Research on the effect of internal markets summarised by Le Grand et al (1998) showed that there is no clear evidence that efficiency and quality are improved by competition. Indeed, Lewis and Gillam (2003) argue that additional capacity and the costs of competition will undermine efficiency as they do in all market systems.

Central initiatives in standard setting, monitoring and regulation

Another strategy adopted by the Blair government has been to set national standards and to strengthen systems for monitoring and regulation. As noted, new national targets were set and the performance management system in England modified with the introduction of the star rating system. The aim was to provide incentives for high-quality performance, while naming and shaming poor performers. It is now acknowledged that the system has produced incentives to massage figures and manipulate data (see Audit Commission, 2003; Goddard et al, 2000). The system also offered scope for political manipulation, although an attempt was made to dispel these allegations by transferring responsibility for performance assessment and star ratings to the new Healthcare Commission – the successor body to the Commission for Health Improvement, established during Labour's first term. From 2004 it will audit, inspect and regulate healthcare in the NHS as well as having additional responsibility for regulating private healthcare. It will have responsibilities for overseeing the advanced stages of the NHS complaint system, will take over some of the value for money functions of the Audit Commission, and will take over certain responsibilities from the Mental Health Act Commission. It will also be expected to work with the Modernisation Agency – which seeks to promote service improvements across the NHS.

Alongside the performance management system, national clinical standards have been introduced in the form of national service frameworks (NSFs). These set out service standards for a particular condition or client group. In England, NSFs have been introduced for mental health, coronary heart disease, older people and diabetes. An NSF for children's services is being developed. There is also a national cancer plan and national standards for paediatric intensive care. Each NSF details national standards along with key interventions, targets and plans for implementation. These are developed by expert groups, including patient and carer representatives. Primary care and other trusts are expected to implement NSFs, which are used as benchmarks for assessing the quality of care provided. In general, NSFs have been positively received. However, there is concern that they may not be implemented uniformly across the NHS and may disadvantage condition fields, such as asthma, for example, not designated for an NSF.

Another attempt to strengthen national standards of treatment was the creation of the National Institute for Clinical Excellence (NICE), in Labour's first term. NICE is responsible for appraising and producing guidance on the cost effectiveness of new and existing technologies in England and Wales. Seen as an international leader in disseminating evidence-based practice in a recent WHO report (Devlin et al, 2003), NICE also recommends clinical guidelines for practice and assesses audit methods, thus providing for dissemination to trusts. Initially criticised for being dominated by commercial interests, NICE has paid increasing attention to listening to the views of user groups, and methodologies are being developed to provide evidence from patients and to strengthen the voice of user representatives (Herxheimer and Ziebland, 2003). NICE guidance is now mandatory, though it does not itself make decisions about which treatments should be funded.

Government has also been active in seeking to expand the supply of practitioners and in reshaping the regulatory framework within which they operate. The UK lags behind other comparable countries in the ratio of trained professionals to population and the NHS Plan suggested that large increases in the medical and nursing workforce are required. Although student places have been expanded, health professionals take many years to produce and, in the meantime, problems are being exacerbated by low morale and early retirement. Supply side shortages have political as well as economic repercussions and help to explain government strategy to expand sources of supply through seeking European and overseas providers, and the recent agreements reached with general practitioners and consultants providing generous rewards for full-time NHS practice. Changes are also being made in the division of tasks in healthcare so that the boundaries between what different professions do for patients are no longer impermeable. For example, the role of some nurses has expanded to include the right to prescribe, to share responsibility for care. Furthermore, many professionals now oversee the work of a range of health assistants of various kinds.

These changes go alongside a much stricter regulation of professional practice. Modernisation in this context has brought a shift from a system of self-regulation to partnership regulation. The councils that register professionals have reduced in size to carry out a more strategic role and their lay membership has increased. In 2002 a new body, the Council for the Regulation of Health Professionals, was established with a remit to protect the public. It will conduct annual reviews of each professional council and report to Parliament. The professional councils themselves are extending their remit, with more emphasis on ensuring that the professionals they register remain competent and up to date in their practice throughout their active careers. Many are developing systems for regular revalidation.

Triggered by findings of the Bristol Inquiry and other investigations into poorly performing doctors, the system of 'self-regulation' through registration and assuring the fitness to practice of health professionals has been supplemented by the creation of a range of other bodies. As well as the Health Service Commissioner, who investigates certain complaints from the public about the healthcare they have received, other recently established bodies include the National Patient Safety Agency, which monitors and analyses adverse events in order to learn from mistakes, and the National Clinical Assessment Authority. This helps hospitals and primary care trusts to deal with doctors with performance problems by helping them improve procedures. In addition, as noted above, the role of CHAI has expanded.

The creation of this plethora of bodies has been motivated by a concern for patient safety. Previously, procedures often were geared to protecting professional autonomy and inhibited managers and others from dealing with poor practice. Concerns about mounting negligence claims and the human and financial costs of errors and adverse events have also assumed greater importance. Detractors have argued that the various bodies have roles that overlap and conflict and in the case of CHAI, developmental objectives may conflict with those related to protecting the public from poor practice. Supporters comment that each body has a different role and, for the first time, informal linkages provide a network of communication that may prevent harm to patients (see Walshe, 2003).

Conclusion

The period covered by this review has, unlike the previous decade, seen additional resources channelled into the NHS. There has also been intense policy activity on the demand and supply sides. Policies have aimed to respond to, and harness, the expectations of healthcare users. Although the NHS remains free at the point of use, speedy access and a service geared to recognising individual needs and preferences have been emphasised. After years of paternalist practice, and stoicism by members of the public in the face of lengthy waiting times for treatment, a more active consumerism may have an impact on service providers; this has been aided by the activities of health consumer groups, which have been extensively involved in the policy process. Whether this will lead to greater inequalities in service use and whether those who use health services will also wish to act as volunteers on patient and public involvement forums is, as yet, not known.

Most policy activity has focused on the supply side of health care, using a variety of carrots and sticks to improve performance. In England, the internal market has edged towards the health maintenance organisation model with funds allocated to the populations within primary care trusts; purchasing is on the basis of diagnostic groups so that costs can be compared between providers. In England also, a plurality of public and private sector providers has been seen as a way of overcoming manpower shortages, using existing facilities and increasing competition through the development of specialist units. Again, whether shorter waiting times and faster and lower cost throughput will be achieved at the expense of equity is not known. But this is not new: inequalities in the distribution of healthcare has been a persistent problem.

It is worth pointing out that the English reforms are in marked contrast to what is happening in Wales and Scotland, where there has been a move towards more integrated healthcare systems. Indeed, trusts are to be abolished in Scotland. Quality and performance management systems have also developed differently in other parts of the UK, and there are different structures of patient and public involvement (for example, CHCs survived in Wales). Differences in entitlements have also emerged between the various parts of the UK, notably with regard to long-term personal care for the elderly and eligibility for free eye and dental checks. It is possible that these variations will be seen as an appropriate means of accommodating the diverse politics and economics across the different UK nations. On the other hand, they may create countervailing pressures for uniformity, as citizens in some parts of the UK seek parity with others.

The final theme in this paper has been the modernisation of long-standing NHS practices through forms of regulation that have made certain areas of activity more transparent, in an attempt to strengthen accountability. Clinical activity, the outcomes of clinical interventions, clinical decision making, the processes of professional regulation and the way trusts and hospitals are governed have all become more open to scrutiny. The fact that this has been costly and, on occasions, has led to manipulation and the massaging of figures, does not detract from the general advantages of a more open form of health service governance. As a consequence of these measures, the politics of healthcare has shifted, with greater potential for user influence within the cloak of state control through funding and regulation.

References

Allsop, J. and Mulcahy, L. (2001) 'Dealing with clinical complaints', in C. Vincent, (ed) *Clinical risk management: Enhancing patient safety* (2nd edn), London: BMJ Books, pp 497-518.

Appleby, J. and Coote, A. (2002) *Five year health check: A review of government health policy 1997-2002*, London: King's Fund.

Appleby, J., Harrison, A. and Devlin, N. (2003) *What is the real cost of more patient choice?*, London: King's Fund.

Audit Commission (2003) *Achieving the NHS Plan*, London: Audit Commission.

Baggott, R. (2004) *Health and health care in Britain* (3rd edn), Basingstoke: Palgrave.

Baggott, R., Allsop, J. and Jones, K. (2004) *Speaking for patients and carers: Health consumer groups and the policy process*, Basingstoke: Palgrave.

Bristol Royal Infirmary Inquiry (2001) *The inquiry into the management of care of children receiving complex heart surgery at the Bristol Royal Infirmary – Final report* (The Kennedy Report), London: The Stationery Office.

Carvel, J. (2003) 'Quick fix: interview with Harry Cayton', *Society Guardian*, 10 December, p 6.

de Lusignan, S. (2003) 'The national health service and the internet', *Journal of the Royal Society of Medicine*, vol 96, pp 490-92.

Devlin, N., Parkin, D. and Gold, M. (2003) 'WHO evaluates NICE', *British Medical Journal*, vol 326, pp 777-78.

DoH (Department of Health) (1991) *The Patients' Charter*, London: DoH.

DoH (1993) *Changing childbirth*, London: The Stationery Office.

DoH (1997) *The new NHS: Modern, dependable*, Cm 3807, London: The Stationery Office.

DoH (1999) *Clinical governance: Quality in the new NHS*, London: DoH.

DoH (2000) *The NHS Plan: A plan for investment, a plan for reform*, Cm 4818, London: The Stationery Office.

DoH (2001) *The expert patient: A new approach to chronic disease management for the 21st century*, London: DoH.

DoH (2003) *Building on the best: Choice, responsiveness and equity in the NHS*, Cm 6079, London: The Stationery Office.

DoH (2004) *Consultation draft: The NHS: (complaints) regulations* (available at www.doh.gov.uk/makingthingsright).

Goddard, M., Mannion, R. and Smith, P. (2000) 'The performance framework: taking account of economic behaviour', in P.C. Smith (ed) *Reforming markets in health care*, Buckingham: Open University Press, pp 139-61.

Herxheimer, A. and Ziebland, S. (2003) 'DIPEx: fresh insights for medical practice', *Journal of the Royal Society of Medicine*, vol 96, no 5, pp 209-10.

House of Commons' Health Select Committee (2003) (HC 395-I) *2nd report 2002/03, Foundation Trusts*, London: The Stationery Office.

Jacobson, B., Mindell, J. and McKee, M. (2003) 'Hospital mortality league tables', *British Medical Journal*, vol 326, pp 777-78.

Kendall, L. (2001) *The future patient*, London: IPPR.

Klein, R. (2003) 'Governance for NHS Foundation Trusts', *British Medical Journal*, vol 326, pp 174-75.

Le Grand, J., Mays, N. and Mulligan, J. (1998) *Learning from the NHS internal market: A review of evidence*, London: King's Fund.

Lewis, R., Dixon, J. and Gillam, S. (2003) 'Outside choice', *Health Service Journal*, 8 May, pp 24-6.

Lewis, R. and Gillam, S. (2003) 'Back to the market', *International Journal of Health Services*, vol 33, no 1, pp 77-84.

OECD (Organisation for Economic Co-operation and Development) (2003) *OECD health data* (3rd edn), Paris: OECD.

Parry, G.J., Gowd, C.R., McCabe, C.J. and Tarnow-Mordi, W.O. (1998) 'Annual league tables of mortality in neonatal intensive care units: longitudinal study', *British Medical Journal*, vol 316, pp 1931-35.

Robinson, R. (2002) 'NHS foundation trusts', *British Medical Journal*, vol 325, pp 506-07.

Robinson, R. and Dixon, A. (2002) *Completing the course: Health to 2010*, London: Fabian Society.

Smith, R. (2003) 'The failure of two contracts', *British Medical Journal*, vol 326, pp 1097-98.

Tew, M. (1998) *Safer childbirth: A critical history of maternity* (3rd edn), London: Free Association Books.

Walshe, K. (2003) *Regulating healthcare*, Maidenhead: Open University Press.

Wanless, D. (2002) *Securing our future health: Taking a long term view: Final report*, London: HM Treasury.

THREE

Developments in social security

Fran Bennett

Introduction

The editor of a recent book described the debates that the various authors had had about the title, which was *Understanding social security* (Millar, 2003). They had discussed the fact that there was no longer any government department with the name 'social security', and that tax credits had now taken over the functions of various benefits. There was perhaps an argument for abandoning the phrase altogether. However, they persevered with it because they thought that:

> ... the phrase 'social security' does capture other important things, apart from institutional arrangements. The word 'social' indicates that this is a shared system. We are all part of it ... and social security provisions involve various forms of redistribution that are an expression of our values.... The word 'security' highlights one of the key goals, which is to ensure that people are not simply at the mercy of the market, but can meet needs now and plan for the future. (Millar, 2003, p 7)

It is important to continue to use the phrase 'social security' for precisely these reasons. In this chapter, 'social security' is understood in a broad sense to include tax credits and some payments made by employers for social protection purposes (such as maternity pay). The chapter discusses developments in social security during 2003. (For a list of social security reforms from 1997 to 2002, see Brewer et al, 2002.) It describes major reforms under the headings of: new tax credits and the national minimum wage; children and family; pensioners; welfare to work; and housing benefit and administration; and then draws conclusions.

New tax credits and the national minimum wage

The most significant development of 2003 in social security was the introduction from April of 'new tax credits' – working tax credit, child tax credit and childcare tax credit. The vast majority of families with children on income support or income-based jobseeker's allowance will not be transferred to child tax credit until 2004; but their levels of benefit were increased from April to reflect the new, higher tax credit rates.

These new tax credits are the culmination of several years' planning. Commentators may joke about the bewildering speed of recent changes in acronyms. But the government's rejoinder is that when it first came into office the mechanisms did not exist for its preferred system to be implemented; so it had to make interim arrangements. In particular – albeit after a year's gap – children's tax credit replaced the married couple's allowance (and the additional personal allowance for lone parents) in the income tax system. Children's tax credit was a payment for a child/ children, which was withdrawable from couples in which either partner paid higher-rate tax. But it was in place for only a short time before being replaced by child tax credit. The replacement for the in-work benefit family credit – working families' tax credit – also had only a short life.

New tax credits introduce a new concept into financial support for people on low incomes (Whiteford et al, 2003). This involves calculating income over a year, rather than taking a snapshot of resources and either leaving the level of benefit/tax credit the same for a fixed period (as with working families' tax credit) or requiring immediate reporting of changes and consequent adjustments (income support). This alignment of the treatment of income in tax credits and income tax may sound uncontroversial. But research shows that low-income families often budget on a weekly basis and may also have complex finances (Kempson, 1996). Moreover, their family status may change more often than for those on higher incomes (Marsh and Perry, 2003). This new idea has therefore caused some difficulty. Despite this structural change, however, the new tax credits are probably still most accurately described as jointly assessed means-tested benefits. In addition, for international comparisons, part of the expenditure on tax credits must be treated in a similar way to benefits, rather than as foregone revenue, in the national accounts.

Another innovation of new tax credits is that for couples they are jointly owned. With working families' tax credit, couples chose which partner claimed and the credit was then theirs (and was paid to the claimant, either in the wage packet or as a benefit). But new tax credits resemble more closely the new 'joint claims' for income-based jobseeker's allowance. The change to joint claims belies the government's attempts to link tax credits to income tax, and wages, which are both based on the individual. The ill-fated community charge (poll tax) did introduce the idea of 'joint and several liability'; but the concept of joint ownership is relatively untested, and its implementation will need to be closely monitored.

Child tax credit and baby tax credit

The child tax credit rolls up all the means-tested allowances for children, and children's tax credit, into one payment. The government sees it as epitomising 'progressive universalism': "support for all, and more help for those who need it most, when they need it most" (HM Treasury, 2003, para 5.1; see also Brewer et al, 2002). Child tax credit has generally been welcomed as a rationalisation of existing means-tested help for children. It also extends support to some groups (such as students) for the first time. The government claims that child tax credit 'builds upon' child benefit. But in fact child benefit remains completely separate and is ignored in tax credit calculations; and there is some concern about its longer-term future. Child tax credit is made up of two elements – per family and per child payments. Families on anything above a low or modest income only qualify for the per family payment. For them, this is essentially a flat-rate payment, which begins to be withdrawn once joint income reaches £50,000 per year or so. It is mirrored in the additional 'baby tax credit', available for the first year of a child's life.

Child tax credit is paid to the main carer, rather than through the pay packet, reflecting the growing understanding that money via the 'purse' rather than the 'wallet' is more likely to be spent on children's needs (Goode et al, 1998). The couple decides who is the main carer. The government describes this as a transfer of over £2 billion from men to women (DWP, 2003a; HM Treasury, 2003). The most significant transfer occurs in April 2004, when most families on income support and income-based jobseeker's allowance enter the new system. The picture in April, 2003 is more mixed and, for those previously on working families' tax credit, depends on which partner was the claimant (Bennett, 2002a). The per child element of the child tax credit will be increased annually at least in line with earnings for the rest of this parliament; but no such guarantee has been given for the per family payment – or for child benefit.

Working tax credit

For families with children, working tax credit replaces the adult elements of working families' tax credit. But it is simultaneously being extended to some able-bodied childless single people and couples on low incomes, giving them an in-work supplement for the first time. The potential new client group is fairly narrow, however, because of the restrictions of age (25 or over) and working hours (30 per week or more). For employees, working tax credit is for the moment paid via the wage packet. It includes additional elements for disabled people and some over-50s, replacing provisions in the previous tax credits system.

The reception given to working tax credit has been more ambivalent. Although the government was concerned that some childless people were not much better off in work than out (HM Treasury, 2000), some commentators were not convinced of the case for extending means-tested in-work support to childless able-bodied people to tackle either disincentive problems or poverty. There is more public support for in-work additions for those with children than for those without (Hills and Lelkes, 2000). Some saw such in-work supplements (especially for couples) as a substitute for shortcomings and gaps elsewhere in the social protection system – if working tax credit was the answer, it was not clear that the right question had been asked. There was also concern about the possibility of exacerbating the more unattractive features of the UK's 'flexible' labour market, by underpinning low pay and discouraging investment in human capital, and about addressing symptoms rather than root causes of labour market disadvantage (Bennett and Hirsch, 2001).

Anecdotal evidence suggests that take-up of working tax credit among newly eligible childless claimants may be low; if so it would mirror experience with earnings top-up, the experimental benefit for childless people with low incomes in work introduced by the Conservatives. The government has been more vocal about the high volume of child tax credit claims. It argues that routing support through the income tax rather than the benefits system removes stigma. However, paying child tax credit to the main carer makes it less likely to be associated with the tax system.

Childcare tax credit

Childcare tax credit replaces the previous tax credit with the same name, paid as an addition to working families' tax credit. Eligibility for working tax credit is necessary to trigger it; but it will be paid to the main carer alongside child tax credit. More families should become eligible, because of the increased generosity of working tax credit. The government has already had to propose new ways of calculating childcare costs, as parents have found assessing them over the long term too complicated.

New tax credits: shared issues

The major issue arising from new tax credits, however, has not been a policy question but the administrative debacle of their introduction (Treasury Select Committee, 2003). The government admitted that around 800,000 families had not received child tax credit on time, despite claiming it (*Hansard*, 2003a). Many low-income families received nothing for weeks, whereas others received wildly varying monthly amounts, with little explanation. The computer system has been blamed but the government decided to plough on with new tax credits on time rather than postpone their implementation, as it did with the child support reforms (see below).

There will be argument over whether the administrative problems could have been foreseen. Means-testing the per family payment for better-off families – thereby including huge numbers in a complex new assessment procedure for the sake of excluding only one in 10 families – may have been a very costly decision.

Administrative issues are likely to continue to be significant. Apart from the end-of-year reconciliation in summer 2004, with subsequent adjustments for overpayments, there is also the immediate impact of changes of circumstances on entitlement. If a family unit changes – from single person to couple, or vice versa – a new claim is triggered. Thus the initial award of tax credit for a new partnership in 2003-04 will depend on what income each partner had in 2001-02 – perhaps long before they met. The possible permutations become somewhat surreal. Last, although the government claims that new tax credits represent 'light touch' means-testing, the administrative burden – or 'costs of compliance' in business-speak – on claimants may depend more on anti-fraud activity than on day-to-day administration. Figures given in the 2002 Budget showed that the numbers subject to marginal 'tax rates' of over 60% would increase by about half between 2002-03 and 2003-04. The government rightly notes that these figures are somewhat artificial, because under new tax credits increases up to £2,500 per year are ignored, meaning that few people experience a 'poverty trap' like this in reality; indeed incentives should improve for some second earners. However, the scope for resentment at such a high 'tax' rate on moderate incomes is significant.

The government has stated that its longer-term aim is integration of the (income) tax and benefits systems. Integration has previously been advocated by many new ministers and policy advisors – who only realise once they have explored it in more detail that it is neither feasible nor desirable (Clinton et al, 1994). However, there seems to be more coherence and energy behind the idea under this government – and perhaps greater knowledge of the difficulties as well. One objection to what is, in effect, a negative income tax has been that people who pay income tax and those who receive benefits do not overlap much, though the extension of child tax credit up the income scale has now changed that somewhat. Another is that true integration would mean means-testing all benefits, and assessing them on a family basis rather than individually.

National minimum wage

In March 2003, after a review by the Low Pay Commission, the government announced that national minimum wage rates would increase from October. The amounts are quite generous, and the Low Pay Commission has also recommended relatively generous increases for 2004. However, these upratings may only restore the position the government wanted to see when it introduced the national minimum wage. Instead, faulty official data on low pay meant that the minimum wage affected far fewer people than intended (Metcalf, 2002; Dickens and Manning, 2003).

Children and family

New maternity, paternity and parental rights

Some of the most significant changes for children and families in 2003 included the introduction of the new tax credits (see above). But in April the new rights for parents also took effect. For the first time ever fathers became entitled to paid paternity leave – albeit for only two weeks and at a flat rate of £100 per week (the same as the newly increased flat rate of statutory maternity pay and maternity allowance). Women could have six months' paid maternity leave, followed by six months' unpaid leave if desired. A recent review of 22 countries showed that even by July 2001 the UK had improved its relative position in terms of financial support for childbirth, children and parenting (Bradshaw and Finch, 2002). But the long period of unpaid maternity leave introduced this year takes the UK in a different direction from most other industrialised countries, which have focused more on improvements in parental leave.

April also saw the introduction of a right to ask for flexible working hours. This applies to all parents of children under six (or under 18 if disabled), though it is expected to be taken up largely by mothers returning after maternity leave. The employer is obliged to consider the request seriously but does not have a legal obligation to grant it. The government is concerned to try to combat the tendency of working mothers to move to lower-paid jobs just because these offer flexible hours which fit better with their daily schedules. In future, this may lead to more moves to lengthen maternity leave and/or improve parental leave.

The government is going to monitor the impact of these new provisions for three years before introducing any major new provisions. However, it did publish a consultation document suggesting further modifications to promote 'family-friendly' working (HM Treasury and DTI, 2003), and is pursuing some of these.

Child support

The former child support scheme provided a good example of the difficulties of legislating for conditionality and compulsion in tangled areas of human behaviour. Despite the penalty of a benefit cut attached to non-compliance without a good reason, "70 per cent of lone parents on income support were seeking to avoid a child maintenance application" (according to the Parliamentary Under-Secretary of State for Work and Pensions, in *Hansard*, 2003b, col 90WH). After lengthy delays, due to problems with the computer system, the new child support scheme was introduced gradually from March 2003. This consists of a much simplified formula under which the non-resident parent will pay 15% of their income for one child, 20% for two and 25% for three or more; those on low incomes pay a reduced rate and those on benefits with net incomes of under £100 per week pay £5 per week. There is some recognition of second families, though some non-resident parents will get higher assessments (Ridge, 2003). There have been complaints about the initial restriction of the new formula to new cases only, especially since this also applies to the £10 per week disregard of child support for claimants of income support and income-based Jobseeker's allowance (*Hansard*, 2003b, col 85WH).

The new scheme will result in lower average awards for parents with care, because of the new percentage-based formula; but they may well find themselves better off in practice nonetheless, largely due to the new disregard. As with working families' tax credit those on working tax credit will have all their child support disregarded.

51

Child support is increasingly now referred to as 'child maintenance' – as in 'child maintenance premium', to refer to the £10 disregard – while 'child support' seems to be used increasingly to mean the whole gamut of financial support for children. This is a return to previous well-worn vocabulary and is to be welcomed. There is still no 'guaranteed maintenance' scheme in the UK, as exists in some other countries, however. And the argument is still often made that "injecting the CSA [Child Support Agency] into people's lives makes their relationship with their former partners, and sometimes their children, very difficult" (Robert Syms MP, in *Hansard*, 2003b, col 73WH). On the other hand the advantages gained by lone parents who do receive maintenance may be a factor in persuading the government to reassess (again) the balance of financial support for lone- versus two-parent families.

Child poverty and childcare reviews

Several initiatives proposed in 2003 will only bear fruit in years to come. The reviews of child poverty and childcare, announced as part of the new public spending round, suggest that the government is fully aware of the need to make faster progress to achieve its own objectives on child poverty and child development. It has made clear that its child poverty review covers a much broader range of issues than income (HM Treasury, 2003). A review of financial provision for young people was also set up.

Cynics may argue that the most important change in the government's approach to child poverty over the medium and longer term is its choice of measure (DWP, 2003b). While this is not a social security issue, the measure chosen in 2003 may be relevant to future policy choices. The government would claim that it had never specified one measure to judge longer-term success and would point to the many indicators in the annual *Opportunity for all* reports (DWP, 2003a); but most commentators had probably assumed that it would use the most common yardstick – numbers in households on under 60% of median income before and after housing costs (measured on a relative basis). Certainly this was how the public service agreement to reduce child poverty by a quarter between 1998-99 and 2004-05 was to be judged (Sutherland et al, 2003).

We now know what that longer-term measure will be (DWP, 2003c). It is in fact three measures: 'absolute' low income (a poverty line uprated only with prices); relative low income; and material deprivation and relative low income combined. All these measures of low income will be on a 'before housing costs' basis, which is the preferred cross-European measure but which may not make realistic assessments of the impact of housing costs on living standards. They will use a new equivalence scale, which gives a more realistic weight to younger children. Child poverty will be seen as falling when all three indicators are moving in the right direction, according to the government. 'Eradication' will mean that no children suffer material deprivation and that the UK is among 'the best in Europe' on relative low income; but material deprivation has not yet been fully defined.

Child trust fund

The long-awaited detailed proposals for the child trust fund, or 'baby bond', were also announced in October, but only take effect in 2005 (HM Treasury and Inland Revenue, 2003). For every child born from September 2002 onwards the government will give a £250 payment at birth, to be invested with a private sector provider until the child is aged 18; but in another example of 'progressive universalism', children in low-income families under the child tax credit threshold will receive an additional £250. A further (as yet unspecified) payment along the same lines will be made at age seven. In addition, parents and other relatives and friends can make extra payments. The charge that can be applied to the accounts will be limited. Accounts will be opened for those who do not open them themselves.

The laudable idea is to try to tackle the asset inequality with which different young people start their adult life. The government argues that the child trust fund promotes 'security, opportunity and responsibility', and that among other advantages it will "encourage parents and children to develop the savings habit and engage with financial institutions" (HM Treasury and Inland Revenue, 2003, p 1). The government's initial idea of limiting what 18-year-olds could spend the money on proved to be impracticable, so it is not clear that everyone will use it to improve their financial or human capital. However, financial education is part of the package; children will "interact with their own savings or investment vehicle", and the government valiantly hopes that they will "make the best use of the assets" (HM Treasury and Inland Revenue, 2003, p 3).

Press comment suggested that if the fund remains at the level donated by the government it will be highly unlikely to turn into a substantial nest egg at age 18; and that the donations allowed from family and friends (albeit limited to an annual maximum of £1,200) threaten to exacerbate rather than reduce inequality. Civil servants have also suggested that it could be counted against income-based jobseeker's allowance for young unemployed claimants from age 18.

Areas of concern

While this review covers policy initiatives rather than new analysis, it is worth noting that the government appears to be increasingly concerned about the position of various groups, one of which is large families (with some overlap with minority ethnic families) (Willitts and Swales, 2003). This analysis has implications for social security benefits and tax credits, as it identifies a trend – also highlighted by a recent review of financial support for families with children since 1975 (Adam and Brewer, 2004) – towards increased relative support for small families. The political benefits of such a strategy are obvious in theory: if it increases the 'per family' rather than 'per child' payment, a government can announce that all families are benefiting from increased financial support. But this may betray some confusion between the direct and indirect costs of children (Bennett, 2002b), and may lead to less than optimal patterns of support.

Pensioners

Pension credit

October 2003 saw the introduction of the pension credit. This has had a rather odd history. Billed initially, as its name suggests, as one of the new generation of tax credits, it transmuted into another means-tested benefit, subsuming the minimum income guarantee for pensioners and adding an additional tranche of benefit to help those with savings or a small occupational or private pension. It will also be 'light touch', as with new tax credits; indeed, because pensioners' incomes are relatively stable, the government has reduced the need to report certain changes in income during a five-year 'assessed income period'. But to all intents and purposes pension credit is a benefit, and it is not being administered by the Inland Revenue.

Despite the Chancellor's former statement about wanting the next Labour government to achieve "the end of the means test for our elderly people" (Brown, 1993), the introduction of the pension credit was perhaps an inevitable outcome of the government's increased emphasis on market provision and means testing, combined with its concern about disincentives to saving. It now forms part of an increasingly complex panoply of pension provisions. Along with the state second pension, the pension credit is billed as particularly helpful to women, who often have only minimal savings over and above their basic pension. Almost half the pensioner population will be on means-tested benefits as a result of its introduction – thereby doubling entitlement – which some commentators suggest will in itself increase take-up (Agulnik, 2003). The government is concerned about take-up. It has reason to be. Take-up of minimum income guarantee, pension credit's predecessor, was only some 68-76% by caseload in 2000/01 (ONS/DWP, 2003). The National Audit Office report on take-up of minimum income 'guarantee' cited research suggesting that about a quarter of pensioner non-claimants would be 'highly resistant' to being encouraged to claim (NAO, 2002). The new Pension Service is more proactive, and is organised largely in call centres, though there is also a local presence; the government says that pension credit can be claimed with one phone call and has set a take-up target.

Welfare to work

Incapacity benefits

As with other claimants, much of the policy activity around disabled/ incapacitated people on benefits has been about paid employment. The new working tax credit from April incorporates additional payments for disability, subsuming the disabled person's tax credit from the previous tax credits system, with the aim of including disabled people in the same system as others. From mid-2003, a computerised form of medical assessment for incapacity benefits has been trialled (Patterson, 2003). Although the New Deal for Disabled People has helped some people into employment via job brokers, the original programme target of 90,000 job entries over three years may be difficult to achieve (Stafford, 2003). The Work and Pensions Select Committee considers the funding inadequate and the strategy too fragmented. More generally, it also criticises the traditional 'binary split' between capacity and incapacity to work (Work and Pensions Select Committee, 2003).

The government had published its proposals to help people on incapacity benefits back into work in 2002, noting that the numbers on incapacity benefits exceeded the combined total of lone parents and unemployed people on benefit. Its proposals included support to help people remain work focused in the initial period of incapacity; provision to help address barriers to employment; and better financial incentives. The plan was to pilot this approach in late 2003 in six areas (DWP, 2002a); but in mid-2003 an extension of the pilots was announced (CPAG, 2003b). There are also measures to try to promote job retention among this group.

Most commentators agree that those on incapacity benefits have been left behind in the welfare to work programmes so far, despite the New Deal for Disabled People, and that further initiatives are needed. Some non-social security measures may help – including the new Disability Discrimination Act provisions. But Berthoud suggests that greater differentiation is required, both in our statistics and in our thinking about welfare to work measures, between different disabled people (Berthoud, 2003); and Stafford also argues that a more 'individualised' approach would be more successful (Stafford, 2003).

Lone parents

The government announced that under eight pilot schemes starting in October 2004 lone parents would get a £40 per week bonus for a year when they got a job, and £20 extra per week for up to a year while they were actively looking for one. In addition, the housing benefit disregard would be extended to lone parents working 16 hours a week or more (instead of 30), and other 'welfare to work' measures were announced (HM Treasury, 2003). These measures are likely to have been devised by the government to help it achieve its target of 70% employment for lone parents by 2010.

Housing benefit

A major feature of government strategy on housing benefit so far seems to have been to float as many people off it as possible, through tax credits in particular. This process will have continued with the increased generosity of the new tax credits. Another plank of the government's strategy is the introduction of a flat-rate standard housing allowance, varying only by family size, in the deregulated private sector (DWP, 2002b). Following improvements in administration and social rent restructuring this is intended to be the next stage in reform. The new scheme was piloted in 'pathfinder' areas in 2003-04. Claimants whose rent is lower than the allowance can keep the remainder of the money; but they will have to find the difference if the allowance is too low. Another significant change is that for most tenants in the pilot schemes housing benefit will be paid to them rather than their landlords.

Originally the government argued in its 2002 document on housing benefit that with greater choice, greater responsibility would be expected of tenants. Therefore, following a proposal from former welfare reform minister Frank Field MP, the government began consulting in May on proposals to cut the housing benefit of tenants held to be guilty of repeated incidents of antisocial behaviour. But the Queen's Speech on 26 November 2003 contained no mention of this idea. Doubts within and outside government about the fairness and practicality of such a proposal may have led to its abandonment.

Administration

In addition to the administrative chaos of the introduction of new tax credits and the slow take-on of new child support cases using the new computer system, the government has been engaged in another administrative upheaval in the benefits area. However, its avowed intent is to improve procedures in the future. May saw the beginning of a longer-term process in which most benefit claimants are to have their benefits paid direct into bank accounts, rather than by giro or order book. This is meant to be more secure for claimants and cheaper for the government. The original idea was that there would be a 'universal banking service'; but private sector reluctance led to an alternative, of basic bank accounts from private providers supplemented by post office accounts. One embarrassing discovery was that some disabled people were unable to use the 'pin pads' provided in post offices for account-holders and the government had to consult with disability organisations to improve them.

Another administrative change is to make even some of those benefits remaining in the traditional means-tested system 'light touch'. Benefit periods are being abolished for housing benefit and council tax benefit (so that awards may be indefinite, subject to occasional review or major changes of circumstances, rather than benefit having to be claimed annually) – for the 60-plus from 2003, and for those of working age from 2004. From April 2003 a combined claim form tries to ensure that local authorities do not have to go back to claimants to get additional information once someone has claimed a means-tested benefit from central government.

Conclusion

Apart from an announcement about a Bill to introduce the child trust fund, the Queen's Speech on 26 November contained very little about social security. This is not surprising, for two reasons. First, the volume of change in 2003 suggests that a consolidation period is now due. Second, many changes to social security do not require primary legislation but consist largely of incremental changes to regulations and/or administration. In addition, however, political and policy minds are now turning to preparing party manifestos. On 28 November, Labour launched its 'big conversation' with the nation. Any more fundamental reforms to social security provision are now likely to follow the next general election. The 'benefits simplification' project currently under way suggests that change will continue.

References

Adam, S. and Brewer, M. (2004) *Supporting families: The financial costs and benefits of children since 1975*, Bristol/York: The Policy Press/Joseph Rowntree Foundation.

Agulnik, P. (2003) 'The pension service: delivering benefits to older people?', *Benefits 37*, vol 11, issue 2, p 103.

Bennett, F. (2002a) 'Gender implications of current social security reforms', *Fiscal Studies*, vol 23, no 4, pp 559-84.

Bennett, F. (2002b) 'Giving all children a good start: financial provision in pregnancy and the first year of life' (www.ippr.org.uk).

Bennett, F. and Hirsch, D. (2001) *The employment tax credit and issues for the future of in-work support*, York: Joseph Rowntree Foundation.

Berthoud, R. (2003) 'Disabled people and jobs', *Benefits* 38, vol 11, issue 3, pp 169-74.

Bradshaw, J. and Finch, N. (2002) *A comparison of child benefit packages in 22 countries*, DWP Research Report 174, Leeds: Corporate Document Services.

Brewer, M., Clark, T. and Wakefield, M. (2002) 'Social security in the UK under new Labour: what did the third way mean for welfare reform?', *Fiscal Studies*, vol 23, no 4, pp 505-37.

Brown, G. (September 1993) Speech to Labour Party conference.

Clinton, D., Yates, M. and Kang, D. (1994) *Integrating taxes and benefits?*, London: Institute for Public Policy Research (for Commission on Social Justice).

CPAG (Child Poverty Action Group) (2003a) *Campaigns newsletter*, issue no 28, October.

CPAG (2003b) *Poverty* 116, Autumn, p 4.

Dickens, R. and Manning, A. (2003) 'Minimum wage, minimum impact', in R. Dickens, P. Gregg and J. Wadsworth (eds) *The labour market under New Labour: The state of working Britain*, London: Palgrave Macmillan, pp 201-13.

DWP (Department for Work and Pensions) (2002a) *Pathways to work: Helping people into employment*, Cm 5690, London: The Stationery Office.

DWP (2002b) *Building choice and responsibility: A radical agenda for housing benefit*, London: DWP.

DWP (2003a) *Opportunity for All: Fifth annual report 2003*, Cm 5956, London: The Stationery Office.

DWP (2003b) *Preliminary conclusions: Measuring child poverty consultation*, London: DWP.

DWP (2003c) *Measuring child poverty*, London: DWP.

Goode, J., Callender, C. and Lister, R. (1998) *Purse or wallet? Gender inequalities and income distribution within families on benefits*, Report no 853, London: Policy Studies Institute.

Hansard (House of Commons) (2003a) debate, 28 April, cols 53-69, London: The Stationery Office.

Hansard (2003b) debate, 12 November, cols 71WH-92WH, London: The Stationery Office.

Hills, J. and Lelkes, O. (2000) 'Selective universalism and patchwork redistribution', in R. Jowell et al (eds) *British Social Attitudes: The 16th report – Who shares New Labour values?* (1999/2000 edn), Aldershot: Avebury.

HM Treasury (2000) *Tackling poverty and making work pay: Tax credits for the 21st century – The modernisation of Britain's tax and benefit system*, Number Six, London: HM Treasury.

HM Treasury (2003) *Budget 2003: Building a Britain of economic strength and social justice – Economic and fiscal strategy report, and financial statement and Budget report*, HC 500, London: The Stationery Office.

HM Treasury and DTI (Department of Trade and Industry) (2003) *Balancing work and family life: Enhancing choice and support for parents*, London: HM Treasury and DTI.

HM Treasury and Inland Revenue (2003) *Detailed proposals for the child trust fund*, London: The Stationery Office.

Kempson, E. (1996) *Life on a low income*, York: Joseph Rowntree Foundation.

Marsh, A. and Perry, J. (2003) *Family change 1999 to 2001*, DWP Research Report 180, Leeds: Corporate Document Services.

Metcalf, D. (2002) 'The national minimum wage: coverage, impact and future', *Oxford Bulletin of Economics and Statistics* 64, Supplement 0305-9049, pp 567-82.

Millar, J. (ed) (2003) *Understanding social security*, Bristol: The Policy Press/ Social Policy Association.

NAO (National Audit Office) (2002) *Tackling pensioner poverty: Encouraging take-up of entitlements*, HC 37, London: The Stationery Office.

ONS (Office for National Statistics)/DWP (Department for Work and Pensions) (2003) *Income related benefits: Estimates of take-up in 2000/01*, London: National Statistics/DWP.

Patterson, T. (2003) 'Changing claims?', *Benefits* 38, vol 11, issue 3, pp 203-06.

Ridge, T. (2003) 'Labour's reforms of social security provision for families: the implications for children', *Benefits* 37, vol 11, issue 2, pp 87-92.

Stafford, B. (2003) 'In search of a welfare-to-work solution: the New Deal for disabled people', *Benefits* 38, vol 11, issue 3, pp 181-86.

Sutherland, H., Sefton, T. and Piachaud, D. (2003) *Poverty in Britain: The impact of government policy since 1997*, York: Joseph Rowntree Foundation.

Treasury Select Committee (2003) *Inland Revenue matters*, Tenth Report (Session 2002-03), HC 834, London: The Stationery Office.

Whiteford, P., Mendelson, M. and Millar, J. (2003) *Timing it right?: Tax credits and how to respond to income changes*, York: Joseph Rowntree Foundation.

Willitts, M. and Swales, K. (2003) *Characteristics of large families*, In-house Report 118, London: DWP.

Work and Pensions Select Committee (2003) *Employment for all: Interim report*, HC 401, Session 2002-03, London: The Stationery Office.

FOUR

The rise of the meritocracy? New Labour and education in the second term

Sally Tomlinson

Introduction

Education remains the Government's top priority. (DfES, 2001a, p 5)

A New Labour government was re-elected in June 2001 and continued to stress education as a major means of improving the nation's economic competitiveness, while encouraging social cohesion and enhancing individual life chances. However, whereas from 1997 to 2001 it had continued the Conservative government's pre-1997 reforming zeal – when every area of education from early years to higher education had been the target of criticism and legislation – and subjected the education system to further Acts, initiatives and regulations (Tomlinson, 2001, 2003) there was something of a slowdown post-2001. A White Paper on schools appeared two months after the election, with an Education Act incorporating most proposals from it passed in July 2002. A long-awaited White Paper on higher education eventually came out in January 2003, with a highly contested Higher Education Bill produced in January 2004. Lord Judd, a shadow Labour Education Minister, had sarcastically enquired in 1993 whether, after the Conservatives had introduced some 17 Acts in 13 years, "is it now a constitutional requirement that there should be an annual Education Bill?" (*Hansard*, 1993). New Labour had seemed set to continue the practice, but 2003 was a year blessedly free from education acts. The slowdown in legislation – although circulars, initiatives, guidance and advice continued to flow from the centre – was possibly because the contradictions and conflicts resulting from hasty legislation and unpiloted initiatives were gradually becoming more obvious, and the gaps between policy rhetoric and practical reality more evident.[1] In particular, during the year 2002-03, inadequate funding caused immense problems for local education authorities (LEAs) and schools, and assessment problems, especially at A level, caused embarrassment for the government and were partially responsible for the resignation of the Education Secretary of State, Estelle Morris, in October 2002.[2] Morris later explained her reasons for resignation in an article entitled 'Why I said sod it' (Ward, 2003).

On a deeper level there was profound unease that although public education was manifestly improving in terms of quantity – more early years' education, staying on and life-long learning– and in terms of quality as measured by numbers achieving literacy targets and public examination passes, policies of competitive marketisation and part-privatisation under the rubric of diversity were helping to increase rather than diminish inequalities. It was becoming clearer that the achievement of a 'meritocracy' – to which the Prime Minister had committed himself (Blair, 1999) was not compatible with an inclusive society, to which the government was also committed (Blair, 1998). A knowledge-driven economy and a high skills society (DfEE, 1998) were also incompatible with a flexible labour market and low national minimum wage. It was becoming embarrassingly clear that in the global economy low wages and insecure employment were a positive incentive for employers (Lloyd and Payne, 2003). The progressive abandonment of government involvement in social welfare policies and the increased role of the private sector appeared to be an electorally attractive way of reducing public spending, but was creating huge anxieties for large sections of the middle classes, who began to realise that the shifts in costs from the state to the individual might not result in the benefits and privileges previously taken for granted.

This article documents policies that are increasing the overt and covert selection of young people for different kinds of unequally resourced schools and universities; notes the continuing search for improved vocational options, intended to be incorporated into a new over-arching diploma award for all school and college leavers; and considers the encroaching privatisation of Local Education Authorities, schools and education services. 'Modernisation by privatisation' as the Centre for Public Services (2003) has pointed out, is common to all areas of the public sector – providing increased opportunities for the private sector to engage in public service provision and create new markets. The article concludes that the winners in the new meritocracy who have climbed the ladders of opportunity that the government insists it is providing, will be well placed to succeed in a global market economy. The future for those that remain on the lower rungs is more problematic.

Commitment to diversity

By 2001 a hierarchy of schooling was well established, although hierarchies differed in different parts of the country. Overall there was private schooling for some 7% of pupils, who constituted some 26% of those staying to take A level examinations. For the majority in the public education sector even primary schools were often battlegrounds for parents anxious to get their children to the desirable schools. At secondary level there was selection for the remaining 164 grammar schools; the rest 'chose' ostensibly non-selective schools – designated post-1998 as foundation schools, voluntary-aided/controlled schools or community schools. Special schools, catering for some 1% of pupils, were either foundation or community. Most schools that embraced the foundation label were former grant-maintained schools, which had benefited from superior resourcing in the 1990s. Secondary schools continued to be able to 'bid' to become specialist schools – a specialist schools programme dated from 1988 when a Conservative government introduced City Technology Colleges to be funded by business. In the event the 15 CTCs ended up largely funded by taxpayers and by 2003 became part of a City Academies programme. From 1993 a specialist programme attempted to increase 'choice and competition' as schools raising £50,000 in private sponsorship were given matched government funding to specialise in technology, sport, arts and other areas. The New Labour government extolled and extended the specialist schools programme as a way of 'modernising the comprehensive principle', quoted contentious research in an effort to prove that exam results were better in specialist schools (see Edwards and Tomlinson, 2002; Specialist Schools Trust, 2004), and in 2004 gave Cyril Taylor, the advisor responsible for the programme under the Conservatives and already knighted by Mrs Thatcher, a special knighthood for further services to the specialist programme.

A Green Paper published in January 2001 had documented the government's view of its achievements since 1997 and claimed that 'rapid, fundamental reform' had transformed the education service. It asserted that schools needed to move from a 'one size fits all' model to a diversity of institutions and partnerships that would lead to more opportunities and choices (DfES, 2001a). A White Paper produced in September, precursor of the 2002 Education Act, further explained that the specialist school programme would lead to "a diverse system where schools differ markedly from each other in the particular contribution they choose to make but are equally excellent in giving their students a broad curriculum" (DfES, 2001b, p 38). Schools would still be required to offer a national curriculum, which was to be modified to allow more vocational courses and work experience from 14. The paper suggested that some specialist schools could be designated as 'advanced specialist', later modified to 'leading edge' schools. The Beacon schools programme, whereby schools were given extra money for their recognised excellence, was to be expanded, as was the City Academy programme. Academies – effectively part of the private sector – could be set up by private, voluntary or faith groups, but have costs met by the state.

By the end of 2003 there were some 992 specialist schools, with Charles Clarke claiming that there would be 2,000 by 2006 and the Specialist Schools Trust asserting that nearly all schools would be specialist by this date (Smith, 2004). Around 173 specialised in arts, 18 business and enterprise, 4 engineering, 157 language, 12 maths and computing, 24 science, 162 sports, and 443 technology. Schools with a sports specialism tended to be in inner cities and the manager of the Trudex Textile Company, which supplies the bulk of school uniforms in England, noted that sports colleges chose sweatshirts and polo shirts, while arts schools chose traditional uniforms of blazer, shirts and ties. Inner city schools tended to go for sports school status, and performed less well academically, suggesting that a hierarchy of specialist schools was developing. Some 130 schools had been designated as training schools for teachers, with more promised, and 240 schools were to join in a pilot of Extended Schooling open to the community. Diversity was presented in the White Paper as responding to individual needs and to different groups in society. Grammar schools, presumably catering for the needs of their middle class intakes, were to be encouraged to share expertise and form partnerships with non-selective schools, and partnerships were to be encouraged with faith groups, the voluntary sector and business. An expansion of faith schools was to be encouraged, Anglican, Muslim, Sikh and Greek Orthodox being mentioned. Successful schools were to be allowed to expand. All this was repeated in a 2003 paper *A new specialist system* (DfES, 2003a), which also noted that legislation via the 2002 Education Act now required LEAs proposing to build a new school to hold a competition between their bid and bids from private, voluntary, faith, business and other 'interested parties'.

Selection, overt and covert

In 1996 David Blunkett, then Shadow Secretary of State for Education, pledged "no more selection under a Labour government"; in 2003 Schools Minister David Miliband wrote in *The Guardian* that "the ending of the 11+ in most parts of the country was a victory over structural inequality of opportunity" (Miliband, 2003). Yet the 11+ continues in 36 LEAs in England and there continues to be selection of children for different and unequally resourced schools. The private sector is a major source of selection, by both income and ability, and the existence of 164 grammar schools affects the intake of some 500 comprehensive schools. There is permitted 10% selection by aptitude in specialist secondary schools, selection by faith for 700 state-aided religious schools and covert selection by interviews and other means in schools that are their own admission authorities (West and Hinds, 2003). 'Selection by mortgage', as those able to afford it moved house to be near desirable schools, has recently been quantified by estate agents as a £42,000 premium near a 'good' primary school and £23,000 near a secondary school (Garrett, 2003).

Arguments are still made that grammar schools enable educational and social mobility for the 'able' working class child, but the reality is that only 2% of pupils in grammar schools are eligible for free schools meals, compared to 17% in all schools. The highly selective grammar schools, heavily oversubscribed by intensively tutored children, still educate the middle classes and the government encourages philanthropic schemes based on the notion of escape from supposedly less attractive comprehensive schools into selective schools.[3] However, there is now accumulating evidence questioning the benefits of selective education even for the most able pupils. A value-added analysis of public examination results in comparable LEAs concluded that "the differences in progress in comprehensive and selective systems are not particularly striking, although they appear to operate in favour of the former, especially at higher levels of prior attainment" (Schagen and Schagen, 2003, p 580). The first publication of 'value added' league tables in 2004 also showed comprehensive schools adding most value at 16. There is also accumulating evidence that selection lowers standards overall. The widely quoted international PISA study (OECD, 2002) demonstrated that countries with non-selective systems achieved the highest standards of education overall. Kent, famously sticking with selection, has been the subject of studies demonstrating the malign effect of selection on standards, and a study in Northern Ireland documented that selection "was socially divisive, damaged self-esteem, disrupted teaching and reinforced inequality of opportunity" (Gallagher and Smith, 2001, p 79).

However, history is against those who claim that there can be parity of esteem between the developing hierarchy of secondary schools. While grammar and specialist schools continue to offer superior resources and are perceived as 'better' they will continue to be regarded as more desirable, although there is a conspicuous lack of evidence that parents actually want specialist schools. But there is evidence that, offered the choice, parents would prefer a good local comprehensive school, specialising in a full range of learning for all pupils (Benn and Chitty, 1996; House of Commons Education and Skills Committee, 2003a).

The government also continued to encourage within-school selection. An Excellence in Cities action plan was launched in 1999 (DfEE, 1999a) largely as an attempt to retain the middle classes in inner city schools, especially in London. It was also a response to ethnic minority parents' continued concern over the quality of education their children were offered. The programme included setting by ability, creating more Learning Support Units and providing mentors for low ability and disruptive pupils, and 'offering opportunities for gifted and talented pupils' – the highest 5-10% in secondary schools – to attend summer schools, take more extracurricular activities and study for new 'world class tests'. Warwick University won a bid to establish an Academy for Gifted and Talented Youth, at which the fortunate talented would pay for courses. An early evaluation of the programme found white middle class children more likely to be selected as 'gifted' and, in 2003, the OFSTED chief inspector reported that while giving pupils more self-confidence, it had not raised educational standards (Bell, 2003).

Higher education for half?

Hierarchies of desirability in schools has rapidly become matched by hierarchies in higher education. By the 1990s all three political parties backed an expansion of higher education. The success of comprehensive education had resulted in a wider qualified body of potential students and degrees were increasingly needed to obtain jobs that previously lower level qualifications would have secured. The binary line between universities and polytechnics was abolished in 1992 by a Conservative government, which set a target of one third of young people to enter HE by the end of the decade. This had been achieved by the mid-1990s, although "on the cheap" as the Liberal peer Lord Russell pointed out – money for each student and staff salaries being held down. In 1996 the government appointed Ron Dearing to chair a review of higher education (Dearing, 1997) and the incoming Labour government received his report. Dearing recommended raising the participation rate to 45%, with more sub-degree courses offered in Further Education colleges, and a substantial increase in public spending on higher education, with graduates in work contributing 25% of their tuition costs. In 1998 the Teaching and Higher Education Act introduced upfront tuition fees of £1,000, abolished maintenance grants and expanded the student loan programme. Although the government response to Dearing had stressed that wider access for those traditionally under-represented was a major goal, the University and College Admissions Service promptly reported a decrease in applications from mature students, working class students and some ethnic minorities (Goddard, 1999). Whether, and how, far fees and debt deter working class applicants has continued to be contested. Evidence is emerging from Australia that with a graduate tax in operation, working class students choose the cheapest courses (Beckett, 2004). What was missing in much of the debate was a recognition that selection for university is influenced by social class long before students arrive in higher education. Without five good GCSEs students are unlikely to go on to, or be considered for, university entry. In 2000 74% of school pupils with parents in the higher professions obtained these, as against only 29% of pupils with parents in routine manual jobs (*Social Trends*, 2003, p 61).

In 2000 David Blunkett announced that universities would become more diverse – some developing as research universities, some offering a two-year foundation degree, and some able to charge more than the set fee. The Labour election manifesto of June 2001 promised to work towards a target of 50% of students going into HE, and on page 20 promised "we will not introduce top-up fees". Yet the first announcement on higher education, made by Charles Clarke, incoming Secretary of State for Education in November 2002, backtracked from this position, quoting an OECD report which had apparently concluded that graduates earned £400,000 more over a lifetime than non-graduates, and therefore more money should come from students and alumni.

In January 2003 a White Paper on higher education announced that universities would be able to charge up to £3,000 for their courses. Students would no longer pay upfront fees, but repayments for fees and loans would be made through a Graduate Contribution Scheme starting when the graduate earned £15,000. Universities were to prove to an Access Regulator that they had developed bursaries and other measures to encourage disadvantaged students. The notion of variable fees was introduced as "allowing universities the right to secure from graduates larger contributions to the cost of their education" (DfES, 2003b, p 9) – in effect variable fees for different courses. This was regarded by many MPs, academics and others as confirming a hierarchy of institutions, with the top universities charging more and attracting richer students, especially as the paper envisaged most higher education expansion coming via two-year vocational courses that were more likely to attract working class students. The National Union of Students president told the House of Commons Education and Skills Committee that "Differential fees are wrong and will create a two tier, elitist higher education system" (House of Commons Education and Skills Committee, 2003b, para 167, p 66).

For the whole of 2003 acrimonious discussion concerning university funding, top-up and variable fees occupied much space in the media and much political and academic time, with the Prime Minister supporting variable fees. A Bill introduced in January 2004 included variable fees, but with more concessions on support for poor students. It was opposed by over 100 Labour MPs and became part of a challenge to the Prime Minister's authority. In the event the Bill was accepted by parliament on 27 January by just five votes. Universities that eventually charge higher fees, attract endowments and gain more funding for research are likely to become top of a diverse system. The Higher Education Funding Council suggested that diversity within Higher Education Institutions (HEIs) was primarily a matter for each institution to determine, but HEIs had long abandoned the pretence that there was parity of esteem, funding, research possibilities and eventual student employment between universities. The Russell Group of 20 universities, largely recruiting students from private, and selective schools,[4] unashamedly labelled itself the top group, with a Coalition of Modern Universities accepting that as former polytechnics they could not compete on the same grounds. It was unsurprising that an official from the Higher Education Funding Council told the House of Commons Education and Skills committee that "there is a clear perception of a hierarchy of Universities. This hierarchy is well known to students and to employers, and the institution attended makes a difference to your life chances" (House of Commons Education and Skills Committee, 2003b, para 141, p 56).

Vocational options 14-19

Since it took office in 1997, the government has given much time and attention to the education and training of those who were to be part of a skilled and knowledgeable workforce via vocational routes, and much rhetoric was devoted to ways of ending the historic status divide between academic and vocational routes. Education as a means of contributing to the economy, the necessity for lifelong learning and the acquisition of new skills, plus the need to reduce the costs of welfare by moving people into work, were recurring themes in numerous papers and initiatives produced between 1997 and 2000.

Initially, there was continued reliance on the messy system of vocational education provided in schools, in the underfunded Further Education Colleges, by voluntary bodies, and by employers who continued to criticise poor vocational training but were reluctant to provide or pay for skills training. In 1999 a White paper (DfEE, 1999b) set out a new framework and funding of all post-16 education and training – post-14 for the disaffected in work-related education – giving unprecedented centralised control of funding, regulation and inspection to the Secretary of State. By 2000 a Learning and Skills Act had set up a Learning and Skills Council with a Chair (Brian Sanderson, already Chair of Newcastle United Football Club) and members appointed by the Secretary of State. An Adult Inspectorate was to inspect post-19 courses – and post-16 vocational courses. The 10-year-old Training and Enterprise Councils (TECS) were to be abolished and the LSC was to use a budget of some £7 million to provide education, training and leisure for all 16- to 19-year-olds via 47 local Learning and Skills Councils (LSCs).[5] Individual Learning Accounts were to be set up for individuals to pay for training – a scheme abandoned in 2003 when widespread fraud was discovered.

Having legislated for differential post-16 provision, the government then proceeded to produce policy papers on the 14–19 age-group, a highly contested area with many competing vested interests, appearing, as one journalist put it, unable to decide whether the aim of education was "to get as many students as possible into university, or to make sure we have enough plumbers" (Crace, 2002). A consultation paper on extending opportunities for 14- to 19-year-olds appeared in February 2002 (DfES, 2002a) which proposed developing new vocational courses to be available in schools, colleges or with other training providers; increasing the provision of Modern Apprenticeships; and allowing students to progress at different rates but with all courses leading to the award of an overarching diploma. A Matriculation Diploma was suggested[6] to be offered at intermediate, higher, advanced and higher levels, with all existing courses and awards including work-related and citizenship activities, fitting into the Diploma. On the academic side there was a proposal that aspects of the International Baccalaureate could be incorporated into the Diploma;

on the vocational side, colleges were to work towards becoming CoVES – Centres of Vocational Excellence – developing links with local employers.

Predictably, private and selective schools led with the criticism that the 'gold standard' of the A level was to be downgraded. They were given considerable ammunition in August 2002, when charges that A level papers had been incorrectly marked and numbers of students denied university places led to "what was arguably the worst education crisis to hit any recent government" (Smithers, 2003, p 4). The Qualifications and Curriculum Authority took the blame – the Chairman, Sir William Stubbs, resigning with some bitterness, to be followed, as noted, by the Secretary of State herself. A Committee of Inquiry into A level standards was set up, chaired by Mike Tomlinson, who in 2000 had taken over as Chief Inspector at OFSTED for two years, following the resignation of Chris Woodhead. The new Chief Executive of QCA, Australian Ken Boston, made it plain that he favoured A levels (Mansell, 2003). Marking at A level was less contentious in 2003 but some 110,000 papers at Key Stage 3 for 14-year-olds were submitted for remarking.

Following consultation on the February document, a White Paper appeared in January 2003, conceding to the A level lobby that A levels and GCSE would continue but, with what was becoming familiar rhetoric, "a curriculum to combine breadth of study with more flexibility for schools and colleges to tailor programmes to individual needs and aptitudes" (DfES, 2003c, p 4). It rejected the suggestion in the consultation paper that moves to the International Baccalaureate be considered. Compulsory subjects to be studied between 14 and 16 were reduced to English, maths, science, information technology and learning about work and enterprise. Other subjects including foreign languages were to be optional. Eight vocational GCSEs were to be supplemented by new 'hybrid' GCSEs for students to study on either academic or applied tracks. This was yet another attempt to "make applied training as important as academic learning" (DfES, 2003c, p 5). A somewhat contentious proposal was that a 14-19 curriculum should be locally differentiated and linked to local labour markets. Pilot projects known as Pathfinders were to develop partnerships to offer 14–19 education and training. A case study in Lincolnshire was quoted, which, under the direction of the LEA apparently brought together all schools, two Beacon colleges, the local Learning and Skills Council, the local Learning Partnership, the local Education and Business Partnership, Connexions (the updated careers service) the Consortium for Work-Based Learning, HE providers, neighbouring LEAs, adult education and youth services, and Scunthorpe United Football Club (DfES, 2003c, p 12). The stated intention in this paper was to improve the quality of vocational programmes for those not choosing A levels or apprenticeships, but who want or are directed into vocational options. While government intentions were admirable, it remained indisputable that "a major need of the middle classes has always been to avoid the relegation of their children to vocational education and practical training" (Tomlinson, 2001, p 137). The expanded opportunities for vocational courses are highly likely to be embraced by students from lower income families and unless attitudes change these courses will continue to be regarded as lower prestige alternatives to academic courses (Wolf, 2002).

A jigsaw of initiatives

While the search continued for ways of creating a more coherent 14–19 phase of learning, it was becoming obvious that there was no overall strategy for reform. Different organisations and departments were either working in competition with each other or with minimal communication. In March 2003, Mike Tomlinson was asked to chair a working group that would suggest reforms over a 10-year period. The group produced a first consultation report in July 2003 (DfES, 2003d), with a further report due early in 2004. The Tomlinson group faced the familiar inconsistencies – endeavouring to "reinforce the concept of 14-19 as a single phase of learning in place of the widespread perception of 14-16 and 14-19 as two distinct phases" (DfES, 2003d, p 7), while funding, regulation and inspection continued to split the phases, there was still legal school leaving at 16, and a pool of employers ready to take on low paid young people and minimise any training. The group, while rejecting the title of Matriculation Diploma, suggested a framework of Diplomas from entry level to advanced level, to replace existing qualifications, but incorporating specific subjects and occupational and vocational specialisms.

Meanwhile, back at the DfES, a consultation paper *Success for all: Reforming further education and training* (DfES, 2002b) came out in November 2002. The introduction by Charles Clarke claimed that the learning and skills sector was crucial for both social justice and for economic success, and addressed the 4,000 providers of learning and skills funded by the LSC. These included Further Education colleges, sixth form colleges, school sixth forms, specialist colleges, HE institutions providing further education, local authority adult education, voluntary and community providers, the University of Industry, and employers. The largest ever investment in FE and training was promised, after the LSC had undertaken

Strategic Area Reviews of what was locally required and published a National Skills Strategy. The paper reiterated that 14-19 learners should have greater choices of academic and vocational courses, with chances of progression, but otherwise barely referred to the 14-19 education Green Paper already issued and not at all to the fact that responses to this would be published in a White Paper in two months' time. The new Chair of the Qualifications and Curriculum Authority, Sir Anthony Greener, in a 2004 New Year speech, deplored the lack of overview of reforms, describing the 14-19 strategies as "wish-lists ... not strategies" and "a jigsaw of initiatives that do not fit together" (Lepkowska, 2004, p 15).

Privatisation and funding

The radical restructuring of public welfare provision undertaken by the Conservative governments of Margaret Thatcher and John Major was continued under the first New Labour government and intensified during the second term, despite evidence that the introduction of market forces, competition and more privatisation had resulted in increased educational, social and economic inequalities (Pantazis and Gordon, 2000; Ball, 2003). Attempts to involve business in initiatives to help the disadvantaged had not been particularly successful. The Education Action Zones, set up in 1998 after competitive bidding to improve education in areas of disadvantage, were intended to bring private money and business expertise into educational management, overriding LEA expertise and becoming 'flagships' for future public service delivery, as well as revitalising local democracy. In the event, business contributed minimal funding or involvement, while some £200 million came from taxpayers. From 2004 there would be no more funding for the zones, although some would be incorporated into the Excellence in Cities programmes. While there were some improvements in education in the zones, researchers concluded that they had not revitalised local democracy or helped to alleviate disadvantage, at least in the short term (Power et al, 2003).

One policy that has generally been recognised as a success was the Sure Start programme, designed to improve the health, development and education of children up to three years of age in areas of disadvantage. By 2003, some 486 Sure Start programmes were in operation, bringing together midwives, health visitors and play-workers to offer services and activities for some 300,000 children. It is noteworthy that this was one initiative that did not require competitive bidding between local authorities and did not appeal for private funding. Instead, it was supported from the outset by Norman Glass, a senior Treasury civil servant now described as an architect of the programme, who made sure that public money was allocated to the scheme. A Sure Start Unit was set up in 2003 in the DfES, which incorporated early years and childcare initiatives including the provision of increased childcare places and a network of children's centres (Benjamin and Inman, 2000).

A downside of close association with the DfES did become evident during the summer of 2003, when a crisis in the education budget led to some £100 million being diverted from the Sure Start programme to schools. From 1997 the government had undertaken several reviews of ways of financing schools, with changes made to allocations via the Standard Spending Assessment (SSA) and Additional Educational Need Index (AEN), and with funds increasingly being directed from the centre towards competitive initiatives. In 2002 the Chancellor of the Exchequer announced an extra £15 billion for education over three years, but by early 2003, a funding crisis led to bitter arguments between central government, LEAs, schools and unions. Essentially, central allocation of funds to local authorities had not taken account of rises in teachers' pay, pensions and national insurance costs, or the required employment of more teaching assistants. The reduced allocations to schools led to schools being forced to lose teachers – research for the National Union of Teachers suggesting 20,000 jobs lost and less funding for special educational needs services. The government initially attempted to blame LEAs for withholding money from schools, but eventually was forced to concede underfunding and promise schools a 4% rise in funding per pupil for 2004-05. One result of the funding arguments was that suggestions resurfaced that central government should take control of all school budgets, 'nationalising' schools and effectively abolishing LEAs.

Privatisation and modernisation

Successive government policy from the late 1980s had been directed towards minimising the role of Local Education Authorities, requiring them to open up a market in education support services and outsource functions to public–private partnerships. From 1999, LEAs were inspected by OFSTED, the then Chief Inspector Woodhead supporting Conservative proposals to remove all schools from LEA control and asserting that "much of the work done by LEAs is not of democratic significance" (Tomlinson, 2001, p 106). 'Failing' LEAs were at risk of takeovers from the private sector, Islington being the first failed LEA to have day-to-day running of education taken over by a private firm, Cambridge Education Associates. This firm was eventually penalised by the DfES for failing to meet agreed targets on pupil performance. A DfEE paper on *The role of the local education authority in school education* (DfEE, 2000) encouraged LEAs to trade services across local boundaries, and promised extra funding for them to develop partnerships with private firms, even when not criticised by OFSTED. Leeds LEA, labelled as failing, was taken over in 2001 by an intriguingly named 'arm's-length company', Education Leeds, run by the private firm Capita, the Chair of the board of the company, Peter Ridsdale, already being Chair of Leeds United Football Club. Capita was the company appointed by the DfES to run the Individual Learning Accounts for those taking vocational courses, a scheme which collapsed at some cost to the taxpayer after fraud investigations – Capita having apparently failed to set up a proper computer system (Hook, 2003).

Southwark, another failing LEA, was forced to transfer its education services to a private engineering conglomerate, W.S. Atkins, in 2001. By the end of 2002, Atkins' performance in improving educational performance was revealed as 'shambolic' (CPS, 2003, p 19): the number of schools in special measures increased and money was owed to creditors including the postage company that franked the mail. In March 2003 the company pulled out. The LEA then went into 'partnership' with a smaller team from Cambridge Education Associates to sort out the problems. A journalist commented that "what happened in Southwark is a bitter case study in how New Labour's political drive to involve private companies in education or health services can go badly wrong" (Toolis, 2003). Undeterred by engineering firms' failings, the government in 2003 awarded a £2 million contract to another engineering firm which had developed an interest in education – Jarvis Educational Services – to advise on failing schools' improvement. Jarvis, the parent company, was the company under investigation over the Potters Bar rail crash in 2002.

The government, however, remains committed to encouraging the restructuring of LEAs to increase private involvement in a variety of ways. There are approved lists of contractors for the privatised inspectorate, for consultancy services and for providing educational services. There is also considerable recycling of personnel from LEAs to private companies. Schools now have more power to engage in privatising activity. The 2002 Education Act allowed successful schools to form school companies with other schools, borrow money and make a profit selling educational services. Corporate influence and advertising in school has increased. City Academies will be owned and operated by private sponsors, who will also be able to appoint staff and change the curriculum. Bexley Business Academy, opened in 2002, operates a 'business court' with a link to the London Stock Exchange. Most school building projects are now funded via the Private Finance Initiative (PFI) where the private sector pays for construction and is repaid by the state. While private firms move into taking over and running schools, the government is encouraging local education departments to amalgamate with social services departments. In examining motives for this move, Crouch has suggested that these enlarged departments will become vehicles for social casualties, with local education services running residual unpopular schools and pupil referral units (Crouch, 2003, p 44).

The rise of the meritocracy

Encouraging the development of hierarchies in schools and universities under the rubric of diversity and replacing the entitlement National Curriculum from 14 with a differentiated curriculum still split between academic and vocational does make sense in terms of the current requirements of the state to develop a workforce capable of competing in a global economy. This accords with an international agenda, a number of other countries having concluded that a differentiated school system is required to create a stratified workforce which corresponds to economic and business needs. A report produced for the European Commission in 1996 unambiguously asserted that "education systems are required to function as a hierarchical talent filter" (Reiffers, 1996, para 78). Education, as the plethora of education and training documents produced by New Labour testify, is primarily a means by which people are prepared for work at different levels in a flexible labour force, with a curriculum increasingly influenced by business interests and – apparently – football interests. An adjunct to this is that education itself has become a national and global commodity – schools and services can be run, bought and sold for profit.

New Labour's rationale for its policies is primarily that all members of society have a duty to develop their own human capital, which will in turn improve national economic productivity in a global market. But since all cannot acquire the desirable jobs in the high skills knowledge economy there should be meritocratic competition. The government will develop ladders of opportunity for all and remove "ceilings that prevent people from achieving the success they merit" (Blair, 1999). The term 'meritocracy' was coined by the late Lord Michael Young, whose satire *The rise of the meritocracy* (1958) demonstrated that the creation of a class who congratulated themselves that their privileges and superior status are deserved because of pure merit, held considerable dangers. He noted that, despite good intentions, it was difficult to separate individual 'merit', as demonstrated by educational qualifications or supposed high IQ,[7] from birth, wealth, nepotism, bribery, patronage and purchase, and that in any case "merit sanctions selection and a sieving of young people according to education's narrow band of values" (Young, 2001, p 25).

New Labour has not appeared to be conversant with empirical studies showing that for the whole of the 20th century the working class has always had to demonstrate considerably more merit than others to achieve desirable positions and that attempts to provide the structures of inequality within modern societies with a meritocratic legitimation do not succeed (Goldthorpe, 1997). While it makes good sense to appoint people to jobs on their merit, when those who are considered to have more merit than others harden into a new social class, believe they have a right to their privileges and have the means to reproduce their class, social injustice and economic inequality are an inevitable result. By 2001, Young was writing that New Labour's encouragement of a meritocracy had resulted in "general inequality becoming more grievous with every year that passes, and without a bleat from party leaders who once spoke up so trenchantly for greater equality" (Young, 2001, p 25)

In the global economy there is an increasing divide between those who are part of the high skills knowledge economy and those whose supposed lesser 'talents' or lack of merit lead to jobs with less income and status. Belief in a meritocracy can sanction a dysfunctional and polarised society.

Notes

[1] The House of Commons Education and Skills Committee, in their 7th report during the parliamentary session 2002-03, cautioned the Department for Education and Skills against introducing further initiatives until earlier ones had been properly evaluated. This was accepted by the Department in its reply to the committee in December 2003.

[2] After the 2001 election David Blunkett became Home Secretary and Estelle Morris became Secretary of State for Education and Skills. She resigned in October 2002 and was replaced by Charles Clarke.

[3] A favoured scheme is run by millionaire businessman Peter Lampl, who set up the Sutton Trust dedicated to selecting 'bright' council estate children to prepare for selective school examinations. The trust also pays for summer schools for selected children.

[4] The Russell Group, named after its first meeting in the Russell Hotel, London, includes Oxford and Cambridge, whose undergraduate intake comprises around 47% from private education, and Bristol, Durham and Warwick, with around 40% from private schools.

[5] In addition to provision by LSCs, 73 National Training Organisations were to be set up to replace TECs. They were judged a failure and abandoned in 2003 in favour of 23 proposed Sector Skills Councils to oversee skills acquisition.

[6] In 1990 Finegold et al had argued for a 'British Baccalaureate' – a single overarching award at 18 and a unified framework of modular academic and vocational courses. However, the continuation of a divided and divisive system, 14-19, was documented in Tomlinson (1997).

[7] Young forecast that the comprehensive school, with a belief in the educability of all children, would give way to selection. In his imagined scenario, IQs would be tested every few years and the whole population required to carry a National Intelligence Card. Even the children of lords could be demoted because of low intelligence, required to live in council housing and do domestic work – a sad fate (Young, 1958).

References

Ball, S.J. (2003) *Class strategies and the education market*, London: Routledge Falmer.

Beckett, F. (2004) 'This Trojan horse of charging', *The Guardian*, 21 January.

Bell, D. (2003) *Education Review*, vol 1, London: National Union of Teachers.

Benjamin, A. and Inman, K. (2003) 'Far from certain', *Society Guardian*, 8 October.

Benn, C. and Chitty, C. (1996) *Thirty years on*, London: David Fulton.

Blair, T. (1998) 'Forging an inclusive society', *Times Educational Supplement*, 11 September, p 21.

Blair, T. (1999) Speech to Labour Party conference, Bournemouth, October, 8 October 1999.

CPS (Centre for Public Services) (2003) *Mortgaging our children's future*, Sheffield: CPS.

Crace, J. (2002) 'What's the point?', *Guardian Education*, 3 December.

Crouch, C. (2003) *Commercialisation of citizenship: Education policy and the future of public services*, Fabian Ideas 606, London: Fabian Society.

Dearing, R. (1997) *Higher education in the learning society*, London: The Stationery Office.

DfEE (Department for Education and Employment) (1998) *The learning age: A renaissance for a new Britain*, Cm 3790, London: The Stationery Office.

DfEE (1999a) *Excellence in cities*, London: The Stationery Office.

DfEE (1999b) *Learning to succeed: A new framework for post-16 learning*, Cm 4392, London: The Stationery Office.

DfEE (2000) *The role of the education authority in school education*, London: DfEE.

DfES (Department for Education and Skills) (2001a) *Schools: Building on success*, Green Paper, Cm 5050, London: The Stationery Office.

DfES (2001b) *Schools: Achieving success*, White Paper, Cm 5230, London: The Stationery Office.

DfES (2002a) *14-19 Extending opportunities, raising standards*, Consultation Paper, Cm 5342, London: The Stationery Office.

DfES (2002b) *Success for All: Reforming further education and training*, London: DfES.

DfES (2003a) *A new specialist system: Transforming secondary education*, London: DfES.

DfES (2003b) *The future of higher education*, Cm 5735, London: The Stationery Office.

DfES (2003c) *Opportunity and excellence 14-19*, White Paper, London: The Stationery Office.

DfES (2003d) *Working group on 14-19 education. Principles of reform of 14-19 learning programmes and qualifications* (Tomlinson Report), London: DfES.

Edwards, T. and Tomlinson, S. (2002) *Selection isn't working: Diversity, standards and inequality in secondary education*, London: Catalyst Publications.

Finegold, D., Keep, E., Miliband, D., Raffe, D., Spours, K. and Young, M. (1990) *A British baccalaureate*, London: Institute for Public Policy Research.

Gallagher, T. and Smith, A. (2001) 'The effects of selective education in Northern Ireland', *Education Review*, vol 15, pp 74-81.

Garrett, A. (2003) 'Top dollar to be top of the class', *Observer* (Property), 21 September.

Goddard, A. (1999) 'Costs thwart broader access', *Times Higher Education Supplement*, 8 October.

Goldthorpe, J. (1997) 'Problems of meritocracy', in A.H. Halsey, H. Lauder, P. Brown and A.S. Wells (eds) *Education, culture, economy, society*, Oxford: Oxford University Press.

Hansard (1993) vol 550, no 11, p 826.

Hook, S. (2003) 'Learning accounts give us a bloody nose', *Times Educational Supplement*, 11 April, p 45.

House of Commons Education and Skills Committee (2003a) *Fourth report: Secondary education: Diversity of provision*, HC 94, London: The Stationery Office.

House of Commons Education and Skills Committee (2003b) *Fifth report: Higher education*, London: The Stationery Office.

Lepkowska, D. (2004) 'Exam chief slams wish-list waste', *Times Educational Supplement*, 23 January.

Lloyd, C. and Payne, J. (2003) 'What is the high skills society? Some reflections on current academic and policy debates in the UK', *Policy Studies*, vol 24, nos 2/3, pp 115-34.

Mansell, W. (2003) 'Plain speaker Ken keeps faith', *Times Educational Supplement*, 8 August.

Miliband, D. (2003) 'Class that haunts the classroom', *The Guardian*, 18 September.

OECD (Organisation for Economic Co-operation and Development) (2002) *Programme for international student assessment* (PISA study), Paris: OECD.

Pantazis, C. and Gordon, D. (2000) *Tackling inequalities*, Bristol: The Policy Press.

Power, S., Whitty, G., Gewirtz, S., Halpin, D. and Dickson, M. (2003) *Paving a third way: A policy trajectory analysis of EAZs*, Final report to ESRC, London: London Institute of Education.

Reiffers Report (1996) *Accomplishing Europe through education and training*, Study Group on Education and Training, Brussels: European Commission.

Schagen, I. and Schagen, S. (2003) 'Analysis of national value-added data sets to assess the impact of selection on pupil performance', *British Educational Research Journal*, vol 29, no 4, pp 561-82.

Smith, N. (2004) 'Specialist delight as they trounce rest', *Times Educational Supplement*, 16 January.

Smithers, R. (2003) 'On your marks', *Guardian Education*, 29 April.

Social Trends (2003) no 33, London: The Stationery Office.

Specialist Schools Trust (2004) *Educational outcomes and value added by specialist schools*, London: Specialist Schools Trust.

Tomlinson, S. (ed) (1997) *Education 14-19: Critical perspectives*, London: Athlone Press.

Tomlinson, S. (2001) *Education in a post-welfare society*, Buckingham: Open University Press.

Tomlinson, S. (2003) 'New labour and education', *Children and Society*, vol 17, no 3, pp 195-204.

Toolis, K. (2003) 'Will they ever learn?', *The Guardian*, 22 November.

Ward, L. (2003) 'Why I said sod it', *Guardian Education*, 9 January.

West, A. and Hinds, A. (2003) *Secondary schools admissions in England: Exploring the extent of overt and covert selection*, London: Research and Information on State Education (RISE) (available at www.risetrust.org.uk/admissions html).

Wolf, A. (2002) *Does education matter?*, Harmondsworth: Penguin.

Young, M. (1958) *The rise of the meritocracy*, Harmondsworth: Penguin.

Young, M. (2001) 'Down with meritocracy', *The Guardian*, 29 June.

FIVE

The personal social services

Bill Jordan

Introduction

The reform of the personal social services in the UK since the 1970s has followed a clear long-term trajectory. This has led away from the model of services based in a single local authority agency and dominated by a single profession. But the logic for the fragmentation of that agency and that profession, and their recoalescence as parts of other services has been tortuous. This chapter attempts to trace the various ideas and models that have contributed to reforms, and how they have patterned the present outcomes.

The creation of the local authority social services departments in the 1970s owed much to a particular perception of the common needs of certain marginal groups. Large numbers of elderly, disabled, chronically ill and disadvantaged people, and many children and their parents, were seen as calling for a kind of mediation and special attention. They were perceived as needing services to bridge with the major pillars of the welfare state – social security, health, education and housing – and to supply a form of personal response to their subjective experiences and particular requirements. And social workers were thought to have a distinctive range of skills and commitments appropriate for these tasks.

None of these assumptions now holds good. The new logic of reform distinguishes strongly between a number of different roles – market broker, community activator, risk assessor and protector – as well as identifying quite separate needs of the various groups. It delegates the tasks to interdisciplinary teams in which social workers tend to play subordinate parts (although medicine, nursing, psychology and occupational therapy now borrow from the range of skills once thought to be the province of social work). And it derives its rationales from a whole set of diverse principles – the 'choice agenda', 'rights and responsibilities', 'value for money', 'opportunities for all', 'social inclusion' and 'tough love', as well as from specific 'crises' (such as street crime or asylum seeking).

All this has reminded us about a fundamental fact in the history of the personal social services – albeit one briefly challenged in the early 1970s (Titmuss, 1974, chapter 9). In essence these have always been residual elements in social policy. As such they have acted as a kind of laboratory for the social sciences' more lurid theorising – from Malthusian population theory, through Social Darwinism and eugenics to the wilder shores of Third Way rhetoric. Hence they have provided opportunities for experiments in speculative social engineering.

Furthermore, they mark the meeting point between the four kinds of organisations characterising modern societies. Families, voluntary associations, firms and states all have quite different forms of membership, entry and exit rights, territorial bases, property holdings, modes of subscription and resources of power. Hence, where they join together in some common enterprise the result is often messy. There are anomalies and compromises and usually no clear winners or losers. No wonder the Swedish sociologist, Goran Ahrne, listed the personal social services with nepotism, corporatism, taxes and tariffs as examples of uneasiness caused by mixing types of organisation (Ahrne, 1990, pp 139-40).

Finally, these experiments and mixtures bear witness to an uncomfortable paradox of the present age, which underlies the disturbing transformation of our collective world. Those of us who were brought up in the era of welfare states were led to believe that social justice gave rise to a clear demarcation between the sphere of political authority (supplying public goods and social institutions for equitable interactions between citizens) and that of markets (allowing efficient allocations of private goods, and voluntary exchange). Now it is obvious that this was a delusion of the postwar era.

In a world where money, goods and people flow readily across political borders and where individuals form themselves into new kinds of collectives to supply themselves with all kinds of goods, a great range of alternative arrangements is feasible, but all with different price tags and quality labels. Anything can, in principle, be done informally (by families or traditional communities, for instance). The same things can be done by firms, as long as they can exclude non-subscribers (or be paid by governments). And states might, in principle, supply everything – but in practice the only places where they tried to do so have had such discouraging results that they have been abandoned (except in Cuba and North Korea).

The personal social services are the clearest examples to illustrate this fundamental truth of public economics. It might have been about them that Buchanan and Tullock were writing in 1962, when they declared that "the choice between voluntary action, individual or co-operative, and political action, which must be collective, rests on the relative costs of organizing decisions, on the relative *costs of social interdependence*" (Buchanan and Tullock, 1962, p 48). Or, as Niccolò Machiavelli put it rather more elegantly in 1525:

> ... in all human affairs one notices, if one examines them closely, that it is impossible to remove one inconvenience without another emerging.... Hence in all discussions one should consider which alternative involves fewer inconveniences and should adopt this as the better course; for one never finds any issue that is clear and not open to question.

In the personal social service, the 'inconveniences' of a state-led system became clear in the 1970s and 1980s and have pointed the path towards a radically fragmented 'mixed economy of welfare'. One suspects that the 'inconveniences' of public–private partnerships, primary health care trusts and interdisciplinary teams may be more apparent in the decades ahead.

The logic of reform

One way of looking at the reforms of the personal social services since 1989 is that they tried to reduce transaction costs and perverse incentives at the interfaces between the organisational sectors. The local authority social services departments were supposed to act as bridges between marginal families and voluntary associations, commercial companies and the major public services. Instead, they had come to be seen as barriers to efficient interactions. Their constituent politicians and bureaucrats acted as 'rent seekers', trying to mobilise electoral support, to expand their budgets and to create interest groups to perpetuate their regimes among staff and clients (Niskanen, 1975; Tullock, 1980). They were therefore the classic targets for the neo-liberal reform principles of the early 1980s.

In their relationships with families, social services departments were criticised for meshing poorly with the requirements of a flexible system of support. More concerned to maintain armies of homecare and residential staff than to meet the needs of frail people and their carers, or of parents bringing up children in difficult circumstances, they offered standardised measures of assistance, in forms that were far from user-friendly. Both academic research (Challis and Davies, 1985) and the lobbying of service-user groups pointed to the unsatisfactory outcomes of these methods and the scope for improvement if 'care packages' could be negotiated rather than imposed.

In relation to the commercial sector and the public services, these same rigidities and interests were blamed for a whole swathe of wasteful inefficiencies. Social services departments had perverse incentives to select fairly low-cost, fit and able residents for their homes, and to divert those who would benefit more from residential accommodation towards healthcare or to allow them to remain in hospital longer than they needed (Alexander and Eldon, 1979). They also had few positive incentives to respond to pressures from mental health or learning disability facilities in the NHS for community support and care. In response to these barriers, a whole system of funding for commercial care through the social assistance budget had come into being, with even larger perverse incentives for expensive and unnecessary residential accommodation than in the public sector. In services for children, too many still remained in homes, with too little organisational energy devoted to long-term planning for alternatives (Rowe et al, 1989).

Finally, the departments were accused of using blunt instruments to assess risks and hence of deploying resources inappropriately in many cases. This was most obvious in the field of child protection, where they were criticised for failing to identify the most serious threats of harm and to coordinate information from other agencies (DHSS, 1982, 1988). But it also applied to all other service groups, where there was little coordinated attempt to relate priorities for provision to risk factors, in the allocation of support and care.

Many researchers and professionals offered their support to the directions of change that were indicated by these analyses. But the process of reform has become entangled with two other agendas of public service transformation, which have skewed it in directions not foreseen by those involved in the original critique.

The first of these stemmed from the idea that the collective goods needed by individuals to flourish are not fundamentally different in kind from the private goods they buy in markets. In principle, they can express their preferences in relation to these goods in various ways, of which voting at elections is only one. For example, they can also 'vote with their feet' by moving to a district in which a certain bundle of such goods are available — within the infrastructure of local amenities and utilities such as roads, drains, street lighting, parks and libraries (Tiebout,

1956). They can also choose to join organisations that supply other shared facilities to their members (as in sports and recreation clubs, or cultural societies) in exchange for subscription fees (Buchanan, 1965; Cornes and Sandler, 1986). In the jargon these are called 'clubs'.

This approach was supposed to supplement the ideas embodied in the other critiques of the functioning of public services by looking for ways in which the individual components within social choices could be better revealed. But it also recognised an existing element in social policy outcomes, which was often overlooked in the literature of the public services. Individuals and households did in fact influence patterns and outcomes in both these ways. They moved to the best districts they could afford, partly in order to avail themselves of the local schools and hospitals, which were often superior to those in poorer ones. And they joined private 'clubs' and membership schemes of various kinds, not just for recreational and cultural amenities but also for health, education, housing and pensions (Jordan, 1996, chapters 4 and 5).

All this was particularly clear in the field of social care, where better-off people were able to construct their own infrastructures of collective goods by buying whatever they needed in the way of day and domiciliary services, by joining a voluntary association or by moving into a residential facility of their choice. But it was a far cry from this to creating a set of public services in which such mechanisms could reveal collective preferences. The people who needed support and care were the most likely to be too poor and isolated to know what was available; and it was manifestly absurd to expect those whose defining characteristics were their reliance on others even for domestic mobility and who seldom had the opportunity to move outside the confines of a house or residential centre, to 'vote with their feet'.

The task was therefore to invent an artificial set of institutions that would mimic the action of individuals and households, shifting costlessly between clubs and jurisdictions in search of the best collective goods for their accommodation costs, taxes and subscription fees. The division of the social services departments into 'purchaser' and 'provider' sections was aimed to accomplish part of this. But in addition, the strong incentives given to purchasers to turn to the commercial and voluntary sectors for social care services, and the extra funds made available from the social assistance budget, were supposed to create more market-like conditions in the public sector, with the purchasing function acting as proxy for the choices of service users and carers, revealed through assessment interviews.

The second agenda was concerned with fiscal discipline and the reining in the public sector 'rent seeking'. If social choice could become more like market choice, not only would preferences find a clearer and more precise expression but those who supplied collective goods would be forced to compete with each other, so the price would be driven down (Oates, 1972, 1999). If purchasers with limited budgets were required to seek their packages of care from a range of such suppliers, the result would be best value for each pound of local taxpayers' money (Davies, 1992). All that was needed was to transform the spendthrift culture of the old-style buro-political regime into a leaner, meaner managerial system that would monitor the placing of contracts and the compliance of providers.

But this aim was in some tension with the goal of flexibility, which drove the research-led reform agenda. The Kent study and other projects had shown how combinations of family care, informal support and ad hoc assistance, often from local sources, might be optimal, with this aim in mind (Challis and Davies, 1985). When the Dutch and German personal social services came to be funded by social insurance payments, beneficiaries of social care payments were allowed to choose between paying family carers, employing care assistants and nurses from small local cooperatives, buying care from large companies, or contributing to the costs of public care. The new system in the UK sanctioned purchasing authorities to agree block contracts, allowing large firms to make economies of scale, but often replicating the inflexibilities of the old public services by fitting service users into broad categories of need or simply filling up existing places which were currently unused (Harris, 2003).

Finally, although the reforms of children's services made no mention of either of these economistic agendas of public choice and fiscal prudence, there was inevitably a spillover from the principles of managerialism, contractualism and 'best value' into this section. Many local authorities adopted purchaser–provider structures for children in need and their families, regardless of its appropriateness for purpose. And the best value agenda plus budgetary constraint led to mass closure of residential placements and other in-house schemes in favour of a new range of private, voluntary and other outsourced solutions.

The Third Way

The advent of the New Labour government in 1997 did not challenge any of these agendas of reform. Rather, it addressed the problems that had arisen in implementing them. There were many unintended consequences of the new institutional structures and perverse incentives of a different kind. In a bewildering set of new initiatives, new partnerships, units, zones and action areas, new targets and quality measures, the government tried to correct the faulty interfaces and interactions between these sectors. And it was more determined and radical in its perception of the local authority departments as the barriers to more efficient and equitable outcomes and in creating alternative professional teams and agencies, which took away many of the tasks previously associated with social work and the personal social services (Jordan with Jordan, 2000).

New Labour recognised an impasse within social policy which had never been adequately addressed by its Conservative predecessors. In their efforts to cut back the social security budget and to break the power of trade unions, they had smashed up the twin systems that protected unskilled workers during the postwar era. Without these, marginal individuals, groups and communities had come to depend on informal activities of all kinds – including petty crime, drug dealing, prostitution, begging and (above all) doing undeclared work for cash while claiming benefits. They also relied on informal networks of mutual care, assistance and exchange among kin, neighbours, communal, ethnic and faith-based systems of solidarity (Jordan, 1996, chapter 5).

Such communities and activities were stubbornly resistant to conventional social policy approaches; and they were also a heavy drain on public expenditure. The enormous expansion of means-tested schemes for income support under the Conservatives was matched by the rise in prison populations, one-parent families and the growth of spending on various programmes for drug dependence, mental illness, suicide attempts, self-harm and family violence. Thus the Conservatives incurred extra costs to the public service budgets, which largely matched the savings they had made on social security, housing and employment. New Labour was ready to take a new approach to the links between these problems by a radical reinterpretation of the relationship between citizens and government.

As with all such shifts in the conceptualisation of the state and subjects (the Speenhamland system, the Poor Law of 1834, Lloyd George's insurance scheme and the Beveridge Plan) this required a new version of the interactions between frontline officials and those who attracted their attention. In this case the government made it clear that both sides were to be transformed, from bureaucratic providers and passive recipients to activating, tutelary and enabling counsellors, and to self-responsible, motivated and autonomous agents (DSS, 1998, p 26).

This sounded remarkably like an idealised version of the transactions between social workers and the clients in 1950s US textbooks. Indeed the new advisers and support workers in the newly named and rebranded agencies were expected to have many of the skills and attributes of social workers. For instance, those who counselled claimants of Jobseeker's Allowances were to arrange and negotiate 'tailor-made packages of work and training' for them (DSS, 1998, p 26). And those dealing with social inclusion and the transformation of deprived communities were supposed to empower and mobilise them to improve their own social and physical environment.

This new thinking was in line with approaches pioneered under the Clinton administration in the USA. Researchers and project-leaders there had come up with the finding that self-esteem, self-improvement and a trajectory towards autonomy were essential elements in the success of programmes for recovery from various forms of deviance and victimhood (Cruikshank, 1994, 1996, 1999). They translated this into a general requirement of all aspects of social policy to be more demanding and challenging of recipients of public support and services. In exchange for these, and as a condition for entitlement, they were to be expected to show effort, planning and motivation towards 'independence' (Rose, 1996).

But it was clear that, although New Labour seemed to derive much of its new thinking from notions of personal development and empowerment that had first emerged in social work, the very last people to be entrusted with these new programmes were local authority social workers and their departments. Instead they were divided up between various new and transformed agencies and initiatives—the New Deals, the Social Exclusion Unit, the Employment Zones and Action Teams, the National Asylum Support Service, Sure Start and the Children's Fund, and countless new Health and Social Care partnerships (Jordan with Jordan, 2000).

These agencies were to forge new relationships with the commercial and voluntary sectors to achieve these purposes. They were explicitly encouraged to facilitate relationships linking up marginal individuals and groups with the mainstream economy and with voluntary agencies by specific schemes of training and employment; by subsidising their wages (especially through the tax credit systems) and by encouraging new initiatives targeting specific problems such as homelessness, truancy and drug dependence; and by regenerating deprived districts.

The spirit of these active and inclusive programmes was reflected only somewhat dimly in the new standards and guidelines for the public services in social care and child protection. Although the same principles were to be applied, there was recognition that – in terms of the aims of empowerment towards autonomy and self-development – these services were residual. Many of the most disadvantaged, disabled and deviant members of the population would be left to rely on these services of support and both they and staff would therefore occupy a kind of ghetto, left behind by the self-actualising majority and the agencies which served their collective needs.

The government set out its agenda for modernising the personal social services in a White Paper (DoH, 1998). It is one of the few documents that actually defines the Third Way in relation to a policy domain. It located this path as lying between the commercialisation of social care characterising the Conservative reforms, and the near monopoly held by local authorities in the 1960s and 1970s. However, this new direction was indicated by very general ethical principles, without any indication of how these were to be reconciled when conflicts between them occurred. These principles include such statements as "care should be provided to people in a way that supports their independence and respects their dignity", "every person – child or adult – should be safeguarded against abuse, neglect or poor treatment whilst receiving care", and "people who receive social services should have an assurance that the staff they deal with are sufficiently trained and skilled for their work" (DoH, 1998, para 1.8).

The difficulty, of course, is that notions of 'dignity' and 'independence' are derived from mainstream cultures of individuals 'making something of themselves' through projects of self-development in work and personal relationships. Increasingly, the ideal cultural standard for such projects has become an autonomous being, forming partnerships of 'negotiated intimacy' in domestic units on equal, discursively regulated terms (Giddens, 1991; Beck and Beck-Gernsheim, 1995). On the one hand, these membership groups explicitly aim to abolish dependency of all kinds – ideally individuals should each have a portfolio of assets (skills and property rights) that allows them to be self-sufficient. On the other hand, equality is sustained, at least partly, by individuals being in a position to leave the unit and set up with another or others elsewhere (Jordan, 2004, chapters 2 and 3).

So, dependency on others is not something that can be dealt with merely rhetorically, or by wishful thinking. In the case of children, the culture of equal autonomy and negotiated intimacy can identify a clear task – to prepare them for their roles as similar autonomous, self-improving adult citizens. This is the theme linking initiatives like Sure Start (pre-school provision for children in deprived districts) and the Children's Fund (for those of school age), with the agendas of education and training. But it does not supply an adequate version of specific interventions in the lives of families in crisis, children in long-term need of basic stability and attachment, or child protection tasks. While the financially independent among the frail elderly and those with disabilities are assumed to be able to combine informal (family and neighbourly) care and paid care in the ways they choose, those without the means to do so become the targets of policies beset by both monetary and human dilemmas.

For example, the White Paper acknowledged that the regime of its predecessor government had led to local authority purchasers focusing intensive packages of care on those frail and disabled individuals seen as most at risk of entering residential homes. But it recognised a case for more low-level support; to try delay such crises, yet to provide *both* low-risk *and* high-risk interventions, would clearly involve increased expenditures, at least in the short run; and the whole emphasis of previous policies had been on better risk assessment to focus on those most immediately in jeopardy (DoH, 1998, chapter 2).

One solution canvassed in the White Paper was to make more widespread use of 'direct payments' to individuals, to arrange their own combinations of care provision. These and other similar systems have in fact expanded. They represent an attempt to get back to the flexibility and choice lost with block contracts and standardised packages. They also indicate the need for service users to have access to the information they require to become competent consumers in the market for care (see final section).

Coordination between services

The most recent phase of the 'modernisation' process again addresses the interactions between the services and professions, in social care for adults, education, childcare, child protection and justice for juveniles. Instead of seeking to identify and minimise barriers to cooperation between these organisations in the public sector, and their voluntary and commercial counterparts, the government has prescribed a whole series of arrangements through which there would be active collaboration. In this it has redrawn the map of health and social care and announced its intention to redraw that of education and childcare also.

The 2001 Health and Social Care Act gave the government powers to direct local authorities, health authorities and healthcare organisations to pool their budgets, especially where services were failing. In the same year 'one-stop' health and social care services were established, with staff working together, and primary and community healthcare teams as part of a single network. The NHS Modernisation Agency (2001) had among its tasks to challenge traditional boundaries between agencies, professions and teams. Care trusts allowed health and social services to form a single organisation to provide closer integration and to commission and deliver health and social care.

These organisational and managerial innovations, which constantly emphasise the goals of generalising both 'best practice' and 'best value', assume that interagency and interprofessional collaboration is largely a matter of breaking down the resistances and mutual misunderstandings which have arisen from previous separate departmental developments and interests (Leathard, 2003). In fact this is possible mainly because the role of social work in social care is narrowed to a technical one, of assessing individuals for specific packages of support and care, in the most cost-effective forms. In this way it becomes a natural and rational extension of healthcare and nothing more.

What is lost in this process is the distinctive contribution of a perspective on wider social relations and in the collective dimension of human flourishing. The point of social work was supposed to be that it identified the *social* element in the private problems and perplexities of citizens. If this was too often perceived in terms of need for *public* provision or *political* action, it was a characteristic weakness of the era in which social work became an integral part of the welfare state. But in principle there were important insights and positive interventions at stake, which are in danger of being lost, at least in the field of adult social care.

This is because, in the processes of joining up social care facilities better with health services (both the NHS and private suppliers), they become more disconnected from the other partnerships, initiatives and agencies with which they were formerly linked. For example, health and social care have now lost virtually all their ties into such processes as urban regeneration, widening participation and social inclusion. They also become disconnected from services for children, even more from the probation service, which is to be part of prisons.

The services for children too are to be reorganised and modernised, in the light of the damaging revelations of Lord Laming's Report on the death of Victoria Climbié (Laming, 2003). That enquiry revealed yet another example of failure to coordinate between agencies and local authorities, in this case a child brought to the UK from the Ivory Coast by her great-aunt (a French citizen), and moving with her and her partner between various London boroughs during a period of less than two years in the country. Police, hospital staff and social workers missed what seemed, in retrospect, to be clear evidence of the physical and emotional abuse that led to her death, and the churches she attended also failed to take action to protect her. The case epitomised the flaws in a network of overstretched and understaffed services, with health and social services relying extensively on agency workers, many recruited from abroad. Writing about the tragedy, in his Foreword to the Green Paper, *Every child matters*, Tony Blair (2003, p 2) declared,

> ... we are proposing here a range of measures to reform and improve children's care – crucially, for the first time ever requiring local authorities to bring together in one place under one person services for children, and at the same time suggesting real changes in the way those we ask to do this work carry out their tasks on our and our children's behalf.

The aim of new organisational systems is to link together the universal services which every child uses, so as to maximise children's developmental potential and protect them from abuse. It aims to cover all services for youngsters up to age 19, and to address educational problems, youth offending and antisocial behaviour as well as childhood illnesses and teenage pregnancies.

The bases for these coordinated services will be "full service extended schools", to be "open beyond school hours to provide breakfast clubs and after-school clubs and childcare, and have health and social care support staff also". In addition to extra resources for out-of-school activities, child and adolescent mental health services, speech and language therapy and reforming the youth justice system (new community sentences, intensive supervision and fostering schemes), the government plans to make more use of parenting orders, to require better supervision and support of truanting or offending children (DfES, 2003).

All this will be reinforced by measures familiar from the field of adult care – a lead professional from one of the services to be a kind of 'care manager' for a 'coherent package' of services to address each child's problems, multidisciplinary teams in schools and children's centres, and a common assessment framework for all the agencies and professions. The whole new approach will require the appointment of Directors of Children's Services at a local authority level (accountable for education and social services responsibilities), a lead council member for children, and Children's Trusts. Finally, the system will be overseen by a Minister for Children, Young People and Families (the first appointment, Margaret Hodge, having run straight into trouble over her stewardship of a London borough council in relation to the abuse of children in its care).

All this implicitly recognises that the Department of Health has failed to provide an adequate lead in issues of childcare and child protection.

In entrusting both youth justice and services for children in need to the system in charge of education, the government intriguingly follows a fairly successful but now no longer operative precedent – the German Democratic Republic.

Conclusion

Looking back over the reform process of the past 15 years, there are certain lessons that even the most diehard defender of the old social services departments could not evade. The perception of what marginal groups with special needs had in common, and what social work could offer them, rested on the conflation of several issues and roles, which have now been usefully distinguished and separated. In so far as the modernisation process has achieved this, it has been a useful exercise.

The first role is that of market broker, or perhaps more accurately *market coach*. Even better off and well-connected citizens are often ill prepared for the onset of a disabling illness, the birth of a child with a physical handicap or learning disability, or the development of a mental illness. However much we may have gained 'autonomy' and 'choice' over arranging our own healthcare, we may well discover that we are not fully protected against the costs of these conditions or fully informed about the options open to us. Hence, we rely on advice from well-informed, sensitive and skilled professionals who can offer support during a period of painful transition, during which we are especially vulnerable.

There is no reason why such a professional should be a social worker rather than a nurse or a psychologist, but whoever it is should be aware of the implications of interdependence in family and community, rather than simply brokers of commercial contracts for the individual in need of domiciliary, day or residential care. In other words, the market coach needs also to be an expert in the issues of autonomy and reliance on others, not only between individuals and commercial organisations but also in the family, neighbourhood and wider community (Davies et al, 2000; White and Harris, 2001).

Second, there is a role for a community activator (the French term is *animateur*), who is capable of mobilising groups, neighbourhoods and wider populations to identify their needs, and take action to meet them. The government has accumulated a great deal of experience by now in putting money into such target groups and communities, in working with local activists and associations and in linking up professional teams with specific projects and sources of support.

This is where the emancipatory agendas of the 1960s and 1970s still survive, albeit in attenuated forms. There is evidence of gradual progress in government thinking, on topics like social exclusion, urban renewal, early-years education and family support, and a move towards getting resources directly into the hands of members and residents and giving them expert help to achieve their goals. This means trusting people to be able to identify collective ways to improve their quality of life and using professionals to enable them in that process (Jordan with Jordan, 2000, chapter 6).

Here the successes of initiatives like Sure Start and the Children's Fund point to a broader interpretation of the functions of the personal social services. Instead of being confined to the activities of professional social workers and their assistants with specific needy groups, they come to be seen to embrace a whole range of involvements, with collective as well as individual aspects of the lives of citizens. Of equal significance is the breaking down of the traditional barriers between the 'social' and the 'economic' spheres. When New Labour drew on the concepts and skills of social work for its New Deals on employment and training, it was recognising that these divisions no longer made much sense. More recently the notion of Social Enterprises (DTI, 2002) straddles the barrier between economy and society, and encourages those who engage with people in disadvantaged situations to be both entrepreneurial and emancipatory – an impossible combination in the rather narrow, sub-Marxist world of community development in the 1960s and 1970s (Jordan with Jordan, 2000, chapter 7).

Finally, the role of protecting vulnerable and dependent individuals from abuses by those with power over them is seen to require special modes of analysis and skills of intervention. It is not enough to monitor such risks in an anxious but uninvolved way; they demand both an engagement and a firmness that differentiate them from the roles of either market broker or community activator. Researchers have been able to elucidate these issues in potentially practice-friendly ways (Parton, 1997), but it remains for organisations to discover ways of enabling practitioners to translate these insights into reliably consistent interactions with service users.

But cutting across this clarification of a number of different and important roles for the personal social services, and the far broader remit for them in the new landscape of interdisciplinary agencies and teams, are the big issues identified in the introduction to this chapter. Despite the effort and resources put into the agendas of choice, equal opportunities and social inclusion, the fact remains that inequalities have scarcely narrowed under New Labour, as concentrations of poverty and deviance persist. Furthermore, new and worrying conflicts have escalated, such as those between deprived white and minority ethnic communities in Bradford, Burnley and Oldham, which erupted in rioting in 2001 and have been further evidenced in the electoral successes of the BNP. There are also the mobilisations around populist social issues, which manifest themselves in bloodthirsty rage against paedophiles or the scapegoating of asylum seekers.

All of these phenomena seem to relate to the tendency of our society to polarise alternative modes of membership and collective action. The first is that of personal development, individual autonomy and social belonging through the self-responsible and self-actualising processes of the 'choice agenda' (Jordan, 2004). It derives from the widening moral and political sovereignty of individuals. Citizens with the necessary skills and resources can indeed meet most of their needs by shifting their affiliations between organisations that behave like markets and by joining communities of choice. They rely on exit rights and portable portfolios of assets to make up their own social infrastructure, with little reference to the wider needs of the whole community. It is for these that New Labour's Social Contract, and its modernisation programme, seem to have been primarily designed (DSS, 1998, p 80).

On the other hand, among those with no realistic prospects of assembling such a portfolio of personal and financial assets, more traditional loyalties and interdependencies of blood, territory, ethnicity and faith, lock them even more strongly into their communities of fate. Belatedly, the government's new emphasis on 'community cohesion' starts to ask questions about whether the barriers between groups loyal to the particularities of kin, clan, race, caste, religion and nationality can be overcome through the 'choice agenda', the New Deals or even the social inclusion initiatives (Home Office, 2001). The old welfare state idea of 'balanced communities' begins to resurface.

There are, after all, many terrible precedents for what happens when whole districts start to function through loyalties of this kind, including one within these islands. Among the deprived communities with the strongest bonds between their members, those of Northern Ireland testify to the dangers of this kind of cohesion, where bridges with the wider economy, society and polity have been dismantled or burnt (Leonard, 1994). The personal social services do still represent one potential element in policies for bridging between such enclaves, but they should not be expected to be effective on their own.

References

Ahrne, G. (1990) *Agency and organization: Towards an organizational theory of society*, London: Sage Publications.

Alexander, J.R. and Eldon, A. (1979) 'Characteristics of elderly people admitted to hospital, Part III Homes and sheltered housing', *Journal of Epidemiology and Community Health*, vol 33, pp 91-5.

Beck, U. and Beck-Gernsheim, E. (1995) *The normal chaos of love*, Cambridge: Polity.

Blair, T. (2003) 'Foreword', in *Every child matters*, DfES Green Paper, London: The Stationery Office, pp 1-2.

Buchanan, J.M. (1965) 'An economic theory of clubs', *Economica*, 32, pp 1-14.

Buchanan, J.M. and Tullock, G. (1962) *The calculus of consent: Logical foundations of constitutional democracy*, Ann Arbor, MI: University of Michigan Press.

Challis, D. and Davies, B. (1985) 'Long-term care for the elderly: the community care scheme', *British Journal of Social Work*, vol 15, pp 563-79.

Cornes, A. and Sandler, T. (1986) *The theory of externalities, public goods and club goods*, Cambridge: Cambridge University Press.

Cruikshank, B. (1994) 'The will to empower: technologies of citizenship and the war on poverty', *Socialist Review*, vol 23, no 4, pp 29-55.

Cruikshank, B. (1996) 'Revolutions within: self-government and self-esteem', in A. Barry, T. Osborne and N. Rose (eds) *Foucault and reason: Neo-Liberalism and rationalities of government*, London: WCC Press, pp 301-50.

Cruikshank, B. (1999) *The will to empower: Democratic citizens and other subjects*, Ithaca: Cornell University Press.

Davies, C., Finlay, L. and Bullman, A. (eds) (2000) *Changing practice in health and social care*, London: Sage Publications/Open University Press.

Davies, H. (1992) *Fighting leviathan: Building social markets that work*, London: Social Market Foundation.

DfES (Department for Education and Skills) (2003) *Every child matters,* Green Paper, London: The Stationery Office.

DHSS (Department of Health and Social Security) (1982) *Child abuse: A study of inquiry reports 1973-1981,* London: HMSO.

DHSS (1988) *Working together: A guide to interagency co-operation for the protection of children from abuse,* London: HMSO.

DoH (Department of Health)(1998) *Modernising social services, promoting independence, improving protection, raising standards,* Cm 4169, London: The Stationery Office.

DSS (Department of Social Security) (1998) *A new contract for welfare,* Cm 3805, London: The Stationery Office.

DTI (Department of Trade and Industry) (2002) *Social enterprise: A strategy for success,* London: The Stationery Office.

Giddens, A. (1991) *Modernity and self-identity: Self and society in the late modern age,* Cambridge: Polity.

Harris, J. (2003) *The social work business,* London: Routledge.

Home Office (2001) *Community cohesion: A report of the independent review team chaired by Ted Cantle,* London: Home Office.

Jordan, B. (1996) *A theory of poverty and social exclusion,* Cambridge: Polity.

Jordan, B. (2004) *Sex, money and power: The transformation of collective life,* Cambridge: Polity.

Jordan, B. with Jordan, C. (2000) *Social work and the third way: Tough love as social policy,* London: Sage Publications.

Laming, Lord (2003) *The Victoria Climbié inquiry,* Cm 5730, London: DoH.

Leathard, A. (2003), 'Policy overview', in A. Leathard (ed) *Interprofessional collaboration: From policy to practice in health and social care,* London: Brunner-Routledge, chapter 2.

Leonard, M. (1994) *Informal economic activity in Belfast,* Aldershot: Avebury.

Machiavelli, N. (1525) 'Discourses on the first ten volumes of Titus Livius', in *Machiavelli: The chief works and others,* A. Gilbert (ed) 1965, Durham: Duke University Press, Chapter 2.

Niskanen, W.A. (1975) 'Bureaucrats and politicians', *Journal of Law and Economics,* vol 18, pp 617-43.

Oates, W.E. (1972) *Fiscal federalism*, New York, NY: Harcourt Brace Jovanovich.

Oates, W.E. (1999) 'An essay on fiscal federalism', *Journal of Economic Literature*, vol 27, pp 1120-49.

Parton, N. (ed) (1997) *Child protection and family support: Tensions, contradictions and possibilities*, London: Routledge.

Rose, N. (1996) *Inventing ourselves: Psychology, power and personhood*, New York, NY: Cambridge University Press.

Rowe, J., Hundleby M. and Garnett, L. (1989) *Child care now: A survey of placement patterns*, London: BAAF.

Tiebout, C. (1956) 'A pure theory of local expenditures', *Journal of Political Economy*, vol 64, pp 416-24.

Titmuss, R.M. (1974) *Social policy: An introduction*, London: Allen and Unwin.

Tullock, G. (1980) 'Rent seeking as a negative sum game', in J.M. Buchanan, R.D. Tollison and G. Tullock (eds) *Toward a theory of a rent seeking society*, College Station, Texas: Texas A. and M. University Press, pp 3-25.

White, V. and Harris, J. (eds) (2001) *Developing good practice in community care*, London: Jessica Kingsley.

Part Two:
Social policy in the wider context

'Scottish solutions to Scottish problems'? Social welfare in Scotland since devolution

John Stewart

Introduction

This chapter examines aspects of social welfare in Scotland since devolution. In this section there is an outline of the devolution settlement. We then briefly examine the historic background to Scottish social welfare and the significance of welfare issues to the movement for devolution. Following this we look at what the Scottish Executive (put crudely, Scotland's 'government') is broadly trying to achieve. The focus next is on education and health, the two main areas of devolved social welfare powers. Particular stress is laid on 'policy divergence' although as we shall see there are constraints on what the Executive can do. Finally we assess what point the Scottish welfare state has reached and what might be its future trajectory. Like its counterpart (more accurately, superior) in London, the Scottish government has been extremely busy in producing policy documents and initiatives. What follows is thus highly selective (for a fuller account, see Stewart, 2004).

In May 1999 the Scottish people voted in elections to the first Scottish Parliament for nearly 300 years. Some form of political devolution had been part of New Labour's programme in 1997 and, as discussed below, there were close links between the demand for political devolution and social welfare issues. Shortly after Blair's accession to power the Scots were asked in a referendum whether there should be a Scottish Parliament; and, if so, whether it should have tax-raising powers. Both these questions were answered in the affirmative, resulting in turn in the 1998 Scotland Act.

What did devolution entail and what were its immediate outcomes? First, elections to the Scottish Parliament involve a measure of proportional representation. Consequently, after the elections of both 1999 and 2003 the largest party, Labour, has had to go into coalition with the Liberal Democrats. Another significant result has been the election of representatives from smaller political parties and groupings such as the vociferous Scottish Socialist Party. All this has led, Davies argues (2003, p 1), to the 'Europeanisation' of Scottish politics. Second, the main opposition party has been not the Conservatives but the Scottish National Party (SNP), which has positioned itself on the political centre-left. Third, the devolution settlement consciously sought to engender a more consensual form of politics than was seen to take place in Westminster. Given the necessity for coalition and the number of represented political parties, such an approach would probably have been necessary anyway. Overall, then, the political dynamics of the Edinburgh parliament are thus rather different from those of the London parliament.

Fourth, there are the devolved powers themselves. To put it simply, Scotland has, as Parry suggests (2002, p 315), "a policy system with incomplete responsibilities" concerned primarily with non-cash social services such as health and education. Certain powers are 'reserved' to London, for our purposes the most important being macroeconomic policy and social security. At least in the case of social security this was by no means logically inevitable – there are historical precedents for its devolution (Parry, 1997, p 38). The decision *not* to devolve was therefore a political decision and can be seen as a major constraint on the 'Scottish welfare state'. More generally, the UK Parliament remains sovereign, with the right to overrule the Scottish Parliament, and Scottish law must also conform with European Community law. These limitations to the devolved powers must always be borne in mind.

Finally in this section, there is the question of funding. In essence, money comes from the Treasury in London using the Barnett Formula. This was devised in the late 1970s and first applied to Scotland in 1978 (Glennerster, 2003, p 190). What needs to be noted here in a complicated and contentious issue is that Barnett does not determine total allocation – this derives from the historic 'baseline', that is the funding situation when the formula was introduced – but rather incremental change. Such change is based upon the negotiations of UK departments with the Treasury. These in turn are then applied proportionately, on the basis of population, to Scotland (and Wales and Northern Ireland). This is therefore not directly a needs-based formula. Barnett clearly predated devolution and was consciously part of the devolution settlement. One implication of its workings is that neither the Executive nor its predecessor, the Scottish Office, has had to deal directly with the Treasury: this is done on their behalf by the UK functional departments. Nonetheless, once funding is allocated the Executive has (as did the Scottish Office) the power to exercise discretion as to what it actually does with the money.

Two more points need to be noted about funding and expenditure. First, Scotland has historically spent more per capita on public services than England, in particular. This is notably the case in health and in education. Given that Barnett operates on incremental change, the formula thus institutionalised a pre-existing situation. Second, the Edinburgh parliament has, as noted earlier, the ability to marginally alter the rate of income tax. To date this power has not been used and the dominant political party, Scottish Labour, is at least for the moment committed to staying with this policy. To put it crudely, then, for the most part the Executive spends money that it has had no direct part in raising.

Welfare, autonomy and devolution

Although Scotland and England were joined by the union of 1707 this did not mean that the former was fully integrated with the latter. Important parts of civil society remained in Scottish hands, most notably law, religion, education and local government. As Lindsay Paterson, an educationalist and prominent commentator on Scottish affairs, has famously suggested, Scotland thus retained significant areas of autonomy (Paterson, 1994). Education was one important dimension of this. So, for example, the Scots were and remain much more committed to comprehensive education and a broad curriculum (the contrast here being between Scottish Highers and English A levels) while overwhelmingly rejecting the private sector (see further, Reynolds, 2002). In health policy as in education, Scotland was usually governed by separate legislation, most notably the 1947 National Health Service (Scotland) Act. And also as with education, private sector health care is relatively insignificant, again especially when compared with England (see further, Reynolds, 2002; Greer, 2003).

This autonomy operated in the context of a particular form of governance that also had deep historic roots but can be summed up as favouring consensus, corporatism and central control (or, for critics, cosiness and complacency). It manifested itself in, for instance, a tight central grip in the Scottish NHS over hospital planning in the era of the 'classic' welfare state (Stewart, 2003). Scotland is, moreover, socially and politically if not geographically a small place and this has resulted – both pre- and post-devolution – in what Jervis and Plowden (2001) describe as 'policy villages'. These are characterised by "tight political and professional networks" allowing "for quicker and easier agreement over policy and strategy" (p 4). While not unproblematic, all this appeared to work reasonably well until the 1980s and 1990s.

Scotland remained loyal to the Labour Party during the long period of Conservative rule. Thatcherite welfare reform became increasingly resented on two levels: first, that it was being 'imposed' by an insensitive London administration at variance with Scottish political preferences; second, that it went against the grain of how cherished institutions of Scottish autonomy traditionally worked. Resistance to the Conservative's reform strategy thus began to manifest itself. So, for example, while many English schools took the opportunity to opt out of local authority control, in Scotland only two did so (Pickard, 1999). Similarly, in health policy there was a marked reluctance to go down the 'internal market' route. Greer suggests that one reason for this was cultural antipathy to market mechanisms (Greer, 2003, p 200). The Scottish Conservative Party's electoral wipeout in 1997 is partly attributable to such issues and illustrates how politically sensitive they are for the Scottish electorate.

It is therefore unsurprising that social welfare matters became central to the growing devolution movement. The broadly based Scottish Constitutional Convention, for instance, asserted, as Nottingham notes, a "direct relationship between constitutional reform and good health policy" (2000, pp 175-76). A Scottish Parliament would, so the case went, be better able to tailor health policies to specific Scottish needs. As Nottingham further remarks, Scotland's notoriously poor health record began to take on a "totemic political status", with all post-1979 changes seen as "alien impositions" with "no roots in Scottish experience or need". In education, similar language was employed during the parliamentary debates on the 'right' of schools to opt out of local authority control and, significantly, was used not only by Nationalist but also by Labour and Liberal MPs (Paterson, 1994, p 1). As Paterson puts it (2000, p 48), there was thus "a distinctive Scottish debate about welfare, which in the 1980s became the basis for a new Scottish nationalism". Parry (1998, p 213) suggests that by the eve of devolution "Scotland's welfare state remained more old-fashioned, better-resourced and less privatised than England's, and those involved in it could see the way to a field of action in the Scottish Parliament".

The Scottish Executive and the Scottish welfare state

The Scottish Executive has consistently stressed certain key concerns. First, social welfare policy is to be seen as a totality. While this might be the aim of all governments pursuing welfare reform, the 'policy village' effect noted above makes it much more plausible in Scotland than in England. The emphasis on, where at all possible, a cross-departmental approach also reminds us that categories such as 'health' and 'education' are broadly conceived and seen as parts of an organic whole. Second, a recent Child Poverty Action Group publication argues that, while the matter should not be overstated, "a different language is often mobilised" in Scotland when dealing with matters such as poverty. There is, it continues, "a greater stress on social inclusion (as opposed to exclusion), on partnership, equality, and, importantly, on social justice" (Brown et al, 2002, pp 6-7). This emphasis has been institutionalised in the Scottish Cabinet post of Minister for Social Justice (after the 2003 elections, Minister for Communities). Picking up on our first point, this post has a coordinating function across departments with, as a statement of spring 2002 put it, the brief to "drive the need for social justice solutions across all the Executive's work". The same statement also claimed that "under the new Scottish budget 2003-2006, unprecedented levels of resources are now available to tackle social injustice in Scotland"[1]. The use of words such as 'partnership' also illustrate Scottish governance's more consensual, corporatist approach while the Executive's repeated claim that it aims to 'rebuild' or 'renew' Scotland's welfare services implies a deep level of commitment to these institutions. At least at a rhetorical level, therefore, a case can be made for the Edinburgh administration as a 'defender' of the welfare state, more accurately the 'classic' welfare state of the quarter of a century or so after 1945.

Third, at the launch of the Scottish NHS Plan in late 2000 – notably, in the light of the last point, referred to as 'rebuilding' Scotland's health services – the First Minister commented that it afforded the chance to "address Scotland's needs with greater determination and focus than ever before". Consequently, the Executive sought to "use our power and resources to make a real difference"[2]. This remark exemplifies both the perception that Scotland has its own particular problems and that the Executive has the powers to address them – hence the frequent use of expressions such as 'Scottish solutions to Scottish problems' and the equally frequent assertion that devolution can and does 'make a difference'. Nonetheless, ministers have also been at pains to stress that however much has been achieved since 1999 – and the Scottish Parliament's first term is

---

often referred to as a settling-in period – much more needs to be done. This approach can be read as a commitment to welfare and welfare reform alongside a condemnation of previous underinvestment in public services, as well as a further assertion of Scotland's ability to operate in its own way in these areas.

However, it would be wrong to argue that since 1999 Scotland has simply followed its own path in those welfare policy fields over which the Executive has control. We return to this in the Conclusion, but for present purposes we should note the constitutional constraints on the Scottish Parliament, with Westminster retaining ultimate sovereignty; the financial constraints, with the Treasury in reality holding the purse strings; the political constraints, notably that Scottish Labour is part of the British Labour Party; and the more general context wherein welfare debates in Scotland are informed by those in the rest of the UK and more widely. And, as with any other government, there is the potential in social welfare policy for tensions, contradictions and differences in interpretation. One example of this came during the 2003 elections when the Westminster Education Secretary visited an Edinburgh school being built under a private–public partnership. For the Conservatives, the visit highlighted the "stark differences in education policy between England and Scotland" while for the SNP "the Scottish Labour Party was increasingly being forced down an agenda that was led by London"[3]. The Executive was thus being attacked simultaneously for policy convergence (by the Nationalists) and policy divergence (by the Tories).

Education and health since devolution

We now turn to a selective review of education and health policy since 1999. An early Executive consultative document stressed that raising school standards was its 'number one objective', a claim comparable to New Labour's famous 'education, education, education' (Scottish Executive, 2000, p 3). One of the first pieces of legislation passed by the Edinburgh Parliament was the 2000 Standards in Scotland's Schools Act, which, although recognised at the time as incomplete, nonetheless embraced four important themes. The Act sought, first, to emphasise a child's right to education, an approach which as Munn (2000, pp 127-28) notes, was much more in tune with the 1995 Children (Scotland) Act than with previous educational legislation. There was thus a clear aim of fostering social inclusion, a role frequently ascribed to education by the Executive. Second, the right of schools to opt out of local authority control was formally abolished. Third, the Act set up a framework for continuous improvement in schools (with a very 'New Labourish' setting of targets). Fourth, pre-school provision for all three- and four-year-olds was guaranteed. This is worth dwelling on briefly. For the Executive, 'free, quality pre-school education' helps children learn as they play; builds on learning in the home; develops 'essential skills' for use in later life; and prepares children for the primary sector (Scottish Executive, 2003a, p 4). Emphasis was placed on 'integrated service delivery' and there was an explicit recognition that "services that have traditionally been thought of as providers of *care* are now recognised as playing a role in *educating* young children and nurturing their development" (Scottish Executive, 2003b, pp 13-14). Here we observe the aim of a holistic approach to welfare provision – 'integrated service delivery' – and early intervention. The latter involves education rather than simply 'care' and, as with other parts of the Act and other Executive statements, embraces a human capital approach to education and the young.

The integrated service approach was especially embodied, however, in the New Community Schools scheme, which is consciously seen as embracing not only education but also health and social care. Among its key aims are promoting social inclusion; increasing the educational attainment of students confronted with the 'cycle of underachievement'; and thereby maximising each student's potential. While originally targeted at deprived areas, it was always intended that New Community Schools would become the model for all schools and their experience thus universalised (see, for example, Scottish Executive, 2003c, p 10).

Equally, the Executive's determination to raise school standards on an ongoing basis has been constantly reiterated. There are now 'National Priorities' in education, set up in 2000 and for review in 2005, which, inter alia, set a timescale and targets for the period 2002-2005 (see Scottish Executive, 2000, and, for a further commitment to the National Priorities, Scottish Executive, 2003c). In his parliamentary statement following the 2003 elections the First Minister stressed that "the next four years will be remembered for the steps we have taken to protect our young people, increase their opportunities and give them the best start in life". To these ends there would be, for example, further legislation to allow ministerial intervention to ensure that desired targets were being met[4]. This proposal was portrayed by one Scottish newspaper as a decision to 'take on' Scotland's powerful educational establishment and to employ 'hit squads' to take over failing schools, "a move in line with policies south of the border ... a profoundly Blairite idea"[5]. As we shall see, this was a rather simplistic analysis, but the use of the expression 'Blairite' reminds us that in certain respects the Executive's education agenda bears strong resemblances to that of its southern counterpart. Pre-primary school provision, for example, is a broadly shared policy objective.

Nonetheless, we have already encountered hints of, at the very least, different emphases, even where there are rhetorical similarities. Paterson finds in the field of 'citizenship' education – a big issue in educational and political circles not least for its potential impact on social exclusion – a divergence in the underlying philosophies of the Scots and the English. This derives, he contends, from a Scottish social democratic communitarianism as opposed to Blairite liberalism (Paterson, 2002, p 125).

Are there, then, ways in which post-devolution education policy has enlarged upon existing distinctiveness? Again we need to be selective, but the following five points merit attention. First, there is the issue of student fees. This was debated during the 1999 elections when, it should be noted, their abolition was proposed by all major parties except Scottish Labour. Nonetheless, as from autumn 2000 tuition fees were done away with although it is more accurate to say that upfront tuition fees were abolished, as a graduate endowment scheme was also introduced. The latter is, however, more financially generous than the current English system and Scotland has supplemented this with schemes aimed at encouraging students from low-income families to enter the sector, further evidence of a commitment to social inclusion and equality of opportunity (Rees, 2002, p 106; for brief details of the schemes, Scottish Executive, 2003d, p 29). All this is at least part of the reason for the 50% participation target being achieved – ahead of England – and the further upsurge in applications to Scottish universities for 2003: 2.9% over the preceding year, double the increase south of the border[6].

Second, it can be argued that Scottish education has continued to operate in a consensual, corporatist way. Early in its existence the Executive reached a generous settlement with the teaching profession based on the findings of the McCrone Inquiry. As well as improving pay and conditions this acknowledged the status of Scotland's powerful and publicly supported teaching profession. Reynolds remarks that such a settlement could only have come about in "a relatively supportive educational climate", a climate *not* characterised by the 'harsh rhetoric' to be found in England (2002, p 98). Third, although there are ambiguities here, in general the Executive remains committed to the comprehensive principle and to the Scottish emphasis on breadth of education. In late 2002 the First Minister declared himself "not interested in having a few schools with centres of excellence. My goal is for every school in Scotland to be excellent"[7]. Bromley and Curtice (2003) thus observe that the Executive has "indicated its continuing faith in the principle of comprehensive secondary schools that have a remit to teach equally well across the full range of the curriculum". Furthermore, this approach is backed up by polling evidence, which shows that attacks on the 'bog-standard comprehensive' do not mirror Scottish popular aspirations. Given both the approach of the London government and public attitudes south of the border, Bromley and Curtice identify a 'distinctively Scottish policy' reflecting a 'distinctive strand of public opinion'. As they rightly suggest, this is less noticed but potentially more important than differences over student fees (Bromley and Curtice, 2003, pp 10-11).

Fourth, it is certainly the case that PFI/PPP[8] initiatives have been used to modernise Scotland's schools. Nonetheless, in broader terms the private sector appears to hold little appeal for either parents – the vast majority of Scottish children, over 95%, are educated in public institutions – or the Executive. The Education Minister, in summer 2003, stressed that the Executive had "ruled out using private companies to rescue failing schools, a measure that has been widely used south of the Border". As, one newspaper suggested, this confirmed the Executive's reluctance "to pursue the Blairite reform model for the public sector"[9]. This should be placed alongside the comments noted above which claimed that Scotland was going down the 'Blairite' route. Finally, while the Executive is committed to improving standards and monitoring this process, nonetheless in autumn 2003 it announced the abolition of school league tables and of national testing for 5- to 14-year-olds. The former had been anticipated during the summer 2002 National Debate on education when one of the 'key comments' made was that there was a need to "celebrate success and recognise the negative effect of league tables" (Scottish Executive, 2003c, p 6). As the newspaper in which this story broke commented, abolition would bring Scotland in line with Wales and Northern Ireland. On the other hand, the demise of league tables and of national testing would be seen as "creating a bigger gap between the Scottish Executive's and the Blairite vision of school education"[10]. In fact, this proved more problematic than anticipated as restricting parents' access to school results would contravene the Freedom of Information (Scotland) Act. Nonetheless, the Executive remained convinced that league tables were, as one spokesperson put it, 'largely meaningless' and reform of the nature and scope of the information was under way in late 2003[11].

Scottish education policy was thus, in important respects, different from that of England prior to devolution and has largely continued on its own path, New Labour approaches to education notwithstanding. To what extent is this true in health policy? Shortly after the 2003 elections *The*

Scotsman remarked that the "gulf between the English and the Scottish arms of the NHS is set to grow"[12]. Earlier the same year the First Minister made a speech on the future of the Scottish NHS in which he made four important points. First, that Scotland had some of the worst health statistics in Europe and that, in part, this was due to individual failure "to take responsibility for our own health". Second, health improvement was not simply a medical matter but had also to do with improvements in social care. Third, the Scottish health services needed "reform to match investment". Crucially, however, this reform was to "go with the grain of Scotland". Finally, the First Minister stressed his commitment to the founding principles of the NHS as enunciated in 1948 while also suggesting that these had to be adapted to "building a health service for this new century"[13]. Here, then, was a perceived need for a change in Scottish health culture; a sense of both the need to 'reform' and for this to acknowledge Scottish particularity and the fundamental ethos of the NHS; and a further assertion of the need for a holistic approach to welfare provision.

That Scotland has a poor health record is incontrovertible. Hanlon et al (2003, pp 33, 55, 57) show that despite recent improvements, "Scotland's health status and key determinants of health lag behind comparable countries in Northern and Western Europe"; that Scotland has the worst health of any part of the UK; and that within Scotland itself there are significant health inequalities. Current projections suggest, furthermore, that in health "Scotland is unlikely to change its relative position". While there are many contributory factors to this disturbing situation, the authors note that poverty and inequality play their part, as do cultural matters such as diet and tobacco consumption. It is against this background that the Executive has launched a barrage of health policy documents and initiatives. And, given the significance of health issues to devolution noted above and the nature of the devolutionary settlement whereby health is a major component of the Executive's brief, then as Woods remarks, making a success of health policy "could be an important determinant of public views on the overall achievements of devolution". Being successful in this way, he adds, "is commonly understood to require distinctive policies suited to the circumstances of each country" (Woods, 2002, p 28).

One early, and important, example of the Executive's strategy came with the publication in late 2000 of *Our national health: A plan for action*. This was part of the UK-wide 'relaunching' of the NHS, although there were differences of timing and, more importantly, emphasis from its English counterpart. One report noted, for example, the "strong consensus [that] historical, cultural and epidemiological circumstances [required] a specifically Scottish solution to Scottish health needs and problems"[14]. The plan itself was consciously designed to 'rebuild' the Scottish health services through, for example, the setting of targets such as a 20% reduction in pregnancy rates among 13- to 15-year-olds[15]. Such ideas were adapted and expanded upon in documents such as the 2003 White Paper *Partnership for care*. As its title suggests, this laid great emphasis on cooperative working and a consequent need to move away from the fragmentation caused especially by the market mechanisms of the 1990s. It was also necessary to "bridge the gap between primary care and secondary care and between health and social care", yet another reminder of the aim of holistic welfare. Targets were again emphasised although, significantly, these were to be achieved through a "culture of improvement" rather than a "culture of blame" (Scottish Executive, 2000e). Introducing the White Paper, the Health Minister stressed the Executive's commitment to improving the Scottish NHS, not least through an increase in expenditure over the lifetime of the 2003 parliament from £6.7 billion to £9.3 billion[16]. In the wake of the 2003 election, the Executive reiterated its 'radical agenda' on health, this including specific commitments on waiting lists; the tackling of lifestyle issues such as tobacco consumption; and a Bill to allow Ministers to intervene "as a last resort, to secure quality of care"[17]. This Bill, published in summer 2003, was an important moment in the development of the Scottish health services for a range of reasons (including, it could be argued, the tension between Ministerial interventionism and the repeated rejection of the so-called 'command and control' model of NHS management).

However, we now focus more fully on the issue of policy divergence, and the 2003 Bill is an important way into this topic. Commenting on its provisions, *The Guardian* claimed that with them "Scotland goes its own way on NHS reforms". With devolution now established, the Bill placed "more clear blue water between the health services north and south of the border – by what it leaves out as well as what it contains". The last point was exemplified by the Executive's lack of interest in foundation hospitals[18]. Scrutiny of Executive statements reveals that such initiatives have never figured in its plans, a position made utterly clear by a spokesperson just at the moment when Scottish Labour MPs were, ironically, about to vote for foundation hospitals in the Westminster Parliament. Foundation hospitals were at odds, it was argued, with the Executive's "vision of creating a more integrated NHS in Scotland, where we break down the barriers between primary and secondary care"[19]. This is, of course, a perfectly valid argument in itself as is the suggestion that foundation hospitals simply would not work in Scotland because of geography and population dispersal. But there is, perhaps, more to it in that the Executive has fairly consistently shied away from any close encounter with the private sector. In Scotland there has not been the 'concordat' with the private sector that New Labour has promoted for England, and in such differences Woods (2003, p 6) finds "a prominent example of policy divergence".

Greer (2003, pp 198, 208, 210) suggests that behind all this lies a distinction between advocates of "new public administration" who see public services as being supplied via contracts rather than necessarily directly (for example, through PFI) and advocates of a single NHS. England, he contends, is the "most important site for PFI and its advocates" and the only part of the UK where the government "appears to see private sector involvement as an end, rather than a means". In Scotland, the government "pursues PFI for less ideological reasons, and it shows". Indeed, there is deep-rooted hostility to the whole notion of private sector involvement in health (although for financial reasons there is, as in education, plenty of PFI activity), manifested by the Executive's purchase of the large former private hospital facility at Clydebank. This not only increased NHS capacity but also "expressed a clear policy choice" since, had the Executive wanted to, it could simply have come to a contractual arrangement with this institution. In short, Scotland is seeking to rebuild the "unitary NHS with strong planning and service integration", while by contrast, England pursues "market-based service organisation and private participation".

The Executive's attitude towards foundation hospitals is a major, if often rather underplayed, dimension of Scottish particularity post-devolution. What has been widely publicised, of course, has been the implementation of the 'free' personal care for the elderly. This came about, though, in a rather curious way (for fuller accounts, see Simeon, 2003; Age Concern Scotland, 2003). The majority recommendations of the Royal Commission on Long-Term Care – the Sutherland Commission – were initially rejected not only by New Labour in London but also by Edinburgh. These recommendations centred on the argument that, when it came to the elderly, no distinction could be made between medical and social care. As things currently stood, however, the former was free at the point of delivery while the latter was means-tested. The basis of New Labour's rejection of Sutherland was that families and individuals should continue to make provision for their old age; that universal personal care would disproportionately benefit those who least needed it, the middle-class elderly – so there should be targeting; and that the costs were too high.

The Executive's initial rejection, however, was reversed (see Scottish Executive, 2001, for the arguments behind this). In early 2002 the Community Care and Health Act (Scotland) introduced 'free' personal and nursing care for the elderly, a move described by one set of analysts as "one of the most distinctive as well as one of the most controversial policies to be introduced by the Scottish Executive" (Curtice and Petch, 2003, p 30). It is now also heralded as a major achievement by the Executive itself. What does this tell us about post-devolution welfare policy in Scotland? First, and obviously enough, we find here a clear case of policy divergence, with personal care being provided on a universal basis in Scotland and on a selective basis in England. And as Simeon (2003, p 220) puts it, there is now a 'public perception' that Scottish pensioners are better off than those elsewhere in the UK. Looking at the process as a whole, Woods (2002, p 44) remarks that it clearly illustrates "the dilemmas facing health (and other public) policy making in the devolved administrations". It arose from a "UK government enquiry; its proposals fall predominantly within the competence of the devolved administrations, but the resources available to them are the Barnett consequences of policy decisions taken in Whitehall".

Second, the measure was clearly intended to facilitate the integration of health and social care. This has not, however, proved all that easy. Age Concern Scotland has found, for instance, that there remains a 'lack of clarity' about what actually constitutes free personal care and consequently what services can, and cannot, be provided (see further, Age Concern Scotland, 2003, pp 21-2). Third, free personal care has been popular with the Scottish public but investigation has shown that it would have been popular in England too (Curtice and Petch, 2003, pp 46-7). Its implementation is thus less to do with differences in popular attitude and more to do with how governments view welfare provision and their relationship with their electorates. On this issue at least, therefore, devolution is 'working' in the sense that the Executive is responding to public desires. We should also note here the impact of the highly vociferous campaign organised in favour of Sutherland by bodies such as Age Concern Scotland and the relative ease with which its representatives could gain access to influential members of the Executive – 'policy villages' again.

Fourth, the creation of this policy saw overtly political factors coming into play. At first the Executive – or, more specifically, its Labour members – appeared to follow London's lead. It then, however, undertook a policy reversal, partly because of public pressure but also because the other main parties were in favour of free personal care and were pressing for its implementation, with the governing coalition at one point threatened by a Liberal Democrat rebellion. It is also possible that this reversal owed something to the desire of an incoming (although politically short-lived) First Minister to assert Scottish distinctiveness. Fifth, the UK government was not happy with Edinburgh's new policy. There was a very public dispute with the Department for Work and Pensions over Attendance Allowances, the net effect of which was that the costs to the Executive of implementing free personal care were increased. London's attitude can be seen either as a point of constitutional principal or as resistance to a policy with which the UK government disagreed. Given that the Treasury is ultimately the paymaster for Scottish social welfare, this clearly raises important issues about the possibility of such a clear divergence happening again[20].

Finally, the whole episode of free personal care raises fundamental issues about the direction of the welfare state north and south of the border. Bauld (2001, p 36) points out that distinctively Scottish policy on free personal care "poses challenges for the future of community care policy across the UK". Player and Pollock (2001, p 252) argue that the London government's rejection of the Sutherland Report constituted a "severing of the 1948 social contract" – that is, the fundamental principle of universalism which purportedly underpinned the postwar welfare state. In the Scottish situation, by contrast, Simeon (2003, pp 231-2) suggests that in going its own way on free personal care we have an instance of Scotland "expanding the welfare state". She further, and rightly, notes that the proposal was defended "as the fulfilment of the NHS principle of universal access from cradle to grave, free at the point of delivery. *It was not defended in the name of a uniquely Scottish need*" (my emphasis). This would thus put devolved administrations in the position of defenders of the welfare state against the retrenchment of London. Curtice and Petch (2003, p 40) similarly comment that the whole issue was largely an argument about the underlying principles of the welfare state – universal or selective. Blair (2002, p 34) detects a "sustained drive ... to facilitate distributive social justice for older people in Scotland" while Parry (2002, p 318) argues that this episode, like that of student fees, illustrates the possibility of "conceptual challenges to the Blair/Brown orthodoxy". Given also the sense in which England has been seen as a 'diverger' not just on this issue but also in other policy areas, then the idea of a devolved administration 'defending' or even 'expanding' the welfare state takes on particular significance, and, in conclusion, it is to this we now turn.

Conclusion

Greer (2003, p 213) remarks that not only has there been divergence in health policy between Scotland and England since 1999 but that there has been an "even greater divergence in ... values". He thus predicts that in a few years the health systems of the constituent parts of the UK will look very different and, like other commentators such as Woods, notes that England is the "likely diverger". This is because, Greer continues, "England is the only country trying explicitly to reinvent its health services, and is certainly the only one that might reinvent the NHS out of existence". He concludes that this "alone might strike people in Northern Ireland, Scotland and Wales as a reason for devolution".

Scotland has not, of course, taken an entirely different course from the rest of the UK since 1999, even in those welfare areas over which it has competence. For one thing, the Scottish First Minister and the British Prime Minister both belong to the same political party and operate in broad terms within its programme. It is sometimes argued that Scotland is a bastion of 'Old Labour' but this is too simplistic. While Scottish Labour does indeed use the rhetoric of social inclusion and social justice, by the same token the language of wealth redistribution is, by and large, absent. New Labour characteristics such as the setting of targets and an emphasis on 'modernisation' can also be found in Executive pronouncements and policies. Much is also made of broader processes such as globalisation and its demands for a 'knowledge economy'. And, of course, we always need to bear in mind the limitations of the devolution settlement.

Nonetheless, as Greer's comments suggest, there is something going on and we finish with the following six observational and analytical points. First, in certain welfare fields Scotland historically had a degree of autonomy and it was primarily these that were handed over to the Edinburgh parliament. Second, this pre-existing autonomy had allowed for a degree of policy divergence prior to devolution, and in important respects this has increased since 1999. This has been justified not only historically, but as necessary to deal with particularly Scottish concerns. In this context it is interesting to note that the Executive, as part of its health strategy, has addressed cultural and behavioural matters, so acknowledging that previous high levels of expenditure on health have not of themselves resulted in improved health outcomes. Third, the reasons for this policy divergence are complex, but at least in part they revolve around a popular, professional, and political ethos that is broadly supportive of the public sector and its provision of, for instance, education and healthcare. Equally there is, in such areas, a related scepticism about, or even hostility to, the private sector. Explaining the existence, and persistence, of this ethos is of itself a complex matter, but we should note that it is historically rooted and philosophically attuned to what we have seen Paterson describe as "social democratic communitarianism".

Fourth, and leading on from the previous points, we have noted several commentators suggest that in welfare policy it has been Blair's government, not the devolved administrations, which have 'diverged' – from, that is, the 'classic' welfare state of the postwar era. Fifth, this in turn raises the possibility of tension between London and the devolved administrations centred round, for example, the issue of equity. Put crudely, why should pensioners in Edinburgh be 'advantaged' in ways that those in London are not? Furthermore, what would the implications be of Edinburgh actually using its tax-raising powers, or of significant changes to the Barnett Formula? The answers to these questions are not straightforward but they do raise key issues about welfare provision across what is in some respects still a unitary state. Finally, it seems likely that because of the nature of its politics and the structure of the devolution settlement, Scotland will for the foreseeable future have a parliament dominated by the centre-left and with strong centre-left opposition. It seems equally likely that in the social welfare areas over which it has control it will continue, at least to some extent, to pursue its own agenda. While it currently seems improbable that the next British general election will result in a Conservative Party victory, this cannot be ruled out in the future. Overall, then, as devolution unfolds there is the potential in the short- and long-term not only for further policy divergence but for social welfare to be an increasingly contested area between London and the devolved administrations.

Notes

[1] www.scotland.gov.uk/library5/social/emsjs-00.asp.

[2] www.guardian.co.uk, 14 December 2000, 'Plan to "rebuild" NHS in Scotland'.

[3] www.thescotsman.co.uk, 24 April 2003, 'Opposition highlights Labour's "great divide"'.

[4] www.scotland.gov.uk, 28 May 2003, 'Parliamentary Statement by the First Minister on the Executive's Programme for 2003-2004'.

[5] www.theherald.co.uk, 28 May 2003, 'Failing schools face takeover by McConnell's hit squads'.

[6] www.thescotsman.co.uk, 18 July 2003, 'More apply to Scottish universities'.

[7] www.bbc.co.uk, 5 November 2002, 'McConnell's schooling vision'.

[8] Private Finance Initiative, now renamed Public Private Partnerships.

[9] www.thescotsman.co.uk, 28 June 2003, 'Private sector "will not bail out schools"'.

[10] www.theherald.co.uk, 25 September 2003, 'School league tables to be scrapped'.

[11] www.thescotsman.co.uk, 5 November 2003, 'MSPs lose battle on school leagues'.

[12] www.thescotsman.co.uk, 14 May 2003, 'Cancer care and devolution'.

[13] www.scottishlabour.org.uk, 11 February 2003, 'First Minister, Jack McConnell: Building a Health Service for this New Century: Speech at Ninewells Hospital in Dundee'.

[14] www.guardian.co.uk, 12 December 2000, 'Why Scotland wants its own NHS plan'.

[15] www.scottishlabour.org.uk/health.html

[16] www.scottishlabour.org.uk, 27 February 2003, 'Health Minister, Malcolm Chisholm: "Partnership for Care"'.

[17] www.scotland.gov.uk/library5/pfbs.pdf; and www.scotland.gov.uk, 28 May 2003, 'Parliamentary Statement by the First Minister on the Executive's Programme for 2003-2004'.

[18] www.guardian.co.uk, 27 June 2003, 'Scotland goes its own way on NHS reforms'.

[19] www.thescotsman.co.uk, 8 July 2003, '"Obsessional" reform fails to improve NHS'.

[20] www.guardian.co.uk, *The Observer*, 14 October 2001, 'London blocks £23m care cash for Scots'; Woods (2002, p 45); Simeon (2003, pp 219, 225).

References

Age Concern Scotland (2003) *'Free for All?': Age Concern Scotland's report into free personal and nursing care*, Edinburgh: Age Concern Scotland.

Bauld, L. (2001) 'Scotland makes it happen', *Community Care*, 18-24 October, pp 36-7.

Blair, S.E.E. (2002) 'Free personal care for older people: is this Scotland's bid for distributive justice in later life?', *Scottish Affairs*, vol 39, pp 19-38.

Bromley, C. and Curtice, J. (2003) 'Devolution: scorecard and prospects', in C. Bromley et al (eds) *Devolution – Scottish answers to Scottish questions?*, Edinburgh: Edinburgh University Press, pp 7-29.

Brown, U., Scott, G., Mooney, G. and Duncan, B. (eds) (2002) *Poverty in Scotland 2002: People, places and policies*, London: CPAG/Scottish Poverty Information Unit.

Cunfice, L. and Petch, A. (2003) 'Does the community care?', in C. Bromley, J. Curtice, K. Hinds and A. Park (eds) *Devolution: Scottish answers to Scottish questions?*, Edinburgh: Edinburgh University Press.

Davies, S. (2003) *Inside the laboratory: The new politics of public services in Wales*, London: Catalyst Forum.

Glennerster, H. (2003) *Understanding the finance of welfare: What welfare costs and how to pay for it*, Bristol: The Policy Press.

Greer, S. (2003) 'Policy divergence: will it change something in Greenock?', in R. Hazell, (ed) *The state of the nations 2003: The third year of devolution in the United Kingdom*, London: UCL Constitution Unit, pp.195-214.

Hanlon, P., Walsh, D., and Whyte, B. (2003) 'The health of Scotland', in K. Woods and D. Carter (eds) *Scotland's health and health services*, London: TSO, pp 31-61.

Jervis, P. and Plowden, W. (2001) *Devolution and health: Second annual report*, London: UCL Constitution Unit.

Munn, P. (2000) 'Can schools make Scotland a more inclusive society?', *Scottish Affairs*, vol 33, pp 116-31.

Nottingham, C. (2000) 'The politics of health in Scotland after devolution', in C. Nottingham (ed) *The NHS in Scotland: The legacy of the past and the prospect of the future*, Aldershot: Ashgate, pp 173-90.

Parry, R. (1997) 'The Scottish parliament and social policy', *Scottish Affairs*, vol 20, pp.34-46.

Parry, R. (1998) 'The view from Scotland', in H. Jones and S. MacGregor (eds) *Social issues and party politics*, London: Routledge, pp 194-213.

Parry, R. (2002) 'Delivery structure and policy development in post-devolution Scotland', *Social Policy and Society*, vol 1, no 4, pp 315-24.

Paterson, L. (1994) *The autonomy of modern Scotland*, Edinburgh: Edinburgh University Press.

Paterson, L. (2000) 'Scottish democracy and Scottish utopias: the first year of the Scottish parliament', *Scottish Affairs*, vol 33, pp 45-61.

Paterson, L. (2002) 'Scottish social democracy and Blairism: difference, diversity and community', in G. Hassan, and C. Warhurst (eds) *Tomorrow's Scotland*, London: Lawrence and Wishart, pp 116-29.

Pickard, W. (1999) 'The history of Scottish education, 1980 to the present day', in T.G.K. Bryce and W.M. Humes (eds) *Scottish education*, Edinburgh: Edinburgh University Press, pp 225-34.

Player, S. and Pollock, A. (2001) 'Long-term care: from public responsibility to private good', *Critical Social Policy*, vol 21, no 2, pp 231-55.

Rees, G. (2002) 'Devolution and the restructuring of post-16 education and training in the UK', in J. Adams and P. Robinson (eds) *Devolution in practice: Public policy differences within the UK*, London: IPPR, pp 104-14.

Reynolds, D. (2002) 'Developing differently: educational policy in England, Wales, Scotland and Northern Ireland', in J. Adams and P. Robinson (eds) *Devolution in practice: Public policy differences within the UK*, London: IPPR, pp 93-103.

Scottish Executive (2000) *Improving our schools: A consultation paper on national priorities for schools education in Scotland*, Edinburgh: Scottish Executive.

Scottish Executive (2001) *Fair care for older people: Care development group report: Executive summary and summary of recommendations*, Edinburgh: Scottish Executive.

Scottish Executive (2003a) *Factsheet: Education*, Edinburgh: Scottish Executive.

Scottish Executive (2003b) *Education and training in Scotland: National dossier 2003: summary*, Edinburgh: Scottish Executive.

Scottish Executive (2003c) *Educating for excellence: Choice and opportunity: the Executive's response to the national debate*, Edinburgh: Scottish Executive.

Scottish Executive (2003d) *Education and training in Scotland: National dossier 2003: summary*, Edinburgh: Scottish Executive.

Scottish Executive (2003e) *Partnership for care: Scotland's health white paper*, Edinburgh: Scottish Executive.

Simeon, R. (2003) 'Free personal care: policy divergence and social citizenship', in R. Hazell (ed) *The state of the nations 2003: The third year of devolution in the United Kingdom*, London: UCL Constitution Unit, pp 215-35.

Stewart, J. (2003) 'The National Health Service in Scotland, 1947-1974. Scottish or British?', *Historical Research*, vol 76, no 193, pp 389-410.

Stewart, J. (2004) *Taking stock: Scottish social welfare after devolution*, Bristol: The Policy Press.

Woods, K. J. (2002) 'Health policy and the NHS in the UK 1997-2002', in J. Adams and P. Robinson (eds) *Devolution in practice: Public policy divergences within the UK*, London: IPPR, pp 25-59.

Woods, K. (2003) 'Scotland's changing health system', in K. Woods, and D. Carter (eds) *Scotland's health and health services*, London: TSO, pp 1-29.

SEVEN

The primacy of ideology: social policy and the first term of the National Assembly for Wales

Paul Chaney and Mark Drakeford

Introduction

Writing in the first few months following the granting in 1999 of limited self-government to Wales and Scotland, policy specialists commented that "the full effect of these changes has yet to be seen, but there is clear potential for a significant and long-lasting impact on the future shape of social policy" (Sykes et al, 2001, p 3). Others have variously chosen to refer to a "sub-national opportunity space" (Bulmer and Burch, 2002, p 21) or to explore the extent to which 'devolution' has the potential to deliver better governance (Chaney et al, 2001). As the following evidence shows, quasi-federalism in the UK has important implications for social policy. Here we explore the social policy record for the National Assembly for Wales during its first term (1999-2003). Our task is threefold. First, it will be argued that the Welsh Assembly is, if it is anything, a *social policy body*. Second, that the government of the Assembly has gone about discharging its social policy responsibilities in a way that has an explicit set of articulated, ideological principles, which mark out that agenda as distinctive. Third, we aim to demonstrate that this distinctiveness has not been confined to policy formulation but has also been translated into the detail of policy implementation and regulation.

The scope and powers of the Assembly: a social policy body?

The powers of the National Assembly for Wales, as framed in the 1998 Government of Wales Act[1], amply illustrate the asymmetrical character of devolution in the United Kingdom (Sandford, 2002; McCrone, 2002), for the Welsh Assembly (in contrast to the Scottish Parliament) lacks both primary legislative and tax-varying powers. A growing number of observers have highlighted the deficiencies in the present constitutional arrangements for Wales (see, for example, Rawlings, 2003a, 2003b)[2]. Hazell (2003, p 298) puts it this way: "the settlement is precarious, because it is completely dependent on the goodwill of the British government to find legislative time (always in short supply) and their willingness to accommodate Welsh concerns". Regardless of one's position on this contentious issue, it is clear that the current constitutional arrangements *do* provide "greater scope for substantive divergence" – and "ever more policy innovation" (Keating, 2002, p 14). As Rawlings (1998, p 487) observes, "the logic of devolution is diversity. As a general principle, the [UK] government expects [Westminster] Bills that confer new powers and relate to the Assembly's functions ... will provide for the powers to be exercised separately and differently in Wales". Central to such a purpose are the civil servants charged with policy development. Parry (2003, p 2-3) highlights the "smaller base of policy-making capability" in Wales when compared to England. Yet he goes on to note that such issues are now being addressed and that Wales presents "the most interesting arena for civil service reform in the UK". In assessing the social policy record of the first term of the Assembly it is necessary to be clear about the political provenance of such policy. This is directly related to the nature and functioning of the Welsh Assembly. In this respect, major changes have taken place in its short history. Initially, it was conceived as an all-party 'body corporate', but following an internal review in 2001 it now operates on a broadly parliamentary model. Executive power – including, for the present purposes, setting and implementing the social policy agenda – now rests with the executive[3] (WAG, 2001a). During the greater part of the first term of devolved governance this was a Welsh Labour Party–Welsh Liberal Democratic Party coalition (Osmond, 2003), succeeded, after elections to the second term in May 2003, by a Labour-only administration, relying upon a wafer-thin de facto majority of one. Accordingly, it is the Welsh executive's, or to give it its official title, the Welsh Assembly Government's, policy record that we examine here.

In policy terms, the Welsh devolution settlement was based upon five key areas of government being retained by Westminster, accounting – by chance rather by design – for almost exactly half the public expenditure in Wales. Foreign affairs, defence, taxation and social security matters were, in their entirety, reserved to Westminster. Unlike Scotland, Wales no longer has a separate system of criminal law. While the Scottish Parliament, therefore, exercises a wide range of responsibilities for justice matters, in the Welsh case a series of Home Office responsibilities such as policing and asylum policy were retained centrally. From the outset, however, these were blurred by Assembly responsibilities in adjacent areas. These include crime and disorder partnerships, and shared responsibility for youth justice matters. For these reasons this is a policy dimension that has become more contentious as the experience of devolution has gathered pace.

The Assembly has taken on responsibility for economic and industrial development, from the agricultural swathes of mid and west Wales to the industrial concentrations of north and south east Wales. An early belief took hold among media and other opinion makers that these powers were the most significant to be held by the Assembly. Yet such analysis is surely wrong-headed. The powers that the Assembly is able to exercise in the economic field are considerably constrained. In the most general sense the capacity of any government to influence the economy is limited by movements of capital that show scant regard for national location – a factor of particular importance for an economy dominated by post-industrial, inward-investment-driven manufacturing industry and located at the western edge of the European Union (Morgan, 2000). More specifically, the Welsh legislature's powers are part of a complex system of multilevel governance shared by other tiers of government and significant public sector bodies (Bulmer and Burch, 2002). For example, in industry these include the Department of Trade and Industry and, within Wales itself, the considerable independence that has been the prerogative of bodies such as the Welsh Tourist Board and the Welsh Development Agency. In budgetary terms, moreover, the economic development portfolio stands clearly among the second rank of ministerial responsibilities and well below those of health or education. While, arguably, economic development has been one area in which the Assembly has most successfully discharged its responsibilities (Cooke, 2002, 2003) – it is not the policy arena in which it has most scope; that distinction lies in the field of social policy. It will not be possible here to do full justice to the entire range of the Assembly's responsibilities. In summary, however, these include the whole of health policy, education, social services, housing and all other local government functions including social services. Together, these areas comprise over 80% of the Assembly's £11 billion annual budget (WAG, 2003d). In other words, the essence of devolution is that it has created a social policy Assembly for Wales.

Policy and ideology

The second purpose of this chapter is to explore the extent to which the exercise of responsibilities might plausibly be described as having some ideological coherence. It was, and remains, one of the core claims for Welsh devolution that it would bring a new quality to the nature of policy making, by aligning it more closely with the political character of the nation. Thus proponents of devolution in the 1990s invoked Wales's "radical and libertarian socialist instincts" and "an inheritance unmistakably rooted in decentralised libertarian community socialist values of solidarity, social justice and co-operation" (Hain, 1999, p 4). According to this view, these factors were essential to the creation of a new "participatory democracy in which there is the greatest possible involvement of citizens" (Hain, 1999, p 14; Davies, 1999; Chaney and Fevre, 2001).

Accordingly, the Welsh devolution White Paper asserted that "by establishing the Assembly the government is moving the process of decision making closer to the citizen: many more decisions about Wales will be made in Wales" (Welsh Office, 1997, p 15). Certainly, the scale of the Assembly – a membership of 60 and a Cabinet of nine members (all working on the same corridor) – provides some basic advantages in avoiding the tribal departmentalism of Whitehall. The Assembly's founding statute, the 1998 Government of Wales Act, also set out three overarching statutory obligations that cut across all portfolio allocations: to promote sustainability, equality and social inclusion.

If the prospects of coherence were enhanced by some basic elements in the Assembly's makeup, the question remains as to whether this was informed and infused by any sense of a unifying *ideology* running through the exercise of different policy responsibilities. Two key texts are available as raw material for such an enquiry (Morgan 2002, 2003), both in the form of lectures delivered by the First Minister, Rhodri Morgan, one shortly before and the other after the elections marking the end of the Assembly's first term in May 2003. The first, delivered to a social policy audience, took place at Swansea University's Centre for Policy Studies in December 2002. The second, established in memory of former Welsh Secretary Cledwyn Hughes and delivered in Welsh to a society of Welsh speaking socialists, but quoted in English translation here, was titled *Social justice and the Welsh tradition.* Taken together, they amount to an explicit claim for a set of linking principles underpinning social policy making at the Assembly.

The basic strand running through these claims is one that devolution has provided an opportunity to align government action with the political and policy values of the people of Wales. Morgan contextualises these developments by referring to a set of three key "ideological fault-lines" in British social policy over a 50-year period, and places the Assembly government along the spectrum that he traces.

The first of these issues identified was that of universalism against means-testing. Contrasting the achievements of the Labour government of 1945-51 – school-age and higher education opportunities for all, National Insurance, a National Health Service, full employment, family allowances, security in old age through an adequate state pension – with the 'pauperisation' of public services during the Thatcher era of the 1980s, he made the claim that "the actions of the Welsh Assembly government clearly owe more to the traditions of Titmuss, Tawney, Beveridge and Bevan than those of Hayek and Friedman". Shortly before the end of its first term, the Assembly published a 'Bill of Citizenship Rights' in which it attempted to draw together the set of new rights that had been created since devolution. These included the reinstatement of free school milk for infant-aged children, free prescriptions for those in the 16-25 age range, free access to national museums and galleries, and free local bus travel for pensioners and disabled people. In describing these initiatives as 'universal', Morgan also clearly implied a contrast with the approach taken in Westminster. These were 'citizenship' rights, he argued, because they were *unconditional* – they did not require the sort of behavioural compliance that was so characteristic of Blairite social policy – even at its most generous (Butler and Drakeford, 2001). Universal, free at the point of use and unconditional in character, these were services, Morgan argued, which helped to "bind a society together and make everyone feel that they are stakeholders in it".

How does the record of the Assembly stand up against such a claim? The following section will explore this question in terms of policy development and the practical delivery of services, but a preliminary verdict suggests that it was based upon some plausible foundations. Not all Assembly social policy measures share each of the core characteristics outlined. Assembly Learning Grants for students, a major initiative of the first term, were means-tested from the outset[4]. The Communities First programme of community regeneration is spatially rather than universally based. The Tir Gofal scheme for farmers[5] is conditional upon behavioural change in care of the countryside. Yet within the financial constraints that the Assembly faces, the political direction of travel can be regarded as one prioritising 'traditional' Labour Party values. The manifesto upon which the party fought the May 2003 Assembly elections included pledges for universal free use of leisure centre swimming pools for school children and older people, universal free breakfasts in primary schools and the abolition of all prescription charges.

The second key policy debate that Morgan identified he described as "the tension between choice and equality"; he was at pains to draw out an understanding of equality which embraced not simply issues of opportunity but "the fundamentally socialist aim of *equality of outcome*". Market theory, he argued, could easily enough encompass a commitment to equality of opportunity. Thereafter, however, it conceptualised the individual as a consumer rather than a citizen, each pursuing her or his best interests with little regard for wider considerations or, to quote from the speech itself, "as some sort of serial shopper, forever out there in the market place looking for the piece of education policy or health care which best meets their individual needs" (Morgan, 2002, unpaginated).

Even within its own terms, he argued, "the theory of marketisation, when applied to social welfare, turns out to be badly flawed" (Morgan, 2002, unpaginated). Spelling out the Assembly's decision to reject the development of foundation hospitals in Wales, he drew on an analysis that was already well developed among trade union and left-of-centre policy groups:

> my objection to the idea of Foundation Hospitals within the NHS is not simply that they will be accessed by those public service consumers who are already the most articulate and advantaged, and who can specify where they want to be treated, but that the experiment will end, not with patients choosing hospitals, but with hospitals choosing patients. The well-resourced producer will be choosing the well-resourced consumer as the kind of patient they want – the grammar school equivalent in hospitals. In other words, in welfare markets, producer-choice, rather than consumer-choice is too likely to be the outcome. That is why the comprehensive school era is not coming to an end in Wales. Selection of pupils by new specialist or faith schools is not the path we intend to encourage. It fails a test which we try to apply to all our policy development at the Welsh Assembly Government, of meeting the wider public interest. (Morgan, 2002, unpaginated)

In the place of competition which choice models require, Morgan emphasised the advantages of cooperation. In his National Eisteddfod speech, he used the analogy of that tradition itself to illuminate the point that he was making:

> of course, competition at the Eisteddfod is very important. But here it rests on the strongest possible foundations of co-operative effort. Nothing would be possible without the huge efforts which local communities invest each year in making the Eisteddfod a reality. Nothing would be possible without that network of local events in which participants try out their trades before making their way to the peak of a *llwyfan* [stage] performance. Nothing would be possible, in so many of the performances themselves, without the co-operation which finds its shape in a choir, or a recitation group or the intricacies of a traditional Welsh dance. (Morgan, 2003, unpaginated)

In this context particularly, Morgan went on to argue that the third key social policy fault-line lay in cooperation rather than competition as the basis for providing collective goods and harnessing the efforts of individuals to the wider common good. Through cooperation, it would be possible to combine a commitment to equality which avoided the dangers of unresponsive or producer-dominated services. Cooperation strengthened the influence that the citizen might bring to bear on policy making and service delivery. Citing the decision to retain and strengthen Community Health Councils in Wales (at a time when they had been abolished in England), he made it clear the Assembly was committed to increasing the receptivity of public services by "strengthening the collective voice of the citizen" and developing a *new pluralism* in policy making in Wales. Closer engagement between policy makers and frontline practitioners had been matched by new ways of encouraging and responding to participation – through, for example, Cabinet 'open mic' sessions, in which the whole Cabinet attend open public meetings and answer questions from the floor. This, Morgan argued, was an approach that prioritised 'active over passive' participation. It had produced a level of direct contact between the public and the political process which "would have been quite inconceivable in the days before devolution" and which had formed the basis for "those qualities of solidarity, tolerance and mutual respect which the Welsh tradition of participation has long delivered" (Morgan, 2003, unpaginated).

At the start of this section it was argued that, in social policy terms, the key claim for devolution was that it had brought about a new alignment between policy making and the preferences of Welsh voters. First Minister

Rhodri Morgan summed up this preference as resting upon a "simple principle – the belief that government can and must be a catalyst for change and a force for good in our society" (Morgan, 2002, unpaginated). Counterpoising this view with the rampant distrust of government in radical right circles, he contrasted it also with the Westminster view of social welfare services as "a series of ladders, or escalators, designed to help those in need to rise above their circumstances". In Wales, he concluded:

> the inclusiveness which we seek does not depend on drawing in a larger number of the able, enterprising and sainted who will go marching inside the stockade. Rather, it depends upon pushing back the boundaries of the stockade itself to the point where there is no stockade any more. That is how, in Wales, we need to create not only a more inclusive, but a more equal society. (Morgan, 2002, unpaginated)

A distinctive social policy agenda? Formulating and implementing social policy in post-devolution Wales

A better country, the Assembly's latest strategic policy document (WAG, 2003a, unpaginated)[6], restates the foregoing ideological perspectives and details the administration's core social policy objectives as:

> to care for those in need by providing a strategic context in which the care and support of vulnerable groups is delivered to improve their comfort and well being; to support elderly people and facilitate independent living; to get services to work together in an inclusive, partnership, way; to provide an appropriate level of funding and ensure that it is used to optimum effect[7].

By necessity, the following discussion will explore selected examples of both substantive policy developments and the structural innovations in post-devolution governance in order to present a preliminary evaluation of the Welsh Assembly Government's social policy agenda, and determine whether its strategic aims – as articulated in *A better country* – are being addressed.

Before exploring examples of policy it is necessary to outline aspects of the new consultation mechanisms that illustrate the revised and distinctive context in which social policy is now being formulated and developed in Wales and which return to the third of the Morgan themes, that of a new pluralism in policy making (Chaney, 2003). Over recent years, partnership between the voluntary sector and government has become an increasingly common feature of European governance (Harris et al, 2000, p 12). However, the terms of the new statutory partnership with national-level government in Wales are, within a UK context, singular and make the realignment of the sector of particular interest. The partnership's terms are set out in section 114 of the Government of Wales Act. The text of the Voluntary Sector Scheme, the contract drawn up in response to the legal requirement for a partnership between the voluntary sector and the National Assembly, sets out the goal of inclusive governance and importantly states that "the Assembly recognizes ... the role they [voluntary organisations] play in formulating and delivering public policy" (NAW, 2000b, ch 2, para 2.10, unpaginated).

As a result, a series of 21 new consultative third sector networks have been created as part of the Voluntary Sector Partnership Council. The 21 strands of the Partnership Council reflect the breadth of voluntary activity in the country, from environmental issues to the arts. Representatives from all 21 interest networks in the Partnership Council hold regular meetings with Assembly members (AMs), officials and managers at the Wales Council for Voluntary Action[8]. In addition, they exercise their right to hold bi-annual meetings with Assembly Cabinet ministers at which they are able to raise issues of concern to their volunteers.

Further, separate consultative 'equality' policy networks have also developed since 1999, again with statutory underpinnings, in this case associated with the Welsh Assembly's legal duty to promote equality of opportunity. These networks are predominantly comprised of voluntary organisations that represent the interests of marginalised groups. They have been given Assembly funding to support dedicated staff, expand their membership and feed into the policy consultations. The self-stated aims of one, the All Wales Ethnic Minority Association, are "to promote ethnic minority participation in government" and "act as an effective vehicle for consultation, participation and communication between minority ethnic communities and the National Assembly" (AWEMA, 2001, p 2).

In addition to the foregoing consultative networks, the Assembly has created further new policy interfaces in the form of its own subject and regional committees. The latter undertake regular regional soundings around Wales while the former have been described as the Assembly's cross-party policy development engine rooms. Overall, these new structures are still in the process of development and questions remain in relation to a range of issues such as: capacity building, structural complexity, representativeness, and the adequacy of resources. However, as Rees and Morgan (2001, p 91) observe:

> nevertheless it is clear that the new governance structures ... have created multiple points of entry to the policy-making system. In sharp contrast, during the Welsh Office era, political access – principally to the Secretary of State and his two junior Ministers – was highly restricted ... quite simply, the Welsh governance system now enables much greater accessibility, at least to those with the organisational capacity to capitalise on the opportunities which are newly available.

Against this background of the reframing of Welsh governance in order to achieve greater citizen participation, we now turn to examples of the substantive policy developments of the Assembly's first term.

An example of the new participatory dimension to policy development is the Assembly Government's *Strategy for older people in Wales* (WAG, 2003c). This is a three-year programme designed to address the needs of the country's changing demographic structure. This strategy is consonant with the Executive's universalist, non-marketised ideology in its emphasis on "equal access to high-quality services across Wales" (WAG, 2003c, p 23). It has a number of principal aims. These are to: tackle discrimination against older people and promote positive images of ageing; give older people a stronger voice in society; promote and develop older people's capacity to continue to work and learn for as long as they want; promote and improve the health and well-being of older people through integrated planning and service delivery frameworks; promote the provision of high-quality services and support which enable older people to live as independently as possible in a suitable and safe environment; and promote effective planning for an ageing population. In furtherance of these objectives, the Assembly Government has committed itself (during the second term) to creating a firmer regulatory framework than seen in England by establishing the new post of Older People's Commissioner for Wales (WLP, 2003). In 2003, in order to develop the *Strategy for older people* the Assembly created a permanent new and wide-ranging consultative National Partnership Forum for Older People charged with "providing expert and informed advice to the Welsh Assembly Government on the development of its policies for older people" (WAG, 2003c, p 14).

At the other end of the age spectrum, the minister with responsibility for compulsory-age education has stated that: "we shall take our own policy direction to get the best for Wales" (WAG, 2001a, pp 2-3). Referring to ongoing introduction of private sector practices into state education in England, she continued: "it is as a matter of policy that reliance on the private sector has been ruled out for Wales" (WAG, 2001b, unpaginated). Prefacing the Assembly's 10-year education strategy, the minister underlined the divergence of education policy and provision in the two countries by stating that:

> although the forthcoming [UK government Education] Bill will cover both England and Wales, many of its provisions will be enabling in character and the National Assembly will have the discretion as to the extent of their application in Wales ... [where appropriate] we intend that the Assembly will have the power not to proceed with them ... We shall take our own policy direction where necessary, to get the best for Wales. (WAG, 2001a, pp 2-3)

Numerous examples of the post-devolution divergence in education policy exist. They include: the piloting of a new post-16 qualification (the Welsh Baccalaureate – that will be extended to intermediate and foundation stage schooling); the abolition of national tests for seven-year-olds; closer links between primary and secondary schools to raise educational attainment for 11- to 13-year-olds; the introduction of Assembly Learning Grants for students in further as well as higher education; wide-ranging measures to promote equality of opportunity and citizenship in Wales's (separate) National Curriculum; addressing individual learning needs through reform of the curriculum and moving away from rigid timetabling in order to integrate academic and vocation learning qualifications; and an overhaul of special education needs provision (including the creation of Regional Centres of Excellence and a Welsh Special Educational Needs Tribunal). In further contradistinction to policy in England and in order to widen access to higher education through universal, non-means-tested measures, the Assembly has also committed itself to use new powers outlined in the Queen's Speech (November, 2003) in order to proscribe student top-up fees in Wales during the present Assembly term.

In respect of children's welfare, the first term of devolved governance has seen the introduction of Children First, an ambitious programme designed to transform the management and delivery of social services for children in Wales. It aims to work to new all-Wales objectives for children's services (as measured against set performance indicators); establish service delivery partnerships between Welsh central and local government; and instigate the annual evaluation of unitary authority Children First Management Action Plans. In addition, in 2002, the Welsh Executive published its Play Policy Statement signalling future policy development in this area. This is in furtherance of the aims of United Nations Convention on the Rights of the Child that recognises the importance of play. This policy document states that:"the Welsh Assembly Government, in seeking to ensure the full implementation of Article 31 of the Convention, intends that this statement should contribute to creating an environment that fosters children's play and underpins a *national* [Welsh] *strategy for providing for children's play needs"* (WAG, 2002, p 3).

In the second year of devolved governance, the 2000 Care Standards Bill contained 25 UK government amendments that related specifically to Wales. Most noticeable was the commitment to create a Children's Commissioner for Wales. The Assembly health minister referred to this as "a unique policy, tailored to Welsh circumstances. No other part of the UK has a firm proposal to establish a children's commissioner" (NAW, 2000a, unpaginated). The role and functions of the commissioner were influenced by the Assembly's unique statutory duty to promote equality of opportunity for *all* persons and in relation to *all* Assembly Government functions (Chaney, 2004). The official remit for the commissioner sets out the need to:"provide a directly accessible point of contact for children and young people, whose services are bilingual and promote equal opportunities in recognising other individual needs" (NAW, 2000b, p 5).

All of the policies thus far highlighted in this discussion are still in the process of implementation (or formulation, in the case of the medium-to long-term social policy strategies). Accordingly, it is difficult to evaluate their effectiveness in terms of tangible outcomes against set policy aims and targets. One exception is the Children's commissioner. The emerging evidence shows that this office is acting as an independent check on the Welsh Executive. The commissioner's reports have led the Assembly to address a number of priorities. For example, the commissioner's first report led to the establishment of the Welsh Child Poverty Task Group, charged with advising on drawing up an anti-child poverty strategy. Subsequent reports highlighted child and adolescent mental health services. This prompted the health minister to state:

> when the Assembly Government came into office we recognised that mental health services for children and young people had been neglected for a very long time. Mental health services remain largely hidden from public view, coming to political and media attention only at a time of crisis. I am determined not to continue that pattern of neglect and that is why we have developed a ten-year strategy, Everybody's Business. (WAG, 2003b, unpaginated)

Launched in 2001, it aims to coordinate public sector health, social care and education services with voluntary sector agencies in order to increase the effectiveness of the support received by children with learning disabilities as well as those with emotional and behavioural difficulties.

The health minister described the related policy, Adult Mental Health Strategy, as "an opportunity fundamentally to change the day-to-day experience of people with mental health problems in Wales" (WAG, 2001c, unpaginated). The latter policy sets out five principal aims: empowerment – users and their carers integrally involved in planning, development and delivery of mental health services; equity – mental health services should be available to all; effectiveness – mental health services should be available to all and allocated according to need; effectiveness – mental health services should provide interventions that improve quality of life; efficiency – mental health services must use resources efficiently and be accountable for the way that money is spent. Both strategies illustrate the difference that devolution has made to the approach to policy in this area in that they are based on: new needs-based assessments, extensive consultation with citizens and NGOs, and implementation within an all-Wales locus for resource allocation and policy development.

Adams and Robinson (2002, p iii) assert that "as the devolution process evolves, it seems increasingly necessary to speak of the UK's *national health services* rather than of its NHS" (emphasis added). As the following evidence reveals, events in Wales during the Assembly's first term support this conclusion. In addition to the Children's commissioner for Wales, the 2000 Care Standards Act had a further far-reaching impact, for it gave additional powers to the National Assembly to establish a new comprehensive social and health care regulator – the Care Standards Inspectorate for Wales (CSIW). This body commenced work in April 2002 and is further evidence of the divergence in the framework of social and health care service delivery and *regulation* in the UK. A new and distinct body of Welsh law underpins the latter assertion[9]. This stems from secondary legislation passed in relation to a range of social issues. A relevant example associated with the creation of CSIW is Welsh Statutory Instrument No 781 (W92) – The Residential Family Centres (Wales) Regulations 2003. This Wales-only law provides for the National Assembly to make future regulations governing the conduct of residential family centres and associated agencies in Wales.

Resource allocation in relation to caring further underlines the divergence of health and social care policy in Wales and England. From 2001, all nursing home residents in Wales received free nursing care. The Assembly health minister described this development in the following terms: "the model we are adopting for free nursing care is unique to Wales. The consultation clearly showed strong support for the model rather than the 'banding system' introduced in England ... this is a fair, reasonable and affordable contribution from the NHS towards care costs, and means on average a self-funder will receive more than his or her counterpart in England" (WAG, 2001d). Such contrasts alluded to by the minister are further illustrated by the general per capita expenditure on health and personal social care in the two countries. In the first year of devolution spending totalled £1,116 per head in Wales compared to £963 in England (Keating, 2002, p 124).

One of the most significant post-devolution developments in health policy stems from the wholesale restructuring of the NHS in Wales. Under the terms of the 2003 Health (Wales) Act, the five Welsh Health Authorities will be abolished and replaced by 22 Local Health Boards. As Greer (2003a, p 53) puts it: "the UK has begun what amounts to a series of health policy experiments" – one in each national polity. The Welsh 'experiment' contrasts starkly with the national policies pursued elsewhere, its focus reflecting the work of Julian Tudor Hart in that it places emphasis on primary care and public health – or prevention rather than cure. The new Welsh health bodies charged with implementing this new approach are intended to be local partnerships that are coterminous with local authorities and responsible for commissioning care and building local health care capacity.

The role of evidence-based policy making following devolution must not be overlooked for it contrasts with the general approach to social policy adopted by the Welsh Office between 1964 and 1999. Accordingly, with regard to the Welsh health service reforms, the Welsh Assembly Government commissioned Derek Wanless to undertake a review of health and social care in Wales. The Assembly is still formulating its response to the findings of the Wanless Report (Wanless, 2003)[10] but ministers have already made it clear that the Assembly will accept the main thrust of its principal recommendations. These include an acceptance that the solution to the unsustainable pressure faced by acute services in Wales does not lie in more beds and a further pouring of resources into the hospital sector. Rather, hospitals have to be freed up to do their essential work by new efforts to prevent onward referrals from primary care of those patients who do not need secondary services, and a fresh determination to move on from hospitals those people no longer needing in-patient care. Future additional Assembly funding will therefore be directed to improve recruitment and training of the health and social care workforce; enhance intermediate and primary care; invest in information and communication technology; and continue funding for the NHS Incentive Fund.

Overall, these developments signal a new approach to the provision of health and social care in Wales, one that will extend beyond the next decade. This new direction has evident ideological underpinnings. For example, it strongly rejects the Private Finance Initiatives adopted in England (Greer, 2003a, p 211). Rather, as the Assembly finance minister articulated, we see the emergence of a 'Welsh way'. The minister explained this by saying: "we must continue to be prepared to finance a large part of our capital through conventional means ... we aim to maintain the public sector ethos, which we value, in all public services" (NAW, 2001, unpaginated). In short, the new focus, or 'new public health' in Wales, is based on a continuing determination to create a health and not just an illness service and one where equality of access and treatment remains a crucial policy driver. Within that envelope, the focus falls upon improving general practice; concentrating on the core role of acute hospitals, with more comparative performance measurement undertaken across the Welsh health trusts; enhancing the role of small community hospitals; and breaking down divisions between health and social care. Weighed against such ambitions this distinctive approach will need to address a range of challenges, not least the budgetary constraints of the present devolution settlement, the comparatively high levels of morbidity and mortality of the Welsh population, and the historical legacy of poor administration of the health service in Wales. According to Greer (2003b, p 61) devolution has meant that "Wales presents two faces as a health system. One is that of a global leader, attempting a highly distinctive experiment. It has tried to redesign its health services organisation so that local communities and joint working will become the core of the system ... but equally Wales is the inheritor of a messy legacy that is not obviously improving". Although aimed solely at health, his conclusion speaks to the full range of social policy initiatives outlined here: "Wales could well be the country that shows us how to really promote health rather than treat illness ... it's quite a burden to be a global experiment, but well worth it. Rest assured that a success will be known the world over" (Greer, 2003b, p 63).

Conclusion

In terms of governance and policy-making Wales has been the subject of some major changes, notably in the past 40 years. Administrative devolution under the Welsh Office, the territorial ministry of the London-based government, was principally concerned with implementing

Whitehall policies in Wales (Deacon, 2002; Morgan, 2000). The granting of limited self-government for Wales in 1999 has resulted in major discontinuity with these former practices. Instead, there has been a shift towards the formulation and implementation of indigenous *Welsh* policies designed to address Welsh needs. This has profound and long-term implications for the formulation and delivery of social policy, not least because under the present constitutional settlement, the Welsh Assembly is predominantly a *social policy body*. Its responsibilities lie in the key areas of health, education, social services and housing. Thus, to varying degrees, the very success of constitutional reform in this country depends upon social policy innovation and delivery.

However, in social policy terms, in order to assess the significance of the recent constitutional reform and the shift towards quasi-federal government in the UK, one must look beyond the legal, constitutional and budgetary powers because they do not of themselves explain the evident divergence between Wales and England on key areas of policy. Rather, as this discussion has highlighted, it is also necessary to focus on the ideological underpinning of the new and distinctive approach to a range of social priorities seen during the National Assembly's first term. While it is arguably a hazardous undertaking to attempt to characterise a nation in terms of political ideology, the historical evidence shows a greater willingness to embrace socialist and communitarian values at the ballot box than has been the case in England (when considered as a discrete polity)[11]. The first term of the National Assembly must therefore be seen within this context, for the Welsh Executive has attempted to articulate such values in the development of a social policy agenda based upon the following notions: universalism, a rejection of marketisation, and cooperation rather than competition in the provision of collective goods. As the emerging policy evidence reveals, devolution as a minimum has created an enabling context in which these values can be applied to social policy.

A cautionary note is also important here for it is still too early to judge the new Welsh social policy agenda in terms of policy outcomes. This underscores the importance of future policy evaluation mechanisms and research-based policy making. Moreover, the Assembly's first term has shown that political will to progress the social policy agenda has, on a number of occasions, been reined in by the institution's limited legal and fiscal powers[12]. Debate continues on the future trajectory of devolution in Wales. However, some observers point to the divergent nature of social policy following devolution as underlining the case for increased powers to be granted, thereby offering the prospect of even greater scope for innovation in the future[13]. Whatever the outcome of such deliberations, the evidence of the National Assembly's first term points to the way in which ideology and 'democratic' devolution has resulted in, and is likely to perpetuate, a significant and long-lasting impact on the future shape of social policy in Wales and beyond.

Notes

[1] See 1998 Government of Wales Act, S22, schedule 2.

[2] The governmental powers and functions of the Welsh devolution settlement are currently being examined by an official, Welsh Assembly Government endorsed commission – the Richard Commission (see www.richardcommission.gov.uk).

[3] The coalition agreement Putting Wales First (c 2001) summarises the situation: "In law, Cabinet ministers have very few functions in their own right. All functions are vested in and are exercisable by the Assembly, which delegates the great majority of them to the First Minister. He in turn delegates functions to ministers in accordance with their portfolios, they then delegating administrative functions to Assembly officials (via the Permanent Secretary)".

[4] In June 2002 the Welsh Assembly Government launched Assembly Learning Grants (ALGs), designed to help the poorest Welsh students through higher and further education. The grants were awarded on top of the existing student loans in higher education. The average annual grant was £935.

[5] Tir Gofal is a whole-farm agri-environment scheme available throughout Wales since April, 1999. The scheme aims to encourage agricultural practices that will protect and enhance the landscapes of Wales, their cultural features and associated wildlife.

[6] Earlier strategic plans are: Better Wales (1999-2000), Putting Wales First (2001), Plan for Wales (2002).

[7] As summarised: www.wales.gov.uk/subisocialpolicy

[8] The official third sector quango in Wales. See www.wcva.org.uk/

[9] Where appropriate the Welsh Assembly Government has passed secondary legislation to underpin policy implementation. Details of this distinct body of

Welsh law can be found at: www.wales-legislation.org.uk and/or at www.wales-legislation.hmso.gov.uk

[10] see www.wales.gov.uk/subieconomics/hsc-review-e.htm

[11] Unlike in Scotland and England, since the extension of the franchise in the 19th century Wales has never returned a majority in favour of the right of centre – the Tory Party.

[12] In relation to free personal care for the elderly, for example, the Assembly Government Health Minister wrote: "In the absence of any change at the UK level, the National Assembly does not have the legislative powers to implement a policy of free personal care. The Welsh Assembly Government will continue to press the UK Government for the powers to consider the matter in Wales, but will however continue to explore opportunities for alleviating the burden of paying for personal care" (WAG, 2003a, p 6).

[13] "What, it may be asked, of areas such as housing and personal social services? Once again, full statutory powers would sit comfortably with the basic constitutional ideas of responsibility and accountability on this major interface of the citizen and the administration" (Rawlings, 2003b, para 5.19, unpaginated).

References

Adams, J. and Robinson, P. (eds) (2002) 'Executive Summary', *Devolution in practice: Public policy differences within the UK*, London: IPPR.

AWEMA (All Wales Ethnic Minority Association) (2001) *AWEMA Times*, 2 November.

Bulmer, S. and Burch, M. (2002) *British devolution and European policy-making: A step-change towards multi-level governance?*, Manchester: Manchester Papers in Politics: European Policy and Research Unit Series, Department of Government, University of Manchester.

Butler, I. and Drakeford, M. (2001) 'Which Blair project? Communitarianism, social authoritarianism and social work', *Journal of Social Work*, vol 1, no 1, pp 1-19.

Chaney, P. (2003) 'Social capital and the participation of marginalized groups in government: a study of the statutory partnership between the third sector and devolved government in Wales', *Public Policy and Administration*, vol 17, no 4, pp 22-39.

Chaney, P. (2004) 'The post-devolution equality agenda: the case of the Welsh Assembly's statutory duty to promote equality of opportunity', *Policy & Politics*, vol 32, no 1, pp 58-74.

Chaney, P. and Fevre, R. (2001), 'Ron Davies and the cult of "inclusiveness": devolution and participation in Wales', *Contemporary Wales*, vol 14, pp 131-46.

Chaney, P., Hall, T. and Pithouse, A. (2001) 'New governance: new democracy?', in P. Chaney, T. Hall and A. Pithouse (eds) *New governance: new democracy? Post-devolution Wales*, Cardiff: University of Wales Press, pp 1-28.

Cooke, P. (2002) *Varieties of devolution: Visionary and precautionary economic policy formulation in Scotland and Wales*, ESRC Devolution and Constitutional Change Programme Seminar Papers Series.

Cooke, P. (2003) 'Economy: Wales' precautionary approach', in J. Osmond (ed) *Second term challenge: Can the Welsh Assembly government hold its course?*, Cardiff: Institute of Welsh Affairs, pp 23-36.

Davies, R. (1999) 'Devolution: a process not an event', *Gregynog Papers*, vol 2, no 2, Cardiff, Institute of Welsh Affairs, pp 2-56.

Deacon, R. (2002) *The governance of Wales: The Welsh Office and the policy process 1964-1999*, Cardiff: Welsh Academic Press.

Greer, S. (2003a) 'Health: how far can Wales diverge from England?', in J. Osmond (ed) *Second term challenge: Can the Welsh Assembly government hold its course?*, Cardiff: Institute of Welsh Affairs, pp 89-118.

Greer, S. (2003b) 'Policy divergence', in R. Hazell, (ed) *The state of the nations 2003 – the third year of devolution in the United Kingdom*, Exeter: Imprint Academic, pp 54-72.

Hain, P. (1999) *A Welsh third way*, London: A Tribune Pamphlet.

Harris, M., Rochester, C. and Halfpenny, P. (2000) 'Twenty years of change', in M. Harris and C. Rochester (eds) *Voluntary organisations and social policy in Britain*, Basingstoke: Palgrave, pp 112-31.

Hazell, R. (2003) 'The devolution scorecard', in R. Hazell (ed) *The state of the nations 2003 – the third year of devolution in the United Kingdom*, Exeter: Imprint Academic, pp 214-29.

Keating, M. (2002) 'Devolution and public policy in the United Kingdom: divergence or convergence?', in J. Adams and P. Robinson (eds) *Devolution in practice: Public policy differences within the UK*, London: IPPR, pp 84-106.

McCrone, D. (2002) 'Devolution: Inter-institutional relations in the UK', evidence given by David McCrone to the Select Committee on the Constitution, House of Lords, 15 May, Papers of the Institute of Governance, University of Edinburgh.

Morgan, K.O. (2000) 'A Europe of the regions? The multi-level polity: subsidiarity in the European Union', Report based on Wilton Park Conference WP 617 on A Europe of the Regions? 13-17 November, 2000, ESRC Devolution and Constitutional Change Programme Seminar Papers Series.

Morgan, R. (2000) *Check against delivery*, Aberystwyth: Institute of Welsh Politics.

Morgan, R. (2002) 'Making social policy in Wales', Lecture by the First Minister Rhodri Morgan to Centre for Policy Studies, Swansea University, December.

Morgan, R. (2003) 'Social justice and the Welsh tradition', Lecture by First Minister Rhodri Morgan to Cymdeithas Cledwyn, National Eisteddfod of Wales.

NAW (National Assembly for Wales) (2000) *Voluntary sector scheme*, Cardiff: NAW.

NAW (2000a) Jane Hutt, AM, Plenary Debate on the Children's Commissioner, *The Official Record*, 7 June (www.wales.gov.uk).

NAW (2000b) *A Children's Commissioner for Wales: the report of the Health and Social Services Committee*, Papers of the Assembly Health and Social Services Committee (www.wales.gov.uk).

NAW (2001) Edwina Hart, Finance Minister – statement on investment through partnerships in Wales, *The Official Record*, 13 December (www.wales.gov.uk).

Osmond, J. (2003) 'From corporate body to virtual parliament: the metamorphosis of the National Assembly for Wales', in R. Hazell (ed) *The state of the nations 2003 – The third year of devolution in the United Kingdom*, Exeter: Imprint Academic, pp 164-87.

Parry, R. (2003) *The home civil service after devolution*, ESRC Devolution and Constitutional Change Programme Policy Papers Series (www.devolution.ac.uk).

Rawlings, R. (1998) 'The new model Wales,' *Journal of Law and Society*, vol 25, no 4, pp 461-509.

Rawlings, R. (2003a) *Delineating Wales: Constitutional, legal and administrative aspects of national devolution*, Cardiff: University of Wales Press.

Rawlings, R. (2003b) Evidence to the Richard commission on the powers and electoral arrangements of the National Assembly for Wales by Professor Richard Rawlings (www. comisiwnrichard.gov.uk).

Rees, G. and Morgan, K. (2001) 'Learning by doing: devolution and the governance of economic development in Wales', in P. Chaney, T. Hall and A. Pithouse (eds) *New governance: new democracy? Post-devolution Wales*, Cardiff: University of Wales Press, pp 87-104.

Sandford, M. (2002) 'What place for England in an asymmetrically devolved UK?', *Regional Studies – Journal of the Regional Studies Association*, vol 36, no 7, pp 74-98.

Sykes, R., Bochel, C. and Ellison, N. (2001) 'The year in social policy', in R. Sykes, C. Bochel and N. Ellison (eds) *Social policy review 13: Developments and debates 2000-2001*, Bristol: The Policy Press, pp 3-19.

WAG (Welsh Assembly Government) (2001a) *Coalition agreement: 'Putting Wales First'*, Cardiff: WAG.

WAG (2001b) *The learning country: a paving document – a comprehensive education and lifelong learning programme to 2010 in Wales*, Cardiff: WAG.

WAG (2001c) Press statement on the learning country, 5 September (www.wales.gov.uk).

WAG (2001d) Health minister's statement on adult mental health strategy, Press release, 25 September (www.wales.gov.uk).

WAG (2001e) Health Minister's statement, Press release, 5 November (www.wales.gov.uk).

WAG (2002) *Play policy*, Cardiff: WAG.

WAG (2003a) *Wales a better country: The strategic agenda of the Welsh Assembly Government*, Cardiff: WAG.

WAG (2003b) *National Assembly for Wales's budget 2004-2005 to 2006-2007: Final budget proposals*, Cardiff: WAG.

WAG (2003c) *The strategy for older people in Wales*, Cardiff: WAG.

WAG (2003d) 'Progress being made on services for children says Jane Hutt', Press release, 5 November (www.wales.gov.uk).

Wanless, D. (2003) *The review of health and social care in Wales: The report of the project team advised by Derek Wanless, June 2003*, Cardiff: Welsh Assembly Government.

Welsh Office (1997) *Llais Dros Gymru – A voice for Wales*, Cm 3718, Cardiff: Welsh Office.

WLP (Welsh Labour Party) (2003) *Working together for Wales: Welsh Labour's manifesto 2003*, Cardiff: WLP.

EIGHT

Attlee versus Blair: Labour governments and progressive social policy in historical perspective

Robert M. Page

Introduction

During his speech to the Labour Party conference in Bournemouth in September 2003 Tony Blair (2003) spoke of the "privilege" of being "the first Labour leader in 100 years" to have held office for six-and-a-half consecutive years. Historic achievements of this kind inevitably lead to comparisons being made between the previous and present record holders. To this end, this chapter will attempt to compare the achievements of the Attlee governments during their six years in office between 1945 and 1951 with those of Blair's New Labour administrations during their first six-and-a-half years in power. Although the focus will be on social policy, attention will also be given to the related sphere of economic policy and the broader 'vision' of each administration.

In comparing the two governments it is useful, as Powell (2002) reminds us, to distinguish between intrinsic and extrinsic assessments:

> Intrinsic evaluation examines performance in its own terms, with reference to stated goals. Extrinsic evaluation is based on a 'third party' specification of criteria, and may result in criticising a government for failing to achieve something that is not an objective, but which the third party thinks should be an objective. (Powell, 2002, p 4)

Conflicting accounts of the success or failure of a particular government can arise in part because of different 'scoring' mechanisms of this kind.

In the first section of this chapter, attention will be given to the record of the Attlee government. This will be followed by a review of the first six-and-a-half years of New Labour rule and, finally, by a discussion of the 'progressive' aspirations and achievements of each of these administrations.

The Attlee government 1945-51

Background

When Clement Attlee was asked to form a government by George VI in May 1945, he might well have allowed himself a wry smile as he reflected on the train of events that had transformed the position of the Labour Party since 1939. Although Labour had gained 38% of the popular vote (securing 154 out of a possible 617 seats) in the 1935 general election, there seemed little prospect of the party achieving an electoral breakthrough in the foreseeable future. The war, however, provided Labour with a unique opportunity to persuade a sceptical public of the progress that could be made if they placed their faith in the 'socialist' policies that the Party had been developing following their catastrophic defeat at the 1931 general election.

After agreeing to join a wartime coalition administration in May 1940 (on the condition that Chamberlain resigned as Prime Minister), Labour ministers made a determined effort to ensure that the military defeat of Germany and the social reconstruction of British society were regarded as complementary, rather than distinctive, activities. Labour representation in Churchill's coalition was far from tokenistic. Sixteen Labour members joined the new government of whom two, Attlee and Greenwood, were given seats in the War Cabinet. During the course of the war their representation increased. By March 1942 the Party had 22 ministers and by 1945 this had risen to 27 (Pearce, 1997). Importantly, Labour had significant ministerial influence in the area of reconstruction (Pearce, 1994).

Throughout the war Labour ministers had to continually reassure their own supporters, especially those on the left, that worthwhile, albeit limited, social and economic advance could be achieved by participating in the coalition government. Their endeavours were not always appreciated. For example, a report prepared by the Party's National Executive Committee in 1941 entitled *Labour in the government* (Labour Party, 1941), drawing attention to the positive impact of increased allowances for children, disabled people and the dependants of service personnel as well as the abolition of the household means-test, was dismissed in *Tribune* as an attempt "to paint cardboard to resemble iron" (quoted in Brooke, 1992, p 58). Criticisms of this kind became less intense after 1942 when reconstruction assumed greater importance following the realisation that the defeat of Germany had become a distinct possibility rather than a faint hope.

Following the publication of the Beveridge Report in 1942, the coalition government embarked on a so-called 'White Paper chase'. Reforms were proposed in areas such as education (1943), health (1944), employment (1944) and social insurance (1944). As Brooke (1995, p 8) points out, "some of this groundwork did lead to legislation, including the Education Act (1944) providing free secondary education to all children, the Distribution of Industry Act (1945), which permitted the state to guide industry to distressed areas, and the Family Allowances Act (1945), which established cash benefits for families with children".

The notion that a growing consensus emerged between the two major coalition partners on economic and social issues after 1942 is clearly open to question (Addison, 1975). While Labour was certainly willing to support a series of pragmatic reforms during the war, this should not be interpreted as a form of ideological conversion. Labour's support for a national minimum, a salaried medical profession, multilateral (comprehensive) schools and economic planning was indicative of an ideological divide between themselves and the Conservatives. As Brooke (1992, p 341) notes, although the Labour leadership "hoped to use the common ground of coalition for Labour's own ends, they did not become mired in a consensual morass. Within the Coalition, Attlee and his Labour colleagues pressed their party's case over both the running of the war economy and reconstruction planning".

Although opinion pollsters had been predicting a Labour victory since 1943, the party was genuinely surprised to be swept to power in 1945. Nevertheless, it was well equipped for government, not least because their leading figures, Attlee, Bevin and Morrison "represented a matchless combination of experience at all levels of government" (Morgan, 1984, p 47).

The record

Economic policy

In its general election manifesto of 1945, the Labour Party stressed the importance of continuing with the interventionist measures that had served the nation so well in wartime. It hoped that these would ensure that "profiteering interests and the privileged rich" were prevented from plundering "the rest of the nation as shamelessly as they did in the nineteen-twenties" (Dale, 2000, p 52). Although it wanted to be regarded as the party of freedom, Labour's support for this principle was not unconditional. "There are certain freedoms that Labour will not tolerate: freedom to exploit other people; freedom to pay poor wages and to push up prices for selfish profit; freedom to deprive the people of the means of living full, happy, healthy lives" (Dale, 2000, p 53).

While Labour remained committed to both nationalisation and planning, there was a lack of unanimity about the precise purpose of either measure. For some, public ownership was essential if the party was to contain the unstable and exploitative nature of capitalism, prevent the concentration of "private economic power, redistribute property and foster industrial democracy" (Francis, 1997, p 68). For others, the purpose of nationalisation was to overhaul inefficient private industries and improve industrial relations (Jay, 1937). In practice, Labour's nationalisation plans, with the exception of the steel industry, satisfied both strands of opinion. "The Bank of England and civil aviation were nationalized in 1946; coal, rail, road haulage, and cable and wireless in 1947; and electricity and gas in 1948" (Thorpe, 2001, p 108). By the end of the 1940s some 20% of the British economy was in public hands (Brooke, 1995). After Cabinet divisions over proposals for the steel industry it was eventually decided to proceed with nationalisation, though implementation was delayed until after the 1950 general election (see Clarke, 1996, pp 224-6).

Labour also lacked any "generally accepted conception of what economic planning was and how it should be implemented" (Thompson, 1996, p 168). Some favoured 'direct' physical controls such as production quotas, rationing and where necessary the direction of labour (see Crossman et al, 1947; Cole, 1950). Others were increasingly persuaded that socialist objectives could be achieved through 'indirect' means such as monetary or fiscal measures. From this perspective it was perfectly feasible to employ Keynesian techniques such as demand management for socialist ends (see Jay, 1937; Brooke, 1996). Although the postwar Labour government used both direct and indirect forms of planning, the latter assumed greater importance from 1947 onwards not least because of a growing acceptance of the advantages of less controlled market activity (Brooke, 1995: Tomlinson, 1997). Significantly, however, this change of emphasis perturbed left-wing ministers such as Bevan as it appeared to signal the abandonment of "a specifically socialist economic policy in favour of Keynesian-inspired expedients, which were at best ideologically neutral, at worst even anti-socialist" (Francis, 1997, pp 34-5).

Unlike the Blair government, Attlee's had to contend with difficult economic circumstances throughout its period of office. At the end of the war the national finances were in a perilous state. Britain had incurred war debts of £3,000m and was heavily reliant on US financial aid in the form of Lend Lease. Exports stood at one third of their prewar level and 40% of overseas markets had been lost. The abrupt ending of the Japanese war in 1945, which led to the suspension of Lend Lease, left Britain with no alternative but to seek further aid from the USA in order to avoid 'draconian cuts' in domestic consumption (Shaw, 1996, p 21). Although the terms of the loan were not nearly as favourable as anticipated (a loan of $3,750m tied to the 'convertibility' of sterling by 1947 and an end to 'imperial preference' – Brooke, 1995), the agreed package did, in conjunction with a Canadian loan of $1,250m, provide short-term economic respite. However, the British economy had not recovered sufficiently to cope with the demands of convertibility in July 1947, in part because of the adverse impact of the three-day week that had been imposed earlier in the year to cope with dwindling coal stocks occasioned by a severe winter (Morgan, 1984). Convertibility was suspended the following month after a significant outflow of dollars; a decision that necessitated further rationing. Britain's economic fragility was further exposed in 1949 when the government agreed to a 30% devaluation of sterling to cope with a downturn in the American economy. Nevertheless, as Brooke (1995, pp 15-16) points out, "1947 and 1949 were not like 1931 for Labour. However grave these crises were, they did not derail Labour's essential commitments. Despite a drop during the fuel crisis, full employment was maintained. Social and economic reform continued along its path".

How successful, then, was Labour's approach to economic policy? Attlee enthusiasts such as Cairncross (1985), Morgan (1984) and Hennessy (1993) have drawn attention to Labour's success in revitalising the British economy in difficult circumstances. Unemployment and inflation remained low, industrial production increased by a third between 1946 and 1951, exports outstripped imports, productivity rose sharply and the growth rate was impressive. These achievements were the result of such measures as "direct controls (e.g. over manpower and raw materials) to steer resources in the direction of the export industries; the deliberate targeting of the US market; the restriction of imports; the dampening of consumer demand and a policy of substituting non-dollar for dollar imports and voluntary wage restraint" (Thompson, 1996, pp 145-6).

Others, in contrast, have been more critical, drawing attention to Labour's failure to develop a medium term economic strategy, which sowed the seeds for subsequent economic decline. According to Dell (1999, p 163), by preserving "the prize of full employment, the government showed itself prepared to distort all other policies, in particular its attitude to price stability, to international trade, to the sterling area and to Europe". In a similar vein, Barnett (1996, p 397) bemoans the fact that "five years after the German war had ended, five years of living on American loans and handouts, no British industrial miracle was under way, not even foundations laid for achieving one in the decade to come".

While such criticisms have some validity, Labour's economic record during this period from its own perspective was highly successful. It achieved most of its objectives and attempted to develop a more progressive type of economic policy. It could be argued, though, that even better results could have been achieved by a speedier recognition that Britain should abandon 'great power' policies, not least in its defence commitments, and adopt a bolder approach to planning (Tomlinson, 1997).

Social policy

The welfare reforms introduced by the Attlee government have proved to be its most enduring legacy. Its two most important legislative initiatives were in 1946, the National Insurance Act and the National Health Service Act. The National Insurance legislation was intended to mark a decisive shift towards the principle of universality rather than selectivity. Under this scheme workers were to be provided with protection against a number of the predictable risks that had been highlighted by Beveridge such as unemployment, sickness, disability, maternity, widowhood and old age. Although Labour's scheme was a decided improvement on prewar arrangements, it proved difficult to devise an effective universal flat-rate insurance scheme (especially one that took no account of variations in rent levels), which would provide claimants with a subsistence income. In consequence, significant numbers of insurees (675,000 by 1948) needed to claim means-tested National Assistance benefits in order to obtain a subsistence income.

In the case of healthcare, the new minister, Aneurin Bevan, recognised that previous coalition plans had failed to address the issue of comprehensive hospital provision (Klein, 2000; Webster, 2002). To resolve this problem he proposed nationalising all existing hospitals. Bevan recognised that his plan "would never have flown" (Glennerster, 2000, p 47) unless he won the support of hospital consultants. Their compliance was secured by a combination of financial inducements, guaranteed representation on new administrative boards and committees, and reassurances concerning continued opportunities for private practice. In the case of the GP-dominated British Medical Association, Bevan faced a much tougher challenge. BMA members only agreed to participate in the new service after he had agreed to amend legislation, ruling out any possibility of a salaried service being imposed by ministerial diktat.

Labour's 1945 manifesto pledge to "proceed with a housing programme with the maximum practical speed until every family in this island has a good standard of accommodation" (Dale, 2000, p 57) proved more difficult to achieve. The depletion of the housing stock as a result of enemy bombing; the limited number of skilled construction workers; the shortfall in the supply of building materials; expenditure cutbacks in 1947; and Bevan's insistence on high-standard local authority construction rather than speculative private sector building, resulted in just 1 million homes being built by 1951 against a target of 4 to 5 million. Moreover, Malpass (2003, p 600) criticises Labour for its failure to develop a broader socialist housing strategy: "instead of a socialist housing policy based on the public ownership of the means of production, Labour opted for a municipal development programme, relying to a large extent on privately owned building firms to deliver production". Although these criticisms are valid, the importance of Labour's achievements in this sphere should not be overlooked. It attempted to provide affordable housing of a good standard to low-income groups. As Morgan (1984, p 170) states, "the main emphasis was placed squarely on those least fortunate, on working-class people without adequate housing and caught in huge waiting lists, seeking housing at low rents, rather than on aspiring middle-class owner-occupiers who saw houses in terms of status and perhaps profit as well as of security".

The Attlee government's education strategy was the subject of much debate following the decision to persist with the tripartite strategy of grammar, secondary modern and technical schooling contained in the 1944 Education Act (Brooke, 1992). Such a move proved unpopular with the National Organisation of Labour Teachers and other sections of the party, who believed that multilateral schools were the best means of promoting the educational advance of working class children. Labour's two education ministers Wilkinson (1945-47) and Tomlinson (1947-51) resisted the pressure to transform the education system in this way, arguing that diverse secondary provision based on 'parity of esteem' would not prove socially divisive, provided that there were no artificial barriers to entry such as fees. Both ministers were particularly keen to retain grammar schools, on the grounds that they offered "working class high achievers the opportunity to compete on equal terms with the products of the independent schools for the prizes of university places and the top jobs in the professions and government service" (Francis, 1997, p 155).

The implementation of the 1944 Education Act proved far from straightforward. Wilkinson had to battle with Cabinet colleagues such as Cripps and Morrison in order to obtain the resources for the additional teachers and new buildings required to implement the raising of the school leaving age to 15 by 1947 (see Morgan, 1984, pp 175-6). It is difficult, however, to take issue with Morgan's (1984, p 177) overall assessment "that education was an area where the Labour government failed to provide any new ideas or inspiration". This was due in part to the fact that most Cabinet members were supportive of educational elitism. There was certainly no desire, for example, to curtail the privileges of the public schools. Indeed Attlee's devotion to his former school was such that he had no compunction about offering ministerial preferment to Old Haileyburians "other things being equal" (Beckett, 2000, p 211).

Assessment

From an intrinsic perspective, it is hard to fault the Attlee government and it is understandable that its achievements in securing full employment and 'creating' the welfare state have come to be regarded by many commentators as little short of monumental (Morgan, 1984; Hennessy, 1993; Thorpe, 2001). According to Rubinstein (2003, p 232):

> it accomplished more than any other peacetime government, arguably before or since, and in many respects represented the culmination of the entire tradition of Britain's reform movement since the Great Reform Act if not before. As well, despite its great achievements, it was an honourable government, composed of honourable men who rarely deceived or dissimulated.

In terms of social policy its achievements were considerable. Although provision was generally of a basic standard and spending tightly controlled (Tomlinson, 1998), Labour's welfare initiatives "provided as never before a secure basis for the lives of the mass of the people who could not provide for all their own needs" (Thane, 2000, p 102).

Extrinsic assessments have focused on some of the shortcomings of Attlee's 'social revolution'. According to one influential critic (Miliband, 1972), Labour's timidity in this regard can be explained by its historic adherence to parliamentarianism, which effectively precluded the introduction of transformative policies (see also Fyrth, 1993, 1995). Even if one rejects Miliband's pessimistic assessment of the inherent weaknesses of progressive parliamentary socialism, the question remains as to whether Labour was fully committed to the creation of a transformative socialist commonwealth. Although the 'ethical' dimension of Labour's approach was alluded to by ministers such as Morrison (see Fielding, 1992, p 138) and highlighted in party publications such as *Labour believes in Britain* (Labour Party, 1949), the next stage in Labour's journey seemed unclear. Indeed much has been made of the fact that Labour's 'crusade' had "lost some of its zeal by the end of the 1940s ... With the 1945 manifesto largely fulfilled, it was not clear how Labour should move on" (Smith, M., 2000, p 115). This uncertainty is reflected in the party's election manifesto of 1950. While it sought to bring about a new moral order in which citizens would be "more kindly, intelligent, free, co-operative, enterprising and rich in culture" (Dale, 2000, p 63), it was not clear how this was to be achieved. It could be said that while Labour had proved successful in "remedying the evils of the past", it had found it more difficult to devise "a challenging agenda for the future" (Pearce, 1994, p 77).

Although Labour held on to power in the 1950 general election, its overall majority was reduced to just five seats. Nevertheless its support held up remarkably well as it did during its subsequent defeat in 1951. Although it lost a number of key marginal seats in 1951, its popularity, as measured by votes cast, remained undiminished (Jefferys, 2002, pp 59-84).

The Blair government 1997-2003

Background

A revitalised Labour party returned to power in 1997 after four consecutive election defeats. This transformation in Labour's electoral fortunes has been attributed to the pioneering efforts of former leaders (Kinnock 1983-92 and Smith 1992-94) who attempted to improve the Party's reputation by jettisoning unpopular policies and revamping its internal structures. It was, however, under Tony Blair's leadership that the so-called New Labour project came to fruition. As Chadwick and Heffernan (2003, p 12) point out, "when Blair announced shortly after the 1997 election that the party was 'elected as New Labour' and would therefore 'govern as New Labour', he was signalling the permanence of the changes to Labour's policy profile and internal organizational discipline".

What, then, are the characteristic features of this New Labour approach? According to Giddens (1998, p 26), New Labour is committed to a Third Way political strategy, which attempts "to transcend both old-style social democracy and neoliberalism". In terms of the former, New Labour has dissociated itself not only from outdated 'fundamentalist' policies such as public ownership, planning and redistribution but also from the statist revisionist strategy devised by Crosland (1956), which 'proved' both "ineffective at promoting growth and containing unemployment" and "inefficient ... in its provision of public services" (Blair, 1998, p 5). While New Labour recognises the virtues of market activity, it has sought to distance itself from neo-liberal orthodoxies in this sphere. As Chadwick and Heffernan (2003, p 15) point out, from a New Labour perspective, "Neo-liberalism and the market fundamentalism it engendered ... has been unable to deal with the economic realities of an unequal, unstable, ever-changing world, particularly when markets are neither self-regulating nor able to promote economic development or provide for social justice".

Importantly, as Blair (2001, p 10) has made clear, New Labour's approach "is not a third way between conservative and social democratic philosophy. It is social democracy renewed". According to Giddens (2002, p 15):

> the new social democracy seeks to preserve the basic values of the left – a belief in a solidary and inclusive society, a commitment to combating inequality and protecting the vulnerable. It asserts that active government, coupled with strong public institutions and a developed welfare state, have an indispensable role to play in furthering these objectives. But it holds that many traditional leftist perspectives or policies either no longer do so, or have become directly counterproductive.

Let us now turn to New Labour's record in government.

The record

Economic policy

Given the difficulties that Labour has encountered with regard to its economic policy in the post-1945 era, both in government and in opposition (Shaw, 1996; Stephens, 2001), it is not surprising that in its 'New' incarnation it has sought to develop a more 'robust' economic strategy. This has involved a rejection of so-called 'tax and spend' and a more positive approach to enterprise and business. As New Labour

Chancellor Gordon Brown (2003a, p 271) argues, "we should celebrate an entrepreneurial climate – encouraging, incentivising and rewarding the dynamic and enthusing more people from all backgrounds and all areas to start up businesses – enabling markets to work better and strengthening the private economy". New Labour has also distanced itself from egalitarian fiscal measures that have been seen to penalise the industrious and the enterprising. According to Brown (1999, p 42), the purpose of redistribution is not to create equality of outcome "irrespective of work, effort, or contribution to the community" but rather to improve the opportunities and life chances of the poor and excluded. It was also recognised that New Labour needed to convince sceptics that it was a Party that promoted the virtue of paid work rather than welfare (see Page, 2003). As another leading New Labour Cabinet minister, David Blunkett, (2001, p 92) asserts, "paid work is the key to productive and fulfilling lives. Of course there are many other worthwhile forms of fulfilment and contribution, not least unpaid parenting. But in modern societies, work is central to an individual's identity, their social status and their ability to exercise real choices in other areas of their lives".

Since 1997 New Labour has taken a number of steps in order to demonstrate its pro-market credentials and its commitment to fiscal and monetary stability. During the first term of the Blair government, the Monetary Policy Committee of the Bank of England was accorded the right, previously 'held' by the Chancellor, to set interest rates; the stringent public spending targets of the previous Conservative government were maintained; borrowing was to be used exclusively for investment rather than for the funding of current expenditure; corporation tax was lowered; and income tax rates were not increased. Indeed New Labour's desire for economic respectability led them to champion such measures as private sector involvement in the financing and operation of 'public' services with the zeal of the religious convert.

While the economic measures undertaken by New Labour have been portrayed by some as slavish adherence to the tenets of neo-liberalism (Hay, 1999; Cohen, 2003), others detect subtler influences at work (Holt, 2001; Keegan, 2003; Annesley and Gamble, 2004). According to Keegan (2003), the economic strategy of New Labour's Chancellor must be judged over the longer term. After demonstrating that he was capable of controlling spending, reducing the budget deficit and redistributing for a purpose during Labour's first term (1997-2002), Brown was then able to "return to the politics of tax and spend, but with nothing like a return to the kind of tax levels experienced during previous Labour governments" (Keegan, 2003, p 252). The introduction of the minimum wage, the redistribution of resources to the working poor and the substantial increases in public expenditure announced in the 2001 budget can all be cited in support of this more progressive interpretation of New Labour's strategy.

The fact that New Labour came through its first term in office with such a positive record of achievement in terms of such conventional economic indices as inflation, employment and growth and secured further electoral success in 2001 (Butler and Kavanagh, 2002; Pattie, 2004) suggests that the 'prudent' policies pursued by Gordon Brown were effective. Such success, however, came with a price. Public spending was lower than it had been during the Major years thereby delaying much-needed investment in key services. Moreover, there was no evidence of any desire to combat growing income inequalities. Indeed, the decision to lower the basic rate of income tax from 23% to 22% in the 2000 budget (albeit to compensate for the withdrawal of mortgage tax relief and the married couples allowance) suggested that New Labour was quite content to preside over growing levels of income inequality (though not poverty) and to maintain its electoral appeal to more 'aspirational' citizens (Gould, 1998).

Social policy

New Labour's decision to adopt a 'third way' approach to social policy, is based in part on its desire to distance itself from the Attlee legacy. While it accepts that the postwar welfare reforms of the Attlee government helped to ameliorate the giant evils identified by Beveridge, New Labour believes that more innovative welfare arrangements are now required to meet such challenges as labour market change, more diverse families and the growth of consumerism. Moreover, reform is also seen as necessary to deal with some of the alleged design flaws of the postwar welfare state such as "dependency, moral hazard, bureaucracy, interest-group formation and fraud" (Giddens, 2000, p 33).

New Labour has placed great emphasis on creating an active rather than a passive welfare state. The Treasury has played such a dominating role in this process that one civil servant felt that his department had been transformed into "the Department of Social Policy" when he returned after a period on secondment (Keegan, 2003, p 244). Following Labour's election victory in 1997, Gordon Brown proceeded to impose a windfall tax on the excess profits of a number of privatised utilities to fund a Welfare to Work programme modelled on Democratic Party initiatives in the USA (King and Wickham-Jones, 1999; Deacon, 2000). Under a variety of New Deal schemes, those benefit recipients capable of undertaking some form of paid work have been encouraged to return to the labour market to avoid the negative effects of long-term dependency. This measure was complemented by the introduction of both a minimum wage and tax credits (including help with childcare costs) to ensure that claimants had a clear financial incentive to return to work.

Another distinctive feature of New Labour's approach to social policy has been its desire to move away from reliance on publicly provided services. It is argued that the public interest can often be better met by the involvement of the private sector as well as "mutuals, social enterprises, not-for-profit trusts and public benefit corporations" in service delivery (Giddens, 2002, p 65). Brown (2003b) has, for example, defended his decision to expand the number of Private Financial Initiatives (PFI) on public interest grounds, arguing that there "should be no principled objection against PFI expanding into new areas where the public sector can procure a defined product adequately and at no risk to its integrity and where the private sector has a core skill the public sector can benefit and learn from". While the private sector has always provided a range of services for public purposes, New Labour's decision to extend commercial involvement in the provision of education and healthcare has led to justifiable concerns about the dilution of a distinctive public realm (Marquand, 1999, 2004; Pollock et al, 2001).

New Labour has also sought to modify Attlee's citizenship model of the welfare state believing that a more explicitly consumerist ethos is now required. According to Blair (2003), the public "want education and health free at the point of use – but they don't want services uniform and undifferentiated at the point of use, unable to respond to their individual needs and aspirations". For example, in an effort to extend choice within the sphere of education New Labour has encouraged the growth of 'specialist' schools, which can demonstrate expertise in an area such as science, languages or sport. Moreover, independent providers have been invited to bid for public funds to establish innovative City Academies in a number of inner city areas. In healthcare, the introduction of foundation hospitals is also intended to ensure that provision better reflects the expressed needs of the local community.

New Labour has also emphasised the need to improve the performance of public services. While it has accepted the case that many services are under-resourced, it has been determined to ensure that any additional funding is tied to improved delivery. In part this reflects its acceptance of public choice ideas concerning the propensity of producers to operate services according to their own needs rather than those of users (see Taylor-Gooby, 2000). Accordingly, it has introduced new Performance

Assessment Frameworks "in services such as the NHS and social services. It has pioneered the government's Annual Reports and PSAs [public service agreements] with SMART (specific, measurable, achievable, relevant, timed) targets. It has stressed the importance of Inspectorates in areas such as health, housing and education, and has 'zero tolerance' for 'failing' schools and hospitals" (Powell, 2002, pp 6-7). While few would take issue with the need to monitor the effectiveness of various forms of public provision, concerns have been raised about the selection, appropriateness and the level of importance attached to such performance indicators.

New Labour's modernised welfare strategy also requires a redefinition of the relationship between individuals, the community and the state (Blunkett, 2001). While the state will still have an important role to play in the funding, and in some cases the provision of services, individuals will be expected to become more responsible for their own welfare and for the collective well-being of their local neighbourhood. Instead of continuing to regard the centralised state as the principal vehicle for the expression of collective interest, New Labour wants to encourage "localities and neighbourhoods" to take "more responsibility for the decisions that affect their lives" (Brown, 2003a, p 267).

In terms of specific social policy initiatives, New Labour has placed great emphasis on improving state education and reducing child poverty. Education was identified as New Labour's key priority in both its 1997 and 2001 manifestos (Labour Party, 1997, 2001). Attempts have been made to improve the educational performance of children living in low-income households by a range of measures including an expansion of free nursery places for three- and four-year-olds and the establishment of Children's Centres and a diverse range of Sure Start programmes. In addition, both primary and secondary schools have been set ambitious achievement targets in relation to pupils' levels of literacy and numeracy. New Labour has also sought to improve the quality of post-16 education by the creation of a Learning and Skills Council and by the introduction of Education Maintenance Allowances in 1999. It has also been seeking ways to increase the numbers of students entering higher education from low-income households.

While it is still premature to evaluate the impact of New Labour's educational reforms, there have been some early signs of improvement, such as the growing proportion of 11-year-olds achieving level 4 or above in Key Stage 2 tests for literacy (75%) and numeracy (72%). Moreover, as Glennerster (2002, p 133) points out, "Not only did average standards of achievement rise, but the gap between the lowest-achieving schools and the rest narrowed in terms of reaching target levels. So, too, did the gap between schools with many poor pupils and those with richer children". However, Glennerster (2002, p 133) also notes that the performance of secondary "schools in poor areas, or with a high percentage of poor pupils, is still dramatically below that of even the average school". Few would question New Labour's desire to improve educational opportunity and social mobility, but the fact remains that progress is likely to be slow when both private schools and some state schools are able to "cream-skim the most able or the least difficult to teach" (Glennerster, 2002, p 133; see also Brighouse, 2000; Collins, 2001).

New Labour has pledged to eradicate child poverty within 20 years (Blair, 1999; DSS, 2000). Again, the Treasury has been the driving force behind this policy. Various initiatives have been undertaken to achieve this objective. These include attempts to boost income levels in poorer households by encouraging parents to return to the labour market, tax credits, enhanced benefit levels, a childcare strategy, Sure Start and the Child Trust Fund.

Early indications suggest that New Labour will meet its interim 'milestone' of reducing child poverty by a quarter by 2004 (Piachaud, 2001; Sutherland et al, 2003; Palmer et al, 2003). However, it is recognised that the government's long-term goal of eliminating child poverty completely will prove more difficult to achieve in the event of an economic downturn or reduced levels of redistribution.

Assessment

From an intrinsic perspective it can be argued that the Blair government has been relatively successful. By engendering a level of economic stability that would be the envy of many previous Labour administrations, it has been able to increase investment in public services, tackle child and pensioner poverty and increase opportunities for the 'socially excluded' through a series of employability measures. As Skidelsky (2002, p 26) notes in an assessment of New Labour's first five years in government, "Britain's world standing has risen, its economy has been well managed and they have dug in to defend a minimum 'left' programme of raising the floor for the poorest, maintaining a public spending level at around 40 per cent of GDP and rallying around the NHS with unprecedented investment". Annesley and Gamble (2004, p 157) also commend the New Labour government for rebuilding "a consensus around the need for a high level of economic activity, universal welfare and public services, and for higher levels of taxation to fund them".

On the debit side, New Labour has been criticised for the overly cautious nature of its programme of economic and social renewal, not least by leading figures in its own party (see Toynbee and Walker, 2001; Cook, 2003; Hattersley, 2003a, 2003b – but see Collins, 2003 for a defence of New Labour's 'inspirational moderation'). The decision to keep to the previous Conservative government's spending plans during the first two years in office and a "Budget announcement (later rescinded) that the [basic] pension would rise by a derisory 75p per week" (Keegan, 2003, p 292) are widely regarded as policy failures. Ministers themselves have also acknowledged that they have been overly managerial and fixated on target setting and delivery at the expense of broader objectives (White, 2003; Waugh, 2003). The decision to launch a so-called 'big conversation' with the British public in November 2003 was an attempt to rectify this particular failure (Labour Party, 2003). New Labour can also be criticised for its promotion of 'populist' penal and asylum policies, which have too often veered in an illiberal direction.

Attlee versus Blair: continuing progressive dilemmas?

To a greater or lesser extent, all Labour governments have been criticised for their limited aspirations and achievements. In part, this reflects differing interpretations about the progressive potential of such governments. Certainly it could be argued that, like all reformist governments, Labour has had to work within tight structural constraints. As Smith (2004, p 212) reminds us, "Labour has never been a radical party in the sense of aiming to overthrow existing political and economic structures. The goals it has attempted to achieve in terms of greater welfare, equality and social justice have been set within the existing institutional, constitutional and economic context". Even if one accepts that progressive parties have to operate within such boundaries, there is still an opportunity to pursue less or more radical agendas.

The Attlee government can be regarded as operating at the more radical end of the reformist spectrum. As Pearce (1994) noted previously, one of the main reasons why the 1945-51 administrations have come to be regarded as the most inspiring and influential in Labour's history owes much to their desire to remedy past evils. Despite inheriting a near broken economy, the postwar Labour government pressed ahead with an impressive series of welfare initiatives that did much to improve the well-being and life chances of the poor and excluded. As Hattersley (2003a) notes, "Attlee's place in history was secured by the creation of the health service and a comprehensive system of social security – two policies implemented with what New Labour would have dismissed as reckless irresponsibility". While the Attlee government was undoubtedly spurred on in its endeavours by a groundswell of popular support, one should not underestimate the extent to which it attempted to shape rather than respond to public opinion (Fielding, 2003, chapter 4). Certainly it could be argued that Labour was far in advance of postwar public opinion in relation to the need to forge a socialist commonwealth (Fielding et al, 1995; Black, 2003a).

In contrast, Blair's New Labour government has been criticised for operating at the less radical end of the reformist spectrum, not least because of its willingness to make an accommodation with Thatcherism (Hay, 1999; Marquand, 1999; Crouch, 2003). As Gamble and Wright (1999, p 4) note, "some of the strongest criticism has come from self-professed guardians of the social democratic tradition, who believe that certain core ideas such as redistribution, universalist welfare and economic regulation, as well as the link between Labour and the trade unions, cannot be abandoned without abandoning social democracy itself". Indeed Hall (2003) contends that New Labour's long-term strategy is to transform "social democracy into a particular variant of free market neo-liberalism".

Those who defend the strategy of accommodation contend that New Labour is merely adopting new means to achieve social democratic goals in the light of changing economic and social circumstances (Smith, M.J., 2000; Rubinstein, 2000; Fielding, 2003). Crucially, New Labour believes that today's more sceptical public needs to be carefully nurtured before it will lend its support to social democratic policies. As Fielding (2003, p 94) notes:

> many of the attributes associated with 1980s individualism had been evident before Thatcher entered Downing Street. Popular hostility to nationalisation had emerged in the late 1940s; the home centred nature of affluent working-class life was obvious in the 1950s and by the early 1970s skilled workers were already unwilling to pay more taxes to help the poor. Thatcher drew these strands together, but she did not create them.

There is evidence to suggest that the public will support some progressive initiatives, but the contingent nature of such support should not be underestimated, not least because "younger people have become less favourable towards increases in public spending and harder in their attitudes towards the benefits system, relative to older generations" (Sefton, 2003, p 25). In such circumstances, New Labour's contention that, in cricketing parlance, 'occupancy of the crease' will yield better long-term gains than a shorter, albeit more entertaining innings, has some merit. "If a progressive coalition can govern Britain for a majority of the time more poverty will be removed and more real change implemented than could ever be achieved by short, sharp, occasional spasms of radicalism" (Gould, 1998, p 394). In short, New Labour could be said to be adopting a long-term 'accommodate to shape' strategy. From this perspective it would be unfair to compare its modest achievements to date with the giant strides made under Attlee.

A second point of comparison raised by Pearce (1994) is whether the Attlee and Blair governments can be said to have provided progressive agendas for the future. When Attlee called the general election in 1951 there was, as Brooke (1995, p 33) reminds us, a feeling "that initiative now lay behind the government and that the best that could be hoped for was the consolidation of its earlier programme". Although the Labour Party remained committed to the pursuit of "social equality and the establishment of equal opportunities for all" (Dale, 2000, pp 77-8), there was little indication as to how this was to be achieved. In part, this was a reflection of a latent antipathy to theorising within Labour circles (Wickham-Jones, 2003). However, it also reflected the social conservatism of the party leadership. As Morgan (1990, p 107) argues, "The Labour government of 1945-51, whatever its reformist aspirations, was never really a group of social radicals. They adhered to the empire: many of them believed in white supremacy: they, or most of them, upheld the extreme penalty of the rope". Moreover, limited emphasis was given to the needs of women not least in the area of equal pay. "For men (and indeed most women) in the Labour Party at this time 'women's issues' were a distraction from the struggle to build socialism" (Francis, 1997, p 212). This failure to develop a longer-term strategy that would enable a socialist 'culture' to take root, left Labour ill-equipped to build the bedrock of public support it needed to make further progress in a post-austerity age (Black, 2003b). Indeed, it could be argued that the difficulties which subsequent Labour administrations experienced in defending the welfare state and the ethic of collectivism were due in part to the inability of the 1945-51 government to provide a second stage route map.

Although even the most fervent New Labour supporters would find it difficult to equate the modest social achievements of the Blair government to date with the 'transformative' measures undertaken during the Attlee years, they might contend that a progressive agenda for the future based on opportunity for all has been developed. The key question, though, is whether a party that embraces the market and gives greater emphasis to individualism and diversity (Goodhart, 2004), not least in order to achieve electoral success in a "post-ideological world" (Kellner, 2003, p 11), can also pursue a progressive 'social democratic' agenda? At present, New Labour's 'accommodate to shape' approach has been heavily weighted towards the former. If it wants to be compared favourably with the crusading Attlee administration, it now needs to develop a long-lasting social democratic 'shaping' strategy in which real gains accrue to the poorer sections of the community. If it fails to do so, future historians may well come to judge the Blair era as one of 'faux' progressivism.

References

Addison, P. (1975) *The road to 1945*, London: Jonathan Cape.

Annesley, C. and Gamble, A. (2004) 'Economic and welfare policy', in S. Ludlam and M.J. Smith (eds) *Governing as New Labour*, Basingstoke: Palgrave, pp 144-60.

Barnett, C. (1996) *The lost victory*, London: Pan.

Beckett, F. (2000) *Clem Attlee*, London: Politicos.

Black, L. (2003a) '"What kind of people are you?" Labour, the people and the "new political history"', in J. Callaghan, S. Fielding and S. Ludlam (eds) *Interpreting the Labour Party*, Manchester: Manchester University Press, pp 23-38.

Black, L. (2003b) *The political culture of the left in affluent Britain, 1951-64*, Basingstoke: Palgrave.

Blair, T. (1998) *The third way: New politics for the new century*, Fabian Pamphlet, No 588, London: Fabian Society.

Blair, T. (1999) 'Beveridge revisited: a welfare state for the 21st century', in R. Walker (ed) *Ending child poverty: Popular welfare for the 21st century*, Bristol: The Policy Press, pp 7-18.

Blair, T. (2001) 'Third way, phase two', *Prospect*, March, pp 10-13.

Blair, T. (2003) 'Progress and justice in the 21st century', inaugural Fabian Society annual lecture, London, 17 June.

Blunkett, D. (2001) *Politics and progress*, London: Politico's.

Brighouse, H. (2000) *A level playing field: The reform of private schools*, Policy Report No 52, London: Fabian Society.

Brooke, S. (1992) *Labour's war: The Labour Party during the second world war*, Oxford: Clarendon.

Brooke, S. (1995) 'Introduction', in S. Brooke (ed) *Reform and reconstruction: Britain after the war, 1945-51*, Manchester: Manchester University Press, pp 1-34.

Brooke, S. (1996) 'Evan Durbin: reassessing a Labour "revisionist"', *20th Century British History*, vol 7, no 1, pp 27-52.

Brown, G. (1999) 'Equality – then and now', in D. Leonard (ed) *Crosland and New Labour*, Basingstoke: Macmillan, pp 35-48.

Brown, G. (2003a) 'State and market: towards a public interest test', *The Political Quarterly*, vol 74, no 3, July, pp 266-84.

Brown, G. (2003b) 'A modern agenda for prosperity and social reform', Speech to the Social Market Foundation, Cass Business School, London, 3 February.

Butler, D. and Kavanagh, D. (2002) *The British general election of 2001*, Basingstoke: Palgrave.

Cairncross, A. (1985) *Years of recovery, British economic policy, 1945-51*, London: Methuen.

Chadwick, A. and Heffernan, R. (2003) 'Introduction: the New Labour phenomenon', in A. Chadwick and R. Heffernan (eds) *The New Labour reader*, Cambridge: Polity, pp 1-25.

Clarke, P. (1996) *Hope and glory, Britain 1900-1990*, London: Allen Lane.

Cohen, N. (2003) *Pretty straight guys*, London: Faber and Faber.

Cole, G.D.H. (1950) *Socialist economics*, London: Gollancz.

Collins, P. (2001) 'A story of justice', *Prospect*, May, pp 28-33.

Collins, P. (2003) 'Inspiring moderation', *Prospect*, September, pp 10-11.

Cook, R. (2003) *The point of departure*, London: Simon & Schuster.

Crosland, C.A.R. (1956) *The future of socialism*, London: Jonathan Cape.

Crossman, R., Foot, M. and Mikardo, I. (eds) (1947) *Keep left*, London: New Statesman.

Crouch, C. (2003) *Commercialisation or citizenship: Education policy and the future of public services*, Fabian Ideas No 606, London: Fabian Society.

Dale, I. (ed) (2000) *Labour Party general election manifestos, 1900-1997*, London: Routledge/Politicos.

Deacon, A. (2000) 'Learning from the US? The influence of American ideas upon "new labour" thinking on welfare reform', *Policy & Politics*, vol 28, no 1, pp 5-18.

Dell, E. (1999) *A strange eventful history: Democratic socialism in Britain*, London: HarperCollins.

DSS (Department of Social Security) (2000) *Opportunity for all – One year on: Making a difference*, 2nd Annual Report, Cm 4865, London: The Stationery Office.

Fielding, S. (1992) 'Labourism in the 1940s', *Twentieth Century British History*, vol 3, no 2, pp 138-53.

Fielding, S. (2003) *The Labour Party*, Basingstoke: Palgrave.

Fielding, S., Thompson, P. and Tiratsoo, N. (1995) *'England arise!' The Labour Party and popular politics in 1940s Britain*, Manchester: Manchester University Press.

Francis, M. (1997) *Ideas and policies under Labour 1945-1951*, Manchester: Manchester University Press.

Fyrth, J. (ed) (1993) *Labour's high noon: The government and the economy 1945-51*, London: Lawrence and Wishart.

Fyrth, J. (ed) (1995) *Labour's promised land: Culture and society in Labour Britain 1945-51*, London: Lawrence and Wishart.

Gamble, A. and Wright, T. (1999) 'Introduction: the new social democracy', in A. Gamble, and T. Wright (eds) *The new social democracy*, Oxford: Blackwell, pp 1-9.

Giddens, A. (1998) *The third way*, Cambridge: Polity.

Giddens, A (2000) *The third way and its critics*, Cambridge: Polity.

Giddens, A. (2002) *Where now for New Labour?*, Cambridge: Polity.

Glennerster, H. (2000) *British social policy Since 1945* (2nd edn), Oxford: Blackwell.

Glennerster, H. (2002) 'United Kingdom education 1997-2001', *Oxford Review of Economic Policy*, vol 18, no 2, pp 120-36.

Goodhart, D. (2004) 'Too diverse?', *Prospect*, February, pp 30-7.

Gould, P. (1998) *The unfinished revolution*, London: Little, Brown & Co.

Hall, S. (2003) 'New Labour has picked up where Thatcherism left off', *The Guardian*, 6 August.

Hattersley, R. (2003a) 'Boldly going nowhere', *The Guardian*, 2 August.

Hattersley, R. (2003b) 'Review of N. Cohen', *Pretty straight guys, The Observer Review*, 7 March, p 15.

Hay, C. (1999) *The political economy of New Labour*, Manchester: Manchester University Press.

Hennessy, P. (1993) *Never again*, London: Vintage.

Holt, R. (2001) *Second amongst equals*, London: Profile.

Jay, D. (1937) *The socialist case*, London: Faber.

Jefferys, K. (2002) *Finest and darkest hours*, London: Atlantic Books.

Keegan, W. (2003) *The prudence of Mr Gordon Brown*, Chichester: Wiley.

Kellner, P. (2003) 'Why ideology is not the answer', *Fabian Review*, vol 115, no 4, Winter, pp 10-11.

King, A.D. and Wickham-Jones, M. (1999) 'Bridging the Atlantic: the Democratic (Party) origins of welfare to work', in M. Powell (ed) *New Labour, new welfare state*, Bristol: The Policy Press, pp 257-80.

Klein, R. (2000) *The new politics of the NHS*, London: Prentice-Hall.

Labour Party (1941) *Labour in the government*, London: Labour Party.

Labour Party (1949) *Labour believes in Britain*, London: Labour Party.

Labour Party (1997) *New Labour because Britain deserves better*, London: Labour Party.

Labour Party (2001) *Ambitions for Britain*, London: Labour Party.

Labour Party (2003) *A future fair for all: Big issues need a big conversation*, London: Labour Party.

Malpass, P. (2003) 'The wobbly pillar? Housing and the British postwar welfare state', *Journal of Social Policy*, vol 32, no 4, pp 589-606.

Marquand, D. (1999) 'Premature obsequies: social democracy comes in from the cold', in A.Gamble and T.Wright (eds) *The new social democracy*, Oxford: Blackwell, pp 10-18.

Marquand, D. (2004) *Decline of the public*, Cambridge: Polity.

Miliband, R. (1972) *Parliamentary socialism: A study in the politics of Labour*, (2nd edn), London: Merlin.

Morgan, K.O. (1984) *Labour in power 1945-1951*, Oxford: Clarendon.

Morgan, K.O. (1990) *The people's peace*, Oxford: Oxford University Press.

Page, R.M. (2003) 'New Labour and paid work: a break with the past?', *Benefits*, vol 2, no 1, January, pp 5-10.

Palmer, G., North, J., Carr, J. and Kenway, P. (2003) *Monitoring poverty and social exclusion 2003*, York: Joseph Rowntree Foundation.

Pattie, C. (2004) 'Re-electing New Labour', in S. Ludlam and M. J. Smith (eds) *Governing as New Labour*, Basingstoke: Palgrave, pp 6-33.

Pearce, R. (1994) *Attlee's Labour governments 1945-51*, London: Routledge.

Pearce, R. (1997) *Attlee*, London: Longman.

Piachaud, D. (2001) 'Child poverty, opportunities and quality of life', *Political Quarterly*, vol 21, no 4, pp 446-53.

Pollock, A., Shaoul, J., Rowland, D. and Player, S. (2001) *Public services and the private sector*, London: Catalyst.

Powell, M. (ed) (2002) *Evaluating New Labour's welfare reforms*, Bristol: The Policy Press.

Rubinstein, D. (2000) 'A new look at New Labour', *Politics*, vol 20, no 3, pp 161-7.

Rubinstein, W.D. (2003) *Twentieth-Century Britain: A political history*, Basingstoke: Palgrave.

Sefton, T. (2003) 'What we want from the welfare state', in A. Park, J. Curtice, K. Thomson, L. Jarvis and C. Bromley (eds) *British social attitudes: the 20th report*, London: Sage Publications, pp 1-28.

Shaw, E. (1996) *The Labour Party since 1945*, Oxford: Blackwell.

Skidelsky, R. (2002) 'Five years Labour', *Prospect*, May, pp 22-6.

Smith, M. (2000) *Britain and 1940: History, myth and popular memory*, London: Routledge.

Smith, M.J. (2000) 'Tony Blair and the transition to new Labour: 1994-2000', in B. Brivati and R. Heffernan (eds) (2000) *The Labour Party: A centenary history*, Basingstoke: Macmillan, pp 143-62.

Smith, M.J. (2004) 'Conclusion: defining New Labour', in S. Ludlam and M. J. Smith (eds) *Governing as New Labour*, Basingstoke: Palgrave, pp 211-25.

Stephens, P. (2001) 'The treasury under Labour', in A. Seldon (ed) *The Blair effect*, London: Little, Brown & Co, pp 185-207.

Sutherland, H., Sefton, T. and Piachaud, D. (2003) *Poverty in Britain: The impact of government policy since 1997*, York: Joseph Rowntree Foundation.

Taylor-Gooby, P. (2000) 'Blair's scars', *Critical Social Policy*, vol 20, no 3, August, pp 331-48.

Thane, P. (2000) 'Labour and welfare', in D. Tanner, P. Thane and N. Tiratsoo (eds) *Labour's first century*, Cambridge: Cambridge University Press, pp 80-118.

Thompson, N. (1996) *Political economy and the Labour Party*, London: UCL.

Thorpe, A. (2001) *A history of the British Labour Party* (2nd edn), Basingstoke: Palgrave.

Tomlinson, J. (1997) *Democratic socialism and economic policy: The Attlee years 1945-1951*, Cambridge: Cambridge University Press.

Tomlinson, J. (1998) 'Why so austere? The British welfare state of the 1940s', *Journal of Social Policy*, vol 27, no 1, pp 63-77.

Toynbee, P. and Walker, D. (2001) *Did things get better?*, London: Penguin.

Waugh, P. (2003) 'Blair admits Labour's "managerial" style leaves voters cold', *The Independent*, 5 July.

Webster, C. (2002) *The national health service* (2nd edn), Oxford: Oxford University Press.

White, M. (2003) 'We got it wrong, admits Blair', *The Guardian*, 5 July.

Wickham-Jones, M. (2003) 'An exceptional comrade? The Nairn-Anderson interpretation', in J. Callaghan, S. Fielding and S. Ludlam (eds) *Interpreting the Labour Party*, Manchester: Manchester University Press, pp 86-100.

NINE

Christian democracy, social democracy and the continental 'welfare without work' syndrome

Kees van Kersbergen and Anton Hemerijck

Introduction: the Christian democratisation of social democracy?

One intriguing observation – at least from a continental perspective – on the British debate on the nature of New Labour concerns what may be called the thesis of the 'Christian democratisation' of British social democracy. David Marquand early on suggested that Tony Blair's aim was to found a "hegemonic people's party appealing to every part of the nation. This may have nothing in common with social democracy, but it is the nearest thing to Christian democracy that modern British politics have known" (quoted in Huntington and Bale, 2002, p 44). Surely, the Labour Party's new social and economic policies converged considerably towards the neo-liberal and conservative policies of the Thatcherite kind, but as Driver and Martell (1998, 2000) point out, this transformation must also be understood as a reaction to the new political reality that Thatcher had helped to create. New Labour must be understood as an "exercise in *post-Thatcherite* politics" as it tries to go beyond both Old Labour and Thatcherism, particularly by adopting communitarianism as an antidote to Old Labour's collectivism and Tory individualism, culminating in an all-pervasive stress on social inclusion.

> New Labour accepts but also departs from Thatcherism. Successful economies, it is argued, cannot live by competitive individualism alone. Economic success requires the government, in partnership with the private sector, to provide the underpinnings for economic growth.

> Despite its embrace of the market economy, New Labour's politics are hostile to what Blair has called the 'politics of self'. Communitarianism is about rebuilding the social cohesion and moral fabric undermined by years of Tory individualism and *laissez-faire*. Much of Labour's economic and social policies are about communitarian inclusions. Divisions must be replaced by the inclusion of all in one nation: government for 'the many not the few'. (Driver and Martell 1998, p 167)

We think that the adoption of a comparative perspective may help to appreciate and understand better this communitarian switch of New Labour and its distinctiveness vis-à-vis conservatism and continental social democracy, because much of New Labour's communitarianism does seem strikingly similar to some of the central tenets of continental European Christian democracy. Part of New Labour's success may then perhaps be explained by the fact that in this way British social democracy has started to capture a political and moral territory that historically has been left unexplored by both the Tories and Old Labour.

However, Huntington and Bale (2002, p 50) argue that only superficially may New Labour be regarded as a hypothetical British Christian democratic party and, looking somewhat closer, reveals major differences: "New Labour's approach to politics – even the politics of community – and policy is too liberal to allow us to place it in the same analytical category as the kind of confessional centre-right parties that play such a large (though declining) role in continental European politics".

Still, there is room for real debate here. According to Seeleib-Kaiser (2002), those who assess new social democracy in terms of neo-liberalism-in-disguise and those who argue that Third Way social democracy clings to traditional goals and values but simply adopts modern instruments, especially active labour market policies, are both wrong. They pose a dichotomy between socialism and liberalism and overlook the role of Christian democracy, which always has been the embodiment of the 'Third Way' between socialism and liberalism.

Seeleib-Kaiser's comparative study of the programmatic transformation of social democratic parties in the Netherlands, Germany, Sweden and Britain in the 1990s suggests that the 'Christian democratisation' of social democracy may be a more general phenomenon. The positions of the parties on social and economic policies are not new, but have simply converged decisively towards the type of goals and instruments that Christian democracy traditionally has fostered. The general trend Seeleib-Kaiser (p 489) finds is towards a redefinition of state interventionism:

"The new social democratic concept of stateness involves, first of all, that the state no longer has the sole responsibility for social equality. Rather, the state should reinforce individual self-responsibility as well as the organisations and communities in civil society" (our translation). This indeed comes down to nothing less than the 'Christian-democratisation' of social democracy.

The 'Christian democratisation' thesis was recently criticised by Frenzel (2003), who offers three arguments to refute it. First, just like there are multiple third ways, there are diverse, nationally specific paths of programmatic development in social democratic parties of which the lowest common denominator concerns social-liberal modernisation. Second, the new social democratic stress is *not* on issues relating to the family and community, but rather on 'utilitarian'-oriented welfare state reform (active welfare state, rebalancing social rights and obligations), active labour market policies (social inclusion), and an appreciation and stronger commitment to the market (welfare to work, politics within markets). Third, the period of classical Christian democracy is over and Christian democratic parties are themselves realigning and converging towards a liberal or an authoritarian direction. According to Frenzel, social democracy is still a distinctive political movement.

This even holds, to some extent at least for British social democracy, as Shaw's (2003) evaluation of New Labour in power demonstrates. Shaw identifies five core social democratic values (but see Powell, 2004). First, *social justice* is still prominent and after the initial retrenchment policies of the first years of government, New Labour "has put increasing emphasis on rebuilding the welfare state" (Shaw, 2003, p 21). Second, the *right to work* and the commitment towards *full employment* are still discernible in Labour's policies. However, in its "reconstruction of the benefit system to render it more responsive to the needs of the labour market, in its insistence on conditionality and its drift towards workfare, the Blair government has ... moved towards an unyielding and hard-nosed attitude towards the unemployed more commonly associated with the right than with the left" (Shaw, 2003, p 22). Third, the ideal of *equality* is still in tact, albeit that government policies show a stronger market orientation, an acceptance of a somewhat wider wage dispersion and more emphasis on equality of opportunity. Fourth, New Labour's labour market policies are now fully oriented towards the promotion of greater labour market flexibility and indicate a clear break with the commitment to *labour protection*. Finally, *social solidarity and collective risk protection* have lost their status as core social democratic values in New Labour, as government policies have abandoned the attachment to universalism based on social citizenship. "Community is detached from social solidarity and collective protection against risk, and is reinterpreted in morally prescriptive terms – the entrenchment of values and norms operating as forms of social control to sustain social cohesion, order and stability" (Shaw 2003, p 22). Especially, with respect to the last conclusion, it seems that there is still ample room for further debate on the 'Christian-democratisation' of social democracy in Britain.

Our modest aim is to contribute to this debate by asking to what extent the thesis of the Christian democratisation of social democracy/ New Labour really makes sense analytically and empirically (and politically, see Van Kersbergen, 2003). Rather than providing a comparison between the ideologies and policies of British New Labour and continental Christian democracy, we propose to look at recent developments on the European continent. Powell (2004) has rightly pointed to the fact that the debate on the transformation of social democracy is confused by a lack of analytical clarity in distinguishing between the various aspects of possible 'renewal' or 'retreat', particularly discourse, values, goals and policy mechanisms. We think this is an important point and we try to pay attention to all aspects. First, we briefly characterise Christian democracy as a social and political actor. Second, we summarise the main features of the continental welfare state regime upon which Christian democracy has had such a momentous impact. Third, we describe how Christian democracies in power in the 1980s and early 1990s attempted to uphold their own legacy: the extended and generous, yet passive, welfare state regime that provides welfare rather than work. Fourth, we analyse how since the second half of the 1990s continental social democracy has tried to break with (unsuccessful) Christian democratic policies. Our thesis is that in the past decade European Third Way social democracy did not 'Christian democratise', but, on the contrary, has tried to 'social democratise' the continental, Christian democratic welfare state regime (Green-Pedersen et al, 2001).

Continental Christian democracy as a social and political actor

Christian democracy is a distinctive political movement that has promoted an equally characteristic political economy and a qualitatively distinctive postwar path to welfare capitalism (Van Kersbergen, 1995, 1999). Ideologically, the religious inspiration of Christian democratic parties has distinguished them from conservative parties, especially with respect to their social concern.

Contemporary Christian democrats shared the conviction that each private, semi-private or semi-public association or institution of society performs indispensable moral, social and economic tasks. In principle, a government should be disinclined to take over the responsibility for these tasks. Nevertheless, this principle of subsidiarity prescribed that political action was mandatory whenever 'lower social organs' (for example, the family, a business, a union) failed to perform their duties. Under such conditions the state had the obligation to intervene in moral, social and economic relations by offering temporary support, with a view to restoring the sovereignty of social associations and their capacity to perform adequately in accordance with their natural function.

On the Christian democratic account, *solidarity* was primarily defined as the attempt to realise harmony between various social groups and organisations with opposed interests. To a large extent, the search for societal 'integration' and accommodation in a plural society has characterised the social and political practice of Christian democratic parties. The basis for social policy practice is found in a distinctive theory of social justice, that – rather than balancing rights and duties – it fundamentally underscored a moral obligation to help the 'weak', 'poor', 'lower strata' or whoever might have been in need of help.

It has been the ceaseless attempt of integrating and reconciling a plurality of societal groups with possibly opposed interests that has made Christian democracy distinctive. Even within its own ranks the Christian democratic movements included various social organisations that had opposed social and political interests. As a result, the movements always needed to be flexible and, therefore, continuously attempted to retain or to increase their capacity to adapt to changing circumstances and to new wishes and demands in their venture of formulating a compromise of antagonistic interests. Christian democracy was in this sense the embodiment of societal accommodation, or at least aspired to become so. The electorate of Christian democracy has traditionally mirrored the social and demographic structure of society.

Christian democratic parties have consequently always had to search for means to conciliate conflicting interests. And it has been the 'politics of mediation', that is, the religiously inspired, ideologically condensed, institutionally rooted and politically practised conviction that conflicts of social interests can and must be reconciled politically via social policy in order to restore the natural and organic harmony of society, that has governed the social and economic practice of Christian democracy in the entire postwar era.

Typically, and crucial for the present purposes, Christian democracy has always promoted a passive or reactive type of social policy which was characterised by the readiness to moderate the harmful outcomes of the imperfect market mechanism by transferring considerable sums of money to families in need, without changing the logic of the market itself. In this sense, the movement has always looked for a feasible middle way between socialist collectivism and liberal individualism. Christian democratic reformism normally aimed at restoring the self-responsibility and self-reliance of social institutions.

Christian democrats came to promote transfer-oriented welfare states, but never embraced a commitment to full male and female employment. This is best illustrated by the fact that active labour market policies were never supported by Christian democratic parties, whereas extensive measures to compensate loss of income for breadwinners, of course, have. Subsidiarity has found its most important organisational expression in how Christian democracy has opposed the transfer of authority and control over social and economic policies to the state. The ideal has always been privately governed, but publicly financed welfare arrangements. Corporatist institutions became the intermediary organs between state and society in the continental welfare state.

The corollary of self-government was self-responsibility. The financing of welfare activities through taxation only, as well as Beveridge-type of flat-rate benefits, ran against Christian democratic policy doctrine. As a result of successful Christian democratic politics, the continental welfare states became strongly characterised by the Bismarckian principle of social insurance, status reproduction and particularism, and modest to considerable generosity of benefits.

With respect to social inequality, Christian democracy promoted distinctive policies, too. An extensive redistribution of societal wealth was considered to disrupt the precarious balance between social groups and associations. Social policy, therefore, was never promoted with a view to establishing a more equal distribution of income. Social policy was not to alter social status, but rather to reproduce it well into retired life. The Christian democratic theory of social justice effectively lacked a conception of individual social rights of citizens. In Christian democratic thought, individuals are, first and foremost, full members of lower social organs that make up society as a whole, not citizens of the national community. Their rightful claim to assistance was therefore not an absolute right derived from their status as citizens, but from their status as members of indispensable classes and other groups.

Social benefits for adult male employees were to replace the family income at the level of the existing status. An unintended, yet conspicuous, consequence of the Bismarckian system was that the continental welfare states developed rather generous benefit structures, especially with regard to families. Benefits for women, on the other hand, were either made dependent on the income of the husband or at least lower than for an adult male worker. In its extreme form, social security systems became sexually differentiated.

Historically, Christian democrats have assumed women to be only marginally present on the labour market and the family to be the prime provider of care. Christian democratic social thought elaborated strong images of the division of labour according to gender: paid and well-protected jobs for men, unpaid domestic labour for women. Such images underlay many policies directed toward the traditional family and reinforced typical male and female employment careers (see Bussemaker and Van Kersbergen, 1994, 1999). Generally speaking, the Christian democratic nations generated distinctive patterns of female labour force participation. The discouragement of female labour force participation and the encouragement of female labour market exit were properties of Christian democratic welfare states.

In sum, the continental European welfare system came thus to be characterised by occupationally distinct, employment-related social insurance, combining (sometimes) very high replacement rates with generally strict levels of employment protection. The system aimed to protect the male breadwinner household (see Sainsbury, 1994; Ostner and Lewis, 1995). Continental social policy was predominantly based on the principle of industrial insurance against occupational risks, financed by earmarked payroll contributions from employers and workers. Strong social partnership traditions extended into the administration of social insurance. The status of labour market policies was strongly correlated with the passive character of Bismarckian social security. In contrast to the Scandinavian welfare state, for instance, the continental regime type lacked a distinctive legacy of active employment policy priorities.

Christian democracy in the 1980s and the 'welfare without work' syndrome

Christian democratic parties in power in the 1980s neither opted fully for the (Scandinavian) social democratic public project of maintaining full employment nor for the neo-liberal market-based accommodation to changes in the international economic order. During the second half of the 1980s the Christian democratic movements in power were increasingly compelled to follow policies of retrenchment and austerity. These policies were characterised by a more or less consistent attempt to preserve the typical form of passive income compensation that Christian democrats had always promoted, albeit on a lower level and without altering the basic logic of the system.

In the 1980s, Christian democratic politicians and policy makers in power in nations such as Germany, the Netherlands and Belgium firmly believed that full employment could only be achieved by a redistribution of existing jobs and early labour market exit. In the continental welfare states, spiralling unemployment in the early 1980s led to a view that strategies of compulsory working time reduction, early retirement and disability leave were socially acceptable alternatives to high levels of unemployment among younger workers. The unintended result, however, was that within less than a decade these temporary measures of labour supply reduction turned into a problem of structural labour market inactivity, with the associate financial crisis of the employment-related social insurance system.

This structural problem became the major socioeconomic and political predicament of the continental welfare states in the 1980s and 1990s. The – by now notorious – 'welfare without work' trap developed into a 'pathology' or 'syndrome' caused by a complex interaction of various political–institutional legacies and policy choices. Its core lies in the combination of four distinct institutional elements: (1) the generosity and long duration of insurance-based income replacement benefits; (2) the mainly 'passive' or compensatory nature of such benefits; (3) their contributory financing; and (4) high minimum wages. Generous insurance entitlements (especially pensions) required high contributory rates on the wages of standard workers, while their jobs were highly protected by labour laws. This is the basic reason for the – sometimes extreme – rigidity of the labour market. Employers were reluctant to hire new (expensive) employees when possible, and incapable of firing personnel when necessary.

There have been three unfavourable consequences for the functioning of the labour market. First, firms were discouraged from continuing to offer traditional (but too expensive) 'Fordist' employment, reinforcing those labour-shedding inclinations already connected with globalisation and post-industrialisation. Second, in order to facilitate productive restructuring, the pressure to extend the facilities for early labour market exit increased and other possibilities such as part-time work remained in the margin. Finally, the logic of the continental regime on the one hand severely hampered the expansion of private service employment because of its high wage floors, and on the other hand proved incapable of expanding public service employment due to the already considerable fiscal overload.

The ensuing unemployment problems were met by measures that largely followed the logic of the regime: further expanding passive schemes of income maintenance (unemployment, sickness, disability) and further encouraging labour market exit through specific early retirement schemes, but also via other provisions originally not designed for this purpose (for example, the disability scheme in the Netherlands, see Hemerijck and Van Kersbergen, 1997). However, such policy reactions required further increases in social charges and in this way reinforced the negative spiral of 'welfare without work'.

This development was particularly disadvantageous for women. Historically already characterised by low levels of female labour market participation, the continental systems – with their high rates of single-income households – failed to promote arrangements allowing women to combine work and family (especially child rearing) responsibilities. Hence, the unfavourable combination of low female labour market participation, high female unemployment and low fertility. The conventional emphasis on 'passive' income transfers and strong job guarantees for male breadwinners became especially problematic when marital instability grew and conventional one-earner households declined.

It was also specifically detrimental to the labour market opportunities of semi- and unskilled workers. The 'Bismarckian' design of the social security systems is to be blamed for this. As the bulk of the welfare budget is financed through payroll taxes (for example, over 70% in Germany), there existed a large wedge between the net wage received by a worker and the gross wage paid by the employer. At the lower end of the labour market, where the net wage of the worker cannot fall below the level defined by (minimum) social assistance, the total burden must be assumed by the employer. In other words, as a direct consequence of social policy design, many workers were not sufficiently productive to earn the cost of their labour back for their employers. The productivity threshold thus turned into an effective 'unemployment trap' for job seekers with low levels of marketable skills. Employment therefore disappeared, especially in those sectors where productivity increases stagnated and the prices of goods and services could not be raised significantly. The result was slackening job growth in the labour intensive private service sector. Christian democratic governments were unwilling to compensate for the undersupply of private sector jobs in labour intensive services through the provision of social services in the public sector. They probably would also have been incapable of doing so, since the fiscal capacity was limited due to the narrow tax base, on the one side, and the costly pension and other social commitments on the other.

Another way of putting the problem is that payroll financing put a premium on high productivity. However, the indirect effect of shedding less productive workers was a substantial increase in the 'tax' on labour, simply because an increasingly smaller number of workers had to provide for an increasing number of inactive citizens. In short, maximising worker productivity resulted in an 'inactivity trap', whereby a virtuous cycle of productivity growth coincided with a vicious cycle of rising wage costs and early exit of less productive workers, all requiring further productivity increases and eliciting yet another round of reductions in the work force through subsidised early exit (Hemerijck and Manow, 2001).

The predicament of Christian democracy and the failure to reverse the downward spiral of inactivity

The specific vulnerability of the continental welfare state and its major political predicament thus came to lie in the difficulty of reversing its own legacy and the in-built policy responses that went with it. Such responses caused a chronic inability to increase the level of labour market participation and decrease the number of social security beneficiaries. As this predicament of structural inactivity was directly related to payroll-based social insurance financing, the problem was to find a politically (and socially) acceptable way to alter this structural feature.

However, reversing this pathological downward spiral of inactivity, under such conditions as de-industrialisation, the rise of the service sector, changing household and labour market patterns and demographic ageing, posed a triple challenge to the Christian democratic guardians of the continental welfare state. First, in terms of policy content, the predicament of structural inactivity required a radical break with the 'normal' policies, particularly the passive breadwinner-biased measures of income compensation, and the introduction of active, gender-neutral strategies of labour market (re-)integration. Second, the political feasibility of such a radical break was heavily constrained by strong social partnership involvement in the administration of the passive social insurance provisions to which Christian democracy were strongly attached. Third, a programmatic break with the income compensation system for the male breadwinner and the transition to a more gender-neutral labour market activation policy ultimately had to be matched by new forms of institutional coordination between social protection and employment provision, functions which in the continental welfare regimes were catered for in completely separated policy areas.

Christian democrats kept defending their own heritage, but the increasing difficulty of doing so in the late 1980s and early 1990s seriously hampered the capacity of continued power mobilisation. As Christian democratic politics and policies became increasingly ineffective, the parties found themselves in precarious circumstances. Crucial was the decay of the politics of mediation. It was this feature that defined the distinction between Christian democracy and conservatism and which facilitated the appeal to a broad section of the voters. The perennial search for an accommodation of social and political conflicts was one of the movement's major electoral assets, determined its 'natural' position in the centre of the political system, but lost its pronounced ideological significance and blurred the electorally favourable distinction between conservatism and Christian democracy.

The golden age of the politics of mediation came to an end. The sources that once provided the media of exchange for social coalitions were rapidly drying up under the impact of increasing international pressures (European integration, internationalisation) and domestic social changes (particularly ageing). The passive, corporatist, transfer-oriented political economies of Christian democratic nations increasingly failed to deliver the goods that provided the currency for the kind of beneficial political exchanges that the parties traditionally nurtured in the attempt to mediate opposed societal interests.

Controversies over the rising costs of the welfare state intensified and these tended to make favourable positive-sum exchanges between different social groups much more demanding. Nevertheless, social and economic policies remained largely rooted institutionally in the postwar paradigm of stable, highly regulated labour markets for male breadwinners, traditional family structures and a relatively balanced demographic structure. The new requirements of flexible labour markets, the transformation of the composition of households, demographic changes, increasing economic interdependence and the need to adjust to the criteria of monetary union in Europe required more fundamental or radical economic and social policy innovations. The existing institutional arrangements, in the context of which social and economic policies were formulated, could no longer remain grounded on the kind of arrangements that Christian democracy conventionally attempted to fashion. But Christian democrats were slow to adapt.

Path breaking reforms and Third Way social democracy in the 1990s

The Christian democratic experience in the past revealed that welfare reform was difficult and almost impossible to turn into a politically attractive electoral position. But the shift to 'competitive corporatism' in wage bargaining in a number of countries and the renewed electoral fortunes of social democratic parties in the 1990s created the political preconditions for more radical endeavours of social security reform (Hemerijck and Schludi, 2000).

As financial viability heavily depended on high levels of employment because of the reliance on payroll taxes, Christian democratic welfare states were particularly vulnerable to increases in inactivity, since this implied an increase in social expenditures and a reduction of revenues at the same time. This created the dilemma of either reducing benefits precisely at a time when more people became dependent upon them, or to raise payroll taxes at a time when firms were particularly sensitive to labour cost increases. This was precisely the type of reforms that Christian democrats experimented with, but with little success and with bad electoral results.

Part of the Third Way renewal of social democracy on the European continent consisted of the discovery that if the logic of the spiral of 'welfare without work' indeed succeeded as it seemed to do, the reverse logic might also hold. In other words, social democrats came to realise that wage moderation – after a first phase of boosting competitiveness in the exposed sector – could help to create more jobs in domestic services, slow down or lower the number of people depending on benefits and hence reduce the social wage component. This would allow governments to use improved public finances to lower the tax wedge at, or near, the minimum and get more low-skilled workers back into jobs. As a result, the *vice* of 'welfare without work' could be reversed into the *virtue* of helping people to adjust to the new realities of post-industrial working life and family relations (Levy, 1999).

Politically, it became of crucial importance that some such perspective of turning vice into virtue became clear before policy makers could prescribe tough measures that were acceptable to the unions and could be defended to the electorate by the social democrats. The promise of job growth had to be realistic and realisable in the near future, before social democrats could risk curtailing drastically social programmes. Social democrats needed a convincing employment story for legitimising further cuts in social insurance benefit levels, narrowing of eligibility criteria and a shortening of benefit periods.

The biggest change social democrats in government in the 1990s brought about concerned the domain of employment policy, breaking with a long tradition of passive, or rather absent, labour market policies. Most conspicuously, a social democratic consensus (as epitomised in the Blair–Schröder paper of 1999; see Bonoli and Powell 2004) was arising that expanding employment levels among women (and increasingly also among older workers) was a *sine qua non* for the long-term sustainability of a welfare state. In most continental welfare states one observes increased spending on active labour market policy since the second half of the 1990s, emphasising the activation content of social insurance instead of exclusively relying on passive transfers. Higher pressures on the unemployed to accept suitable job offers or participate in education went along with the policy change and reinforced activation programmes. However, it turned out to be very difficult to reform the gender bias, and social democrats remained half-hearted in introducing women- and child-friendly policies of affordable access to day care, paid maternity and parental leave, a more equal division of household tasks between men and women and reasonably generous provisions for work absence when children are ill.

In contrast to the traditional built-in policy reflexes, since the early 1990s most social democratic-led governments have attempted to reduce the volume of people moving into inactivity via early exit routes. The reduced labour market opportunities of older unemployed and partially disabled persons are no longer grounds for granting benefits. Administrative controls have been reinforced and benefit replacement rates have been reduced. For instance, in the Netherlands the privatisation of the sickness benefit scheme, the obligation of employers to hire privately owned health service companies and the possibility of the employers to insure disability risks with private insurance companies (in 1998), have all been attempts to bolster employers' incentives to limit the number of sickness and disability benefit claimants. Germany has tried to encourage beneficiaries to return to work, with targeted training and employment policies, including the provision of subsidised jobs for older workers. The result of these policy initiatives in the area of social protection has been a general trend towards later withdrawal from the labour market (Hemerijck and Vail, forthcoming).

The Netherlands in the 1990s has gone furthest in resolving the continental pathology of 'welfare without work' by embracing a new policy agenda centred around 'jobs, jobs, jobs' rather than benefits and transfers or Blair's 'education, education, education'. The 'Dutch miracle' was based on a long-term strategy of organised wage restraint, restriction of access to (and curtailing heavy misuse of) disability pensions and sickness insurance, and promotion of part-time work (Visser and Hemerijck, 1997), politically backed by – for Dutch standards – an unusual coalition between social democrats and conservative liberals, that – between 1994 and 2002 – kept Christian democrats out of government for the first time in over 75 years.

The Dutch experience with long-term wage restraint suggested that the employment effects are the strongest in domestic services that were previously priced out of the regular labour market. The Dutch experience inspired ideas on policy change in other continental welfare states, as it was considered evidence for the view that wage moderation and active labour market policies were beneficial also to the larger and less exposed continental economies. In fact, the expectation was that to the extent that wage developments in the private and public sector were coupled, responsive pay settlements could lower the public sector wage bill, curtail the costs of social security and broaden the revenue bases of the welfare state (Ebbinghaus and Hassel, 2000). Finally, there was some evidence that responsive income policy cooperation allowed for a smoother interplay among income, monetary and fiscal policy, thus stimulating economic growth while keeping inflation low.

In the Netherlands, female labour force participation has increased rapidly, doubling since the early 1970s. The massive entry of Dutch women into the labour market was inherently related to the changing status of part-time work. By the mid 1990s 68.8% of all female workers were employed on a part-time basis in the Netherlands (Visser and Hemerijck, 1997). Dutch employers essentially recruit part-time workers to strengthen organisational flexibility, not to pursue low-price competition as in the UK. In many Dutch households the pay increases resulting from long-term wage restraint were in a way compensated (or even overcompensated) for by additional family income stemming from women's growing job opportunities.

Dutch labour developments have increased the pressure for policy measures allowing working parents, especially women, to combine child rearing and participation in the labour market. So the so-called 'flexicurity' agreements (1995) between the social partners aimed to establish a win-win relation between flexible employment afforded by safeguarding social security, and the legal position of part-time workers and temporary workers in exchange for a loosening of legislation concerning the dismissal of (full-time) employees. The 2000 Working Hours Act gave part-time workers an explicit right to equal treatment in all areas negotiated by the social partners, such as wages, basic social security, training and education, subsidised care provision, holiday pay and second tier pensions. The 2002 Work and Care Bill provided for short-term paid care leave and paid adoption leave. The Dutch experience thus renders an example of how concerted efforts of labour market desegmentation can help avoid problems of labour market dualism and gender marginalisation (Hemerijck and Schludi, 2000).

Social democratic policies to increase the demand for low-skilled workers typically aimed at exempting employers hiring low-skilled workers from social contributions. For Belgium, France and the Netherlands it made sense to use regressive employment subsidies to create a low-wage job intensive service sector (see Hemerijck et al, 2000; Levy, 2000). In these countries with relatively high minimum wages and high gross labour costs, there was a considerable potential for an expansion of low-skilled jobs in services like wholesale and retail trade, personal services, personal and public safety, house improvements, environmental protection, tourism and cultural recreation. Targeted wage subsidies permitted a scenario of 'labour-cheapening' and job growth, without an American-style surge in poverty and inequality. This opened up a wide range of additional, economically viable employment opportunities at the lower end of the labour market.

Notwithstanding the success of employment subsidies in continental welfare states, they were not without problems. As many programmes were targeted on unemployed people out of work between one and three years, employers were inclined to substitute the long-term unemployed for the short-term unemployed, or delay hiring until the subsidy could be collected. Also, it is important to emphasise that a policy of lowering social security contributions for employers hiring low-skilled workers could harm workers and employers' incentives to upgrade skills. This created the danger that the employment subsidies would lock low-skilled workers in a secondary low-wage economy from which they could not escape. The risk was that a 'skill trap' would replace the 'inactivity trap'.

Activation programmes based on individual guidance and training opportunities, primarily targeted on youngsters and low-skill groups, gained in importance over the past decades. Many of the recent policy reforms have triggered important processes of institutional recalibration (Ferrera et al, 2000) – that is, a reconfiguration of the involvement of the social partners and the division of labour between public and private actors and levels of governance in the provision of welfare and promotion of employment. At the interface of the public and the private sector, the proliferation of supply side approaches to labour market policy, providing for one-to-one counselling, came hand in hand with a demonopolisation and regionalisation of public employment services, for instance in Belgium (Cantillon and De Lathouwer, 2001). In the Netherlands, the privatisation of public employment services and liberalisation of the rules and regulation governing private temporary employment agencies extended the use of market-type mechanisms, such as contracting out and organisational reforms, including among other things separating purchasers and providers. Private reintegration services and health and safety at work services were growing. In terms of regulation, these developments shared in a shift away from 'heavy' legislated or rule-governed labour market regulation and employment policy to 'lighter' forms of decentralised coordination, including the social partners, private actors and third-party groups.

Pension reform, especially in the pay-as-you-go systems of Belgium and Germany, made for cumbersome exercises in reform. A dominant approach to improving sustainability of pension systems has been the raise of contribution rates. Changes to indexation rules for pensions are enacted across the board in continental Europe. Germany has moved from gross to net wage indexation. The Netherlands and Belgium have started building up advance-funded reserves within existing pay-as-you-go public pensions. Such funds can be used to maintain adequate pension provision when the baby boom generation retires, while for now putting fiscal policy and thereby the growth potential of the economy on a sounder footing (Esping-Andersen et al, 2002).

Germany has gone furthest with reforms to encourage savings in private occupational pensions through the use of direct transfers and tax advantages. Moreover, German policy makers are planning to support contributions to supplementary pension schemes for low-income earners through state subsidies. But while wage earners are encouraged to pay up to 4% of their income into this additional pillar, German pension policy makers have failed in their attempt to make supplementary private old age provision compulsory, as in the Netherlands (Schludi, 2001). Another weakness of the German pension policy reform – compared to successful efforts in Austria – is that no efforts have been made to harmonise civil servants' pensions with the general scheme.

Conclusion

Our modest aim was to contribute to the debate on the 'Christian democratisation' of New Labour by asking to what extent this thesis makes sense analytically and empirically. After a brief characterisation of

Christian democracy, we looked at the main features of the continental Christian democratic welfare state regime. We argued that contemporary attempts at reforming this welfare state are necessarily directed at problems that are very specific to this regime and we identified the typical political, institutional and social arrangements that caused the so-called syndrome of 'welfare without work'. We showed that Christian democracy in power in the 1980s and early 1990s essentially acted according to the continental regime's own internal logic, following its path of development via in-built policy reflexes. In other words, Christian democracy consistently was upholding its own legacy: the extended and generous, yet passive, welfare state regime that provided welfare rather than work. This reform policy can best be characterised as trying to safeguard 'less of the same'.

The analysis of the continental syndrome of welfare without work, the Christian democratic policy response and the contrast with renewed Third Way social democracy allowed us to explain that, since the second half of the 1990s, social democracy on the European continent did not 'Christian democratise'. In fact, one of the main characteristics of the continental variant of the Third Way has been the attempt to reform the welfare state according to a logic that was explicitly aiming to break with the Christian democratic tradition. In other words European Third Way social democracy tried to 'social democratise' the continental Christian democratic welfare state. In the course of its transformation, Third Way social democracy was inspired by neo-liberalism, as was clearly discernible in its adoption of market-oriented policies such as cuts in personal income taxes, social security retrenchments and increased labour market flexibility, which all aimed at strengthening the economic incentive to work. However, at the same time, strong state intervention in the form of active labour market policies and social investments also became crucial elements in the policy mix of social democratic governments. It was these last policy instruments that were fundamentally at odds with the *differentia specifica* of the Christian democratic continental welfare state regime. Therefore, the core of the Third Way on the European continent was clearly about job creation and labour market participation and in this sense echoed Scandinavian social democratic traditions rather than continental Christian democracy.

One important question is whether those reforms introduced in the second half of the 1990s, and which break with the Christian democratic continental tradition of passive welfare policy, are institutionally robust or that a simple change in the political balance of power is already enough to restore 'old' policy reflexes. We cannot really answer this question, but we do have a suggestion. The recent Dutch experience with renewed

Christian democratic rule seems to indicate that some old policy reflexes are indeed easily restored. The absolute policy priority of the current Dutch coalition between Christian democrats and conservative liberals concerns budgetary restraint. In foreign European policy the Dutch government has behaved as if it were the prime guard of the stability criteria of the EMU, resisting the type of budgetary lenience that Germany and France demand for stimulating employment growth. In domestic politics, active labour market policies such as subsidised jobs and various retraining programmes have been the first victims of the government's retrenchment rigour. This policy is accompanied by a strong normative appeal to 'norms and values' and greater private responsibility for finding jobs and guaranteeing income.

References

Blair, T. and Schröder, G. (1999) *Europe: The third way/Die neue Mitte*, London: Labour Party.

Bonoli, G. and Powell, M. (eds) (2004) *Social democratic party policies in contemporary Europe*, London and New York: Routledge.

Bussemaker, J. and Van Kersbergen, K. (1994) 'Gender and welfare states: some theoretical reflections', in D. Sainsbury (ed) *Gendering welfare states*, London: Sage Publications.

Bussemaker, J. and Van Kersbergen, K. (1999) 'Contemporary social-capitalist welfare states and gender inequality', in D. Sainsbury (ed) *Gender and welfare state regimes*, Oxford: Oxford University Press.

Cantillon, B. and De Lathouwer, L. (2001) 'Report for Belgium', Paper presented at the conference Welfare systems and the management of the economic risk of unemployment, Florence: European University Institute, 10-11 December.

Driver, S. and Martell, L. (1998) *New Labour: Politics after Thatcherism*, Cambridge: Polity Press.

Driver, S. and Martell, L. (2000) 'Left, right and the third way', *Policy & Politics*, vol 28, no 2, pp 147–61.

Ebbinghaus, B. and Hassel, A. (2000) 'Striking deals: concertation in the reform of continental European welfare states', *Journal of European Public Policy*, vol 7, no 1, pp 44–62.

Esping-Andersen, G. with Gallie, D., Hemerijck, A. and Myles, J. (2002) *Why we need a new welfare state*, Oxford: Oxford University Press.

Ferrera, M., Hemerijck, A. and Rhodes, M. (2000) *The future of social Europe: Recasting work and welfare in the new economy*, Oeiras: Celta Editora.

Frenzel, M. (2003) 'Neue Wege der Sozialdemokratie – sozialliberaler Minimalkonsens oder christdemokratische Kopie? Eine Erwiderung auf Martin Seeleib-Kaiser', *Politische Vierteljahresschrift*, vol 44, no 1, pp 86–93.

Green-Pedersen, C., Van Kersbergen, K. and Hemerijck, A. (2001) 'Neo-liberalism, the "third way" or what? Recent social democratic welfare policies in Denmark and the Netherlands', *Journal of European Public Policy*, vol 8, no 2, pp 307–25.

Hemerijck, A. and Manow, P. (2001) 'The experience of negotiated reforms in the Dutch and German welfare states', in B. Ebbinghaus and P. Manow (eds) *Comparing welfare capitalism: Social policy and political economy in Europe, Japan, and the USA*, London: Routledge.

Hemerijck, A. and Schludi, M. (2000) 'Sequences of policy failures and effective policy responses', in F.W. Scharpf and V.A. Schmidt (eds) *Welfare and work in the open economy, vol 1: From vulnerability to competitiveness*, Oxford: Oxford University Press.

Hemerijck, A., Unger, B. and Visser, J. (2000) 'How small countries negotiate change: twenty-five years of policy adjustment in Austria, the Netherlands, and Belgium', in F.W. Scharpf and V. A. Schmidt (eds) *Welfare and work in the open economy. Volume II. Diverse responses to common challenges*, Oxford: Oxford University Press.

Hemerijck, A. and Vail, M.I. (forthcoming) 'The forgotten center: the state as dynamic actor in corporatist political economies', in J.D. Levy (ed) *The state after statism: New state activities in the age of globalization and liberalization*, Cornell: Cornell University Press.

Hemerijck, A. and Van Kersbergen, K. (1997) 'Explaining the new politics of the welfare state in the Netherlands', *Acta Politica* vol 32, pp 258–301.

Huntington, N. and Bale, T. (2002) 'New labour: new Christian democracy?', *Political Quarterly*, vol 73, no 1, pp 44–50.

Levy, J.D. (1999) 'Vice into virtue? Progressive politics and welfare reform in continental Europe', *Politics & Society*, vol 27, no 2, pp 239–73.

Levy, J.D. (2000) 'Directing adjustment? The politics of welfare reform', in F.W. Scharpf and V. A. Schmidt (eds) (2000) *Welfare and work in the open economy, vol 1: From vulnerability to competitiveness*, Oxford: Oxford University Press.

Ostner, I. and Lewis, J. (1995) 'Gender and the evolution of European social policies', in P. Pierson and S. Leibfried (eds) *European social policy. Between fragmentation and integration*, Washington, DC: The Brookings Institution.

Powell, M. (2004) 'Social democracy in Europe. Renewal or retreat?', in G. Bonoli and M. Powell (eds) *Social democratic party policies in contemporary Europe*, London and New York: Routledge.

Sainsbury, D. (1994) 'Women's and men's social rights: gendering dimensions of welfare states', in D. Sainsbury (ed) *Gendering welfare states*, London: Sage Publications.

Schludi, M. (2001) 'The politics of pensions in European social insurance countries', MPIfG Discussion Paper 01/11, Cologne: Max Planck Institute for the Study of Societies.

Seeleib-Kaiser, M. (2002) 'Neubeginn oder Ende der Sozialdemocratie? Eine Untersuchung zur programmatischen Reform sozialdemokratischer Parteien und ihrer Auswirkung auf die Parteiendifferenzthese', *Politische Vierteljahresschrift*, vol 43, no 3, pp 478–96.

Shaw, E. (2003) 'Britain: left abandoned? New labour in power', *Parliamentary Affairs*, vol 54, no 1, pp 6–23.

Van Kersbergen, K. (1995) *Social capitalism. A study of Christian democracy and the welfare state*, London and New York, NY: Routledge.

Van Kersbergen, K. (1999) 'Contemporary Christian democracy and the demise of the politics of mediation', in H. Kitschelt, G. Marks, P. Lange and J.D. Stephens (eds) *Continuity and change in contemporary capitalism*, Cambridge: Cambridge University Press.

Van Kersbergen, K. (2003) 'The politics and political economy of social democracy', *Acta Politica*, vol 38, no 3, pp 255–73.

Visser, J. and Hemerijck A. (1997) *'A Dutch miracle'. Job growth, welfare reform and corporatism in the Netherlands*, Amsterdam: Amsterdam University Press.

TEN

Activation through thick and thin: progressive approaches to labour market activation

Jonah D. Levy

Introduction

In the literature of comparative politics, political economy and globalisation, progressive policy is portrayed typically as an *alternative* to economic liberalisation: social democratic corporatism as an alternative to neo-liberalism (Garrett, 1998); a social investment strategy as an alternative to neo-liberal austerity (Boix, 1998); a coordinated market economy as an alternative to a liberal market economy (Hall and Soskice, 2001). Progressive approaches enable governments to *avoid* economic liberalisation. It is by avoiding liberalisation that progressive governments are able to project sovereignty and give expression to their political values.

I believe that this dichotomous vision rests on a narrow, impoverished conception of economic liberalisation. My central claim is that there is more than one way to liberalise. Economic liberalisation need not be synonymous with the harsh, neo-liberal methods of Ronald Reagan and Margaret Thatcher. It is possible to reconcile liberalisation with concerns about equity and the disadvantaged, depending on how liberalising reforms are constructed. Such progressive liberalising reforms are not simply abstract possibilities but the very real practice of a number of European governments.

I call the progressive approach to economic and social reform a 'new social liberalism'. What is 'new' about the new social liberalism is that it does not simply accept a liberal market order, while compensating the losers (as under the German 'social market economy' or arguments about trade openness and welfare state development). Rather, the 'social' helps define the content of 'liberalism' itself, the character of the more marketised economic order. Under the new social liberalism, the character of the market economy – of the smaller government, lower taxes and more flexible and active labour markets – is itself defined by social principles and concerns for the disadvantaged.

The new social liberal approach to economic and social reform has marked the actions of European governments, particularly left-led governments, in a variety of areas including budget cutting, tax relief and competition in public services. Often, these reforms reflect what I have termed a 'vice-into-virtue' strategy (Levy, 1999). Under the vice-into-virtue approach, savings are extracted, not from virtuous programmes that help the poor and disadvantaged, but rather from the attenuation of 'vices', that is, programmes that concentrate benefits on the affluent, that are marked by patronage or fraud, that are patently dysfunctional or that are at odds with stated programme objectives. For example, in the 1990s Italian authorities eliminated a pension deficit of some 5% of GDP primarily by attenuating 'vices': imposing a minimum tax on the self-employed, who had engaged in widespread evasion; eliminating so-called 'baby pensions' and "seniority pensions" that allowed privileged groups to retire before the age of 40; and slashing subsidies to the pensions of the self-employed, a relatively affluent group.

This paper focuses on one strand of the new social liberalism, labour market activation. The term 'labour market activation' derives from the distinction between so-called 'passive' labour market expenditures that pay people not to work (unemployment insurance, early retirement, etc) and so-called 'active' labour market expenditures that help people find jobs. Labour market activation conveys two main ideas. The first is that people should derive their income primarily from paid employment, as opposed to government transfers. The second notion is that the goal of policy is not simply to minimise unemployment but also to maximize total employment. In other words, in addition to reducing *formal* unemployment, the goal of activation is to move people *outside* the labour force – stay-at-home mothers, disabled workers, early retirees, discouraged workers – into the labour force.

The idea of labour market activation has a long pedigree, dating at least to Swedish initiatives in the 1930s. But, in recent years, the principle of 'work first' has been pursued most aggressively in the United States, where it goes under the rubric of 'welfare to work'[1]. For many European progressives, welfare to work is about as welcome a US import as GMOs or hormone-laden beef. Such initiatives are seen as bad for both the welfare recipients and for labour market participants in general. For those pushed into the labour market, 'activation' entails the transformation of an unconditional right of citizenship into a privilege that is dependent on the goodwill of the caseworker (King, 1999; Handler, 2003). Activated workers are at risk of being coerced, humiliated and deprived of personal dignity and rights (Cloward and Piven, 1971). They can be forced to take substandard jobs at substandard wages, on pain of losing their benefits. In addition to hurting activated workers, these substandard jobs undercut the wages and working conditions of those already in the labour market. In short, activation transforms Marshallian citizens into a reserve army of the unemployed, mobilised on behalf of capital and against the rest of the workforce.

The progressive criticisms point to real risks associated with activation. That said, activation also holds potential benefits to both society and the activated individual (Ellwood, 1988; Field, 1995, 1997; Deacon, 1996, 2002). From a societal perspective, paying people not to work is incredibly wasteful, especially when the recipients of passive benefits are capable of holding jobs. Moreover, the legitimacy of the welfare state can be jeopardised if programmes are perceived as rife with abuses or encouraging behaviour at odds with social norms. When one-seventh of the adult population in Holland is receiving a disability pension, for example, it is only a small step to conclude, in the words of a centre-right prime minister, that "the Dutch welfare state is sick" (Visser and Hemerijck, 1997). Finally, social expectations about work have changed over the years and it could be argued that the welfare state should evolve with the times. If in the 1950s, a 'good mother' was someone who stayed at home full-time with her children, rather than pursuing 'selfish' career interests, today the vast majority of mothers are employed and it seems unfair for mothers on welfare not to have to go to work like everyone else (Orloff, 2001).

It is not just society that stands to benefit from welfare-to-work initiatives but also the activated themselves. A job often brings an increased sense of self-worth and pride. Reliance on earnings as opposed to social transfers reduces personal dependence of the activated individual on the whims of policy makers and caseworkers (although it substitutes a dependence on employers). From a political perspective, people who are employed are a much more sympathetic constituency, making it easier to upgrade benefits subsequently. Activation neutralises a wedge issue, transforming 'them' (the non-working poor) into 'us' (hard-working people who are struggling to get by) (Ellwood, 1988; Weir, 1998). When people who are not working are poor, opponents of government intervention can always argue that the solution to their problem is to get a job; when people who *are* working are poor (or lack health insurance), the case for government support becomes much stronger.

The judgement about the merits of welfare-to-work initiatives depends, to considerable extent then, on how the measures are conceived and implemented. Are recipients abused, forced into lousy jobs? Do they benefit financially from working? Do they receive support and services that they need? Are the expectations for balancing job and family duties realistic?

Although the 1996 welfare reform in the USA has received the most attention, a number of European countries have also acted aggressively to move recipients of income support into the labour force (Lødemel and Trickey, 2000; Gilbert and Voorhis, 2001; Andersen and Jensen, 2002). These initiatives go by a variety of monikers: 'New Deals' in Britain; an 'activity guarantee' in Sweden; the 'activation' or the 'comprehensive approach' in Denmark and Holland. All entail increased surveillance and coercion of claimants to try to induce them to take jobs. That said, there are very significant differences between the US and European approaches.

The progressive, new-social liberal approach to labour market activation is defined by two main features. The first is a concern for the *quality* of employment, for improving the situation of activated workers, not just for the *quantity* of employment. Whereas the neo-liberal approach favours more jobs, the new social liberal approach favours more *and better* jobs, jobs that provide better living circumstances and life chances.

The second feature of the new social liberal approach to labour market activation is a much more extensive, positive role for public policy. The neo-liberal strategy consists primarily of withdrawing state protections so as to increase work incentives and employment opportunities. It is a 'thin' strategy, resting on a relatively limited or 'thin' set of policy instruments. The new social liberal strategy may include some 'thin' measures but it goes much further. It entails positive as well as negative reforms; it offers carrots as well as sticks; and it demands much more of the state as well as of the individual – a plethora of public policies to support workers as they re-enter the labour force. As a result, 'thick' labour market policies are often as expensive, or even more expensive, than the passive labour market programmes that they replace.

This chapter is divided into six sections. The first section analyses the strategic choices confronting progressive parties in an age of economic liberalisation, highlighting the perils of inaction. The second section elaborates the differences between 'thick' and 'thin' labour market activation. The next three sections present a range of labour market activation strategies across three national settings. The USA (the third section) corresponds most closely to the thin, neo-liberal approach, yet even in this instance welfare leavers have made significant gains. Sweden (the fifth section) embodies the thick, progressive approach, while Britain's self-styled 'New Deals' (the fourth section) fall somewhere in between. The final section offers brief concluding remarks.

The perils of inaction: France's Jospin government

The 'new social liberalism' has generally been the product of *a constrained or corrective European left*. For parties of the right - even if the continental European right is different from the Anglo-American right – policies that expand the play of market forces fit well with their basic policy orientation, and the upward redistribution of wealth that accompanies such reforms benefits their electoral base. For parties of the left, by contrast, economic liberalisation challenges fundamental beliefs, while an upward redistribution of wealth harms their supporters. Consequently, the European left has tended to embark on liberalisation with great reluctance, usually as a result of some kind of constraint.

Some constraints are economic, such as Maastricht budget deficit targets, while others are political, such as the need to govern in coalition with centre-right parties. New social liberal reforms have generally been a response by left-led governments to constraints, an effort to pursue liberalisation on terms acceptable to the left, in particular protecting the interests of disadvantaged and low-income citizens. New social liberal reforms have also emerged as a corrective to prior neo-liberal reforms by centre-right governments, accepting a degree of economic liberalisation but trying to harmonise the more liberal economic context with left values and constituent interests.

There is nothing inevitable about the left's turn towards the new social liberalism. Indeed, the traditional leftist response to economic liberalisation has been to resist it. To be progressive is to combat the extension of market forces, not to cultivate the market. From this perspective, left-led governments that engage in liberalising reforms, such as labour market activation, are guilty of the worst kind of betrayal.

A strategy of resistance to liberalisation, while appealing to the leftist rank-and-file, is not without risks. The recent experience of the Jospin centre-left, which governed France from 1997 to 2002, offers a cautionary tale. In the name of progressive principles, Prime Minister Jospin refused to introduce any kind of job search requirements into France's unemployment insurance system and guaranteed minimum income (RMI). Yet a strong majority of French voters, including leftist voters, supported some kind of reasonable job search requirement. Thus the government found itself defending an unpopular status quo. Moreover, Jospin's resistance to reform lent credibility to conservative critiques that he was avoiding hard choices, that he was placating interest groups rather than modernising the country – a charge that damaged Jospin badly in the 2002 presidential election. Finally and most importantly, Jospin's refusal to reform the French unemployment system did not mean that liberalising reform did not happen; rather, it meant that reform was spearheaded by actors other than a government of the left.

In June 2000 the French employer association, the *Mouvement des Entreprises de France* (MEDEF), using a combination of blandishments, threats and divide-and-conquer techniques, rammed through a collective bargaining agreement with several trade unions that overhauled the unemployment insurance system. The reform contained a job search requirement, which was softened subsequently under government prodding. Still, the contours of the reform had been crafted by MEDEF, not the left. In addition, although described as a 'labour market activation measure', the reform provided no money for job training, placement or employment and wage subsidies. The absence of carrots to go along with the stick of job search requirements was all the more remarkable, given that France's unemployment insurance system was running a substantial surplus at the time. As part of the employer-drafted reform, however, the entire surplus was channelled to reductions in payroll taxes, leaving no money for measures to help the unemployed locate and become qualified for jobs. *In the end, then, the Jospin government did not 'do nothing' on unemployment insurance; rather, it allowed the French employer association to do something in its place.* With the election of a conservative government in 2002, the left has ceded the terrain of unemployment reform for at least the next five years.

Defenders of the Jospin government might argue that it is not for governments of the left to enact programmes of the right. Labour market activation is a conservative agenda that hurts society's most vulnerable citizens. If the left is unable to block activation, at least it can avoid being complicit. What this argument fails to understand, however, is that labour market activation need not be synonymous with a punitive, neo-liberal agenda.

Thick versus thin labour market activation

There is more than one way to conduct labour market activation. This section identifies two contrasting approaches to labour market activation – a thin, neo-liberal approach, embodied by the USA, and a thick, progressive approach found in many European contexts. The schematic differences between thin, neo-liberal activation and thick, progressive activation are summarised in Table 1.

The thin, neo-liberal approach attributes unemployment to personal failings or excessively generous benefits, as opposed to broader social and economic factors. The way to reduce unemployment is to withdraw state protections that impede work incentives and employment opportunities. Typically, benefit levels are lowered so that claimants will have more incentive to accept a job. In addition, neo-liberals advocate scaling back alternatives to employment such as training programmes and higher education, which are seen as undermining job search and parking the unemployed temporarily in useless activities. Finally, eligibility rules are tightened in an effort to move people off the public rolls. Claimants are forced to meet with caseworkers more regularly (meetings that can be quite unpleasant) and can lose their benefits as punishment for missing meetings or declining job offerings.

The neo-liberal approach emphasises moving people into jobs, with little regard for the quality of those jobs. The main metric of 'success' under this approach is the reduction in welfare caseloads, as opposed to improvements in the living standards of welfare leavers. A second measure of success is the reduction in government spending, made possible by shrunken welfare rolls. Relatedly, the work–family tensions arising from paid employment, such as childcare and elderly care, are seen largely as a 'private' matter to be handled by the individual, not government. The

Table 1: Thick versus thin labour market activation

Thin	Thick
1. Reduce benefits	1. Allow activated workers to combine government transfers with earnings from employment
2. Tighten job search requirements	2. Reduce taper rates of public programmes; reduce tax rates on labour income
3. Increase coercion, control	3. Substitute universal benefits for means-tested benefits
4. Scale back publicly sponsored alternatives to paid employment' (training, education)	4. Increase opportunities for education and training
5. Treat work–family tensions as a 'private' matter to be handled by the individual, not government	5. Expand services for activated workers, especially childcare

Note: In many cases 'thick' strategies are a supplement to 'thin' strategies rather than an alternative.

neo-liberal approach is thus a thin approach in that it narrows government commitments and supports, demanding that welfare claimants do more to help themselves.

The thick European welfare-to-work strategy increases the obligations and duties on the non-employed, in the manner of a thin American strategy, but there the similarities end. *Whereas the thin strategy seeks to scale back public commitments and protections, the hallmark of a thick, progressive strategy is that it imposes significant obligations and expenditures on society as well as the activated individual.* A thick welfare-to-work strategy seeks to increase human capital and skills, so that claimants can obtain better jobs; to provide quality jobs, not just a quantity of jobs; to guarantee the services necessary for people with limited financial resources to be able to balance work and family responsibilities; and to make work pay, to improve the living standards of those who leave the welfare rolls.

Danish social scientist, Jacob Torfing, distinguishes between 'offensive' (social democratic) and 'defensive' (neo-liberal) approaches to labour market activation (Torfing, 1999). The 'offensive' approach does not just push people into the labour market but also strives to improve their labour market position through training and education. Torfing is right to point to the positive or affirmative role of government in a progressive activation strategy. That said, the range of relevant policies should be drawn more broadly. Other policies critical to progressive activation include: tax reform, high-quality social services (notably childcare), generous treatment of wage earnings, and universal (as opposed to means-tested) benefits.

In a sense, the hallmark of a progressive activation strategy is that it involves much more than labour market policy. A progressive activation strategy is thick; it buttresses the well-being of activated workers with an array of other government programmes, carrots as well as sticks. Indeed a thick, progressive activation strategy may be more expensive than the passive policies that it replaces.

The thin approach to activation: welfare reform in the United States

The thin neo-liberal approach to labour market activation is most closely approximated by the 1996 welfare reform in the USA (Weaver, 1998, 2000; Weir 1998)[2]. The title of the US legislation, the 1996 Personal Responsibility and Work Reconciliation Act (PRWORA), reflects the emphasis on personal failings as the root cause of poverty and unemployment. The law tightened work requirements and imposed time limits on the receipt of benefits – a maximum of two years for any individual episode and five years' lifetime.

The central objective of the 1996 reform was to move people off welfare. Again, the language is revealing: Aid to Families with Dependent Children (AFDC), the welfare programme dating to the 1930s, was replaced by Temporary Aid to Needy Families (TANF). The 50 states administering welfare were required to cut their caseloads by 50% by the year 2002 or else face steep penalties. By contrast, no targets were set for the earnings and living standards of welfare leavers. Indeed states were not even required to collect data on plight of former beneficiaries. Thus caseload reduction was the central metric of success, the standard by which the 50 states would be punished and rewarded.

The 1996 welfare reform was also supposed to save money – in excess of $50 billion over a five-year period, principally from denying benefits to legal immigrants, reducing spending on food stamps and tightening eligibility for Supplemental Security Income (Weaver, 1998). Moreover, the legislation capped the federal government's financial commitment to welfare. PRWORA replaced AFDC's open-ended federal commitment to match state spending on welfare recipients with a block grant: if welfare rolls surged, it would be the states rather than the federal government that would foot the bill. Moreover, since the federal grant is not indexed to inflation, it has declined in real terms by nearly 15% since 1996.

While greatly increasing the obligations on welfare mothers, the 1996 legislation provided little in the way of support services. In moving from welfare to work, claimants often fall between two health insurance stools, earning too much to qualify for Medicaid but holding low-end jobs that do not provide health insurance. Since single mothers, by definition, have children, they also confront increased outlays for childcare. Transportation to and from work represents a further need. Yet the 1996 legislation offered scant help with these challenges. As two scholars wryly note, "Expanded access to assistance for working families was in no way mandated by TANF" (Gais and Weaver, 2002, p 39).

The 1996 reform was not altogether silent on family matters. The legislation sought to promote marriage and discourage teenage and out-of-wedlock births. States were authorised to deny benefits to new children of teen welfare mothers, the so-called 'family caps' provision. In addition, the federal government offered bonuses of up to $20 million per year to the states that made the most progress in reducing illegitimacy rates.

Despite the punitive orientation of PWORA, the US experiment has yielded quite good outcomes, as even centre-left think tanks like the Brookings Institute and the Urban Institute have acknowledged (Sawhill et al, 2002; Weil and Finegold, 2002). According to the Brookings evaluation, welfare caseloads have dropped 60% since their peak in 1994 (Sawhill et al, 2002). The labour force participation rate of single mothers surged from 58% in 1993 to 74% in 2000 – above the 68.5% figure for married mothers. Perhaps of greatest importance, welfare leavers are significantly better off financially, with post-tax-and-transfer incomes rising over 20% for those in the bottom two quintiles. Relatedly, child poverty has dropped to the lowest levels since the 1970s.

Several factors have helped welfare leavers improve their living standards. The most important, of course, was the robust economy of the late 1990s. In a context of full employment and even labour shortages, it was relatively easy to find jobs for welfare leavers, and these jobs paid increasingly well. Low-wage workers have also benefited from a number of supportive public policies. At the state level the combination of rapidly decreasing welfare rolls and a fixed block grant from the federal government created a fiscal windfall that allowed states to boost spending on transitional and work-related services. The share of programme spending consumed by cash assistance fell from 76% in 1996 to 38% in 2001, freeing up substantial resources for in-work benefits (Waller, 2003a, 2003b). Common expenditures include: childcare subsidies, health insurance, transportation allowances and more generous treatment of earnings (higher income and asset disregards, lower benefit withdrawal rates).

Federal policy has also helped welfare leavers. The Earned Income Tax Credit (EITC) was more than doubled during the initial years of the Clinton presidency. The EITC pays a 40% cash supplement for every dollar of earnings up to $10,000 and can be worth as much as $4000 to a household with two or more children. The increase in the EITC predated PRWORA, but the passage of welfare reform created a more favourable political climate for other measures to make work pay, notwithstanding Republican control of Congress. In 1996, the minimum wage was increased from $4.25 per hour to $4.75, then increased again the following year to $5.15. The Balanced Budget Act of 1997 established the State Children's Health Insurance Program (SCHIP), which provides federal funds to states that offer health insurance to children of low-income families.

The reformed US welfare system is not without problems (Sawhill et al, 2002; Weil and Finegold, 2002). Even in the best of times there remains a core of hard-to-employ claimants with multiple disadvantages (lack of education, drug or chemical dependency, abusive family situations, etc). For this group, welfare reform has meant a reduction in benefits that was not very generous to begin with. Another problem is that despite increased spending by the states, support services are still inadequate for welfare leavers. SCHIP may provide health insurance to some children but it generally leaves the parents uncovered at a time when employer-provided insurance continues to contract. Childcare is also a concern. Fewer than half welfare leavers receive help with childcare and this aid is generally confined to a transitional period. Aggravating matters, many welfare leavers have lost Medicaid and Food Stamp benefits to which they remain entitled, due to confusing eligibility rules and dissuasive bureaucratic hurdles.

The greatest concern, no doubt, is the solidity of the US welfare system in a recession. The gains of low-income families have been the product of a fortuitous economic climate and a fiscal windfall for the states, rather than any generous intentions on the part of the framers of the 1996 legislation. Today, all of the states are grappling with massive budget deficits, making cuts in 'discretionary' work-related services unavoidable. Historically, welfare rolls have increased by 9 to 17% for every 1% increase in unemployment (Weaver, 2002, p 98). Although the 1996 reform has dampened welfare take-up, it is clear that even a mild recession can provoke a significant spike in welfare rolls. Equally troubling, as the recession lingers many welfare recipients are bumping up against federal time limits. Employed recipients are also exhausting eligibility because, perversely, periods of in-work benefits count against the federal time limits in the same way as periods spent on passive TANF assistance. What will happen to America's poor and vulnerable families should the recession persist or deepen is the great unanswered question of the 1996 reform.

Despite the uncertainties surrounding the future of TANF, the US case demonstrates that welfare-to-work programmes can have a positive effect on the lives of welfare leavers if conducted in a context of rapid growth and job creation. Moreover, these positive results were obtained almost in spite of the intentions of the framers of welfare reform. Yet as the cases of Britain and Sweden suggest, welfare-to-work programmes need not be conducted in the harsh US manner.

Progressive activation in a liberal welfare world: Britain's 'New Deals'

Recent reforms in Britain illustrate the possibilities for progressive activation, even within a 'liberal welfare world', like that of the USA. Shortly after assuming office in 1997, the New Labour government of Tony Blair launched the first of a series of 'New Deals', designed to move benefit claimants into the labour force (Lødemel and Trickey, 2000; Judge, 2001; UK Government, 2002). The first New Deal targeted those under the age of 25. Subsequently New Deals have been established for workers over 25, older workers, lone parents, partners of the unemployed, and disabled people.

The New Deals were inspired by US welfare reform: they include increased surveillance, mandatory meetings with caseworkers to design a programme for securing a job, and, in some cases, benefit loss as punishment for non-cooperation. To take the first and most developed programme, young people are allowed to receive unemployment benefits for six months, before entering the so-called 'Gateway period', which lasts four more months. During the Gateway, the employment service and its partners work with the unemployed young to improve their employability and find an unsubsidised job. At the end of the Gateway, if claimants are still unemployed they are given four options: (1) a period of subsidised employment lasting six months; (2) a course of full-time education and training; (3) a job with an environmental task force; (4) a job in the voluntary sector. "There is no fifth option", in the words of British officials, meaning that claimants may not remain at home passively receiving benefits. This activity requirement marks a departure from the traditional passive orientation of British welfare benefits.

Despite the broad affinity with US welfare reform, the New Deal initiative differs in several important ways. The first is that it allows for a period of full-time training and other alternatives to paid employment in the private sector. Although the training period is brief by Scandinavian standards (Torfing, 1999), it still provides an opportunity for upgrading skills that is generally unavailable to US welfare leavers.

The second difference is in the degree of coercion applied to the target population. None of the New Deals contains the kinds of invasive, degrading provisions permitted under the US legislation, such as 'family caps' or requirements that teen mothers live at home. In addition, the jobs search requirements vary from one New Deal to the next. Young people under 25 face the tightest restrictions because the government fears that prolonged unemployment will create an unintegrated 'lost generation' and because young people tend to be unburdened by family and caring responsibilities. At the other extreme, lone parents are required only to meet with a caseworker to discuss options. In contrast to the US treatment of single mothers, participation in an activation programme remains voluntary.

A third difference between the British and US activation strategies concerns in-work services. Because Britain has a universal public healthcare system, welfare leavers do not risk losing their health coverage, as happens so often in the USA. A formidable barrier to activation is thereby eliminated. British authorities are working to ease another barrier to employment, the lack of affordable childcare. Britain's activation strategy views childcare, not as a 'private matter' to be managed by the individual but as a public good, a prerequisite for a well-functioning labour market. The government has channelled considerable resources to making childcare more widely available and affordable. Public spending on childcare is slated to triple between 2001 and 2003-2004, leading to the creation of 1.6 million places (UK Government, 2002). Much of the spending takes the form of a tax credit to offset the costs of childcare. The means-tested tax credit can cover as much as 70% of childcare expenses up to £135 per week for one child and £200 per week for more than one (Chote et al, 2003).

Perhaps the most significant difference between the British and American approaches is that the former is part of a comprehensive anti-poverty programme. In 1999, Prime Minister Blair announced the goal of eliminating all child poverty within a generation. Subsequently the British Treasury translated this goal into quantitative targets: a 25% reduction of childhood poverty (measured as 60% of median income) by 2004; 50% by 2010; and 100% by 2020 (Brewer and Gregg, 2001). Because of these targets, the government's activation strategies are being judged less by their impact on employment levels than by their impact on child poverty. Activation is a means to an end, rather than the end itself.

The British government has deployed two main instruments to combat child poverty. The first is the minimum wage. The national minimum wage was re-established in April 1999 at a level of £3.60 per hour. It was raised to £4.20 in October 2002 and is scheduled to reach £4.85 in October 2004 (HM Treasury, 2003a). The British minimum wage is considerably higher than the US minimum wage of $5.15 per hour (£3.43) and the impact on poverty is significant. According to estimates, if the US figure were raised by $1 per hour (still below the British figure), some 1 million people would be lifted out of poverty (Sawhill and Haskins, 2002, p 110).

The second strand of the British government's anti-poverty policies is an array of tax cuts and credits. In contrast to recent US practice, British authorities targeted tax cuts at *low* earners, slashing the bottom tax rate from 20% to 10% while keeping the top rate unchanged at 40%. The Labour government has emulated the US tactic of using tax credits to make work pay, but in line with the emphasis on combating child poverty, the tax credit system is heavily titled toward working *families*. The system has been reformed several times and is extremely complicated (one of the major criticisms). The central thrust, however, is to boost the income of low-wage workers, especially low-wage workers with children. According to the Treasury (HM Treasury, 2003b), changes in the tax and benefit system since 1997 have increased the income of the average family with two children by £1,200 per year and of the poorest quintile of families by £2,500 per year. Some 500,000 children have been lifted out of poverty by these policies (Piachaud and Sutherland, 2002).

In April 2003, the Labour government combined the various tax credits, family allowances and other forms of aid that have arisen over the years into a single programme, the Integrated Child Credit (ICC) (HM Treasury, 2002; Chote et al, 2003). Part of the motivation was administrative simplification. Claimants no longer have to apply to multiple programmes, each with different rules and deadlines, and pretty much the only information that they need is their income, working hours and number of children. The creation of the ICC also allowed the government to eliminate contradictory policies and focus its resources on the working poor, especially working poor families. Finally and perhaps most interestingly, the ICC reflects an effort by the Labour government to build an electoral constituency that will support aid to low-income families. Given the structure of the British economy, the government believes that Britain cannot afford a Swedish-style, generous, universal welfare state. The problem is that if benefits are paid only to the poor, the programmes will lack political support. Labour's gambit, which it labels 'progressive universalism' (Miliband, 1999; HM Treasury, 2002), is that by giving small amounts of aid to everyone it can gain political support for an ICC that concentrates the lion's share of resources on poor families. The ICC provides roughly £16 per week to all families (universal child benefit) and £26 per week to 90% of families (child benefit plus family element of child tax credit), so even the affluent receive something. Low-income families receive considerably more, however. The 50% of families at the bottom of the income scale get an additional £29 per week (per child element of child tax credit) for a total of £55 per week. These families are also eligible for income support and working tax credits worth as much as £90 per week. Taken together, the combination of a higher minimum wage and tax credits raised the minimum weekly income guarantee for a family with one child and one full-time worker by almost one third in four years, from £182 in 1999 to £241 in 2003 (HM Treasury, 2003a, p 90).

The British case shows the possibilities for a more supportive, thick approach to labour market activation within a liberal welfare world and political economy. Like the US welfare reform, Britain's New Deals have tightened the surveillance and pressure on those outside the labour force to take a job. That said, New Labour has been much less coercive in its treatment of single mothers and has allowed claimants to enter training programmes or internships, rather than mandating immediate employment. British authorities have emulated the US practice of extending tax credits to make work pay and relieve family poverty, but have gone further in supporting working families, in part because the goal is to reduce child poverty, not just the welfare rolls. Tax cuts have been targeted at the lowest income brackets rather than the highest; leaving welfare does not mean leaving health insurance as well; and the government has boosted spending on training and especially childcare. More generally, whereas PRWORA aimed to cut spending by over $50 billion, British authorities have made no secret of the fact that the costs of activation may exceed those of passive income support. As a result, the well-being of welfare leavers is less dependent on the vicissitudes of the economy in Britain, more protected by public policy.

Activation in a social democratic welfare world: Sweden

Recent reforms in Sweden extend the 'thick' approach to activation further still. The Swedish strategy has revolved around three sets of policies. The first has been the commitment to traditional 'active labour market policy', as pioneered by Sweden in the 1950s: heavy investments in job training, job matching and geographical relocation for displaced workers (Hort, 2001). This approach was bolstered during the 1990s by the 'Adult Education Initiative', which allowed the unemployed to pursue higher education full-time while still receiving their unemployment benefits. The university population doubled in the 1990s (Björklund, 2000) and many young Swedes were able to re-enter the labour market with a stronger knowledge and skill base.

The second strand of Swedish activation has been a reform of the unemployment insurance system in 1999 (OECD, 2001; Ministry of Finance and Ministry of Industry, Employment and Communications, Swedish Government, 2002). The reform established a so-called 'activity guarantee'. This initiative corresponded more closely to the thin, neo-liberal approach, tightening supervision and increasing the demands on claimants. Even so, the activity guarantee was not entirely coercive. The reform simultaneously increased unemployment benefits by up to 30% and was supported by the LO trade union.

The 'activity guarantee' was designed to remedy the problem of the quaintly named 'benefits carousel'. Formally, unemployment benefits in Sweden expire after two years. In practice, however, whenever benefits were about to end, recipients would be placed in a training programme where they would remain for six months, thereby requalifying for another two years of unemployment benefits. Thanks to this 'carousel', there was no effective time limit on the receipt of unemployment benefits.

Another problem with the 'carousel' was that the unemployed received the attention of public authorities only at the end of their two-year benefit period. The rest of the time they were left to their own devices. This benign neglect by public authorities created opportunities for fraudulent unemployment claims. It also left many unemployed workers isolated, discouraged and depressed.

The 'activity guarantee' broke with the logic of the 'benefits carousel' and lax public supervision. After 100 days of unemployment, claimants are no longer allowed to remain at home. They must be 'active' for eight hours per day, with 'activity' defined as a job, a training programme, a public internship or some other kind of structured routine outside the home. The 'activity guarantee' has helped some unemployed people by providing contact with caseworkers and placement opportunities. It has also made it more difficult to cheat the system. Claimants can no longer receive unemployment benefits while holding a job under the table, since they must account for their actions eight hours per day. Recent Swedish statistics reveal a sharp drop-off in the unemployment rolls at the 100-day mark.

The third dimension of the Swedish activation strategy has centred on carrots instead of sticks. The goal has been to reduce the financial penalties on employment – to lessen the 'poverty trap', as it is commonly called. The thin, neo-liberal strategy for 'making work pay' is to slash unemployment benefits (the principle of 'less eligibility'), while perhaps tendering some kind of tax credit to low-income earners. As we have seen, Sweden increased unemployment benefits rather than cutting them. Consequently, in order to 'make work pay', Swedish authorities also needed to boost the financial pay-off from holding a job.

One way of 'making work pay', in line with standard neo-liberal prescriptions, has been to reduce taxes on labour income. A 7% employee payroll tax, which had been imposed as part of the austerity measures of the 1990s, is being phased out over the four-year period from 1999 to 2003 (Ministry of Finance and Ministry of Industry, Employment and Communications, Swedish Government, 2002). Although few would argue with the need to cut taxes in Sweden, the most heavily-taxed country in the world, the Social Democrats' strategy was not without critics. During the 1990s, the government had raised the top personal income tax rate to 55%, but promised to reduce it below 50% once the economy improved. Given this pledge and given that mobile investors tend to be very sensitive to personal income tax rates, one might have expected the Social Democrats to reduce the top rate once the Swedish budget returned to surplus in 1998. Instead, the government announced that the 55% bracket would be retained permanently and concentrated its tax-cutting efforts on employee payrolls. This approach put money in the pockets of Social Democratic constituents, while also increasing the pay-off for moving from welfare to work.

Swedish authorities have done more than cut taxes. They have also lowered 'taper rates', that is, the rate at which transfer payments are withdrawn when a claimant earns money from work. Swedish policy has always been based on the assumption that the best way to combat poverty is to allow people to combine government transfer payments with earnings from work. This orientation is especially important for single mothers, who often can only work part-time because of their child-rearing responsibilities. Poverty rates among single-parent households have been kept at very low levels by allowing lone parents to combine earnings from a (typically part-time) job with social benefits (Gustafsson, 1995).

The third way in which Swedish authorities have increased the returns to employment has been by phasing out means-tested benefits. Swedish Social Democrats despise means-tested programmes, not only because they see them as stigmatising, but because the means-test functions as an additional income tax, one that is concentrated on the poor. Typically, as a person moves from welfare to work, means-tested benefits are reduced, sometimes drastically. Most Swedish social programmes are therefore organised on a universal basis. In contrast to the USA, the unemployed in Sweden do not have to worry that they will lose healthcare or childcare benefits should they take a job, since these benefits are available to all citizens at little or no cost. Nonetheless, means-tested programmes have always existed around the edges of the Swedish welfare state, and they were expanded in the 1990 as fiscal austerity made it more difficult to provide universal benefits at an adequate level. With the return to more flush fiscal times in the past few years, the Social Democrats have made it a priority to curtail means-testing.

In 2002 a sliding scale for childcare fees was replaced by the 'maximum fee', which limits the maximum parental contribution to about £100 per month, cutting costs for the average family by 40 to 50% (OECD, 2001; Ministry of Finance and Ministry of Industry, Employment and Communications, Swedish Government, 2002). Children of the unemployed also became eligible for public childcare, so that their parents would be able to search for work. The Social Democrats attempted to reform another means-tested programme, the housing allowance. Arguing that housing costs are primarily a problem for households with one income, they proposed to turn the means-tested housing allowance into a non-means-tested benefit for single mothers. Even in 'woman-friendly' Sweden, however, this proposal proved politically unfeasible. As a fallback, the Social Democrats have frozen the housing allowance, allowing it to wither on the vine, while channelling the savings into a universal child allowance that is not means-tested. The result, again, is to phase out means-testing.

The thick, Swedish approach to activation has activated public authorities as well as the non-employed. Under the 'activity guarantee' the non-employed are held accountable for their actions during the workday. But the government is also held accountable. The unemployment benefits of people who genuinely cannot find jobs have been increased by up to 30%. Swedish public authorities have also forged expensive new instruments such as the Adult Education Initiative to boost the human capital and employment prospects of job seekers. Most important, the Social Democrats have retooled public policies across a range of areas to improve the financial returns from employment: lowering taxes on labour; allowing people to combine substantial earnings from work with social transfers; providing high-quality, universal services virtually free of charge; and phasing out means-tested programmes. In short, the thick, Swedish policy has been geared not only to move people from welfare to work but also to improve their welfare in the process.

Conclusion

This chapter has advanced three reasons why progressives should accommodate labour market activation. The first is that resistance may prove futile. As the experience of France's Jospin government illustrates, if progressives are disinclined to reform in line with their principles and constituent interests, other actors with different principles and interests stand ready to act in their place.

The second reason is that labour market activation may benefit the activated individual. In the USA, welfare reform was crafted with little regard for the well-being of welfare leavers. Yet buoyed by a strong labour market and a fiscal windfall for the 50 states, welfare leavers have improved their income by an average of 20%. In addition, many welfare leavers speak of an increased sense of self-worth and capacity. These are not small gains.

The third reason why progressives should take up labour market activation is that the US approach is not the only possibility. The thick activation strategy deployed in Sweden and, to a lesser degree, Britain, moves beyond the thin, neo-liberal agenda of coercion, reduced benefits, and scaled-back state protections. It promotes good jobs as well as more jobs; it increases the income and opportunity of the activated as well as their obligations; and it forces state authorities to rethink and expand their interventions across a range of policy areas, including areas outside formal labour market policy (taxation, social services, and means-tested benefits, to name just a few).

Thick, new social liberal activation is a very different set of policies, with very different economic and social consequences, as compared to thin, neo-liberal activation. For this reason labour market activation should not be seen as inherently opposed to progressive principles and the needs of the disadvantaged. Stated in more general terms, there are varieties of economic liberalisation. Neo-liberalism is a subset of liberalism, not a synonym, and *how* a country liberalises is as important as *whether* it liberalises.

Notes

[1] The two notions are not strictly synonymous. Welfare to work in the USA has centred on single mothers, whereas European labour market activation has usually started with the unemployed young before being extended to older unemployed workers, single mothers and the disabled. In this chapter, for purposes of syntactic variation, I will use the phrases 'welfare to work' and 'labour market activation' interchangeably to designate strategies designed to move claimants from passive programmes, such as unemployment, disability or support for single mothers, to paid employment.

[2] The Bush administration's reauthorisation proposal for TANF in 2002 also reflects a thin neo-liberal approach (Waller 2003a, 2003b). The administration sought to increase work requirements from 30 to 40 hours per week, despite the post-9/11 recession and growing unemployment. Moreover, many training and education activities would no longer count towards the work requirement. According to the Congressional Budget Office (CBO), to meet the new work requirements, states would have to spend an additional $8 to $11 billion over five years, principally on childcare and public works programmes. Yet the Bush administration proposed no increase in funding.

References

Andersen, J. and Jensen, P. (eds) (2002) *Changing labour markets, welfare policies, and citizenship*, Bristol: The Policy Press.

Björklund, A. (2000) 'Denmark and Sweden – going different ways', in G. Esping-Andersen and M. Regini (eds) *Why deregulate labour markets?*, Oxford: Oxford University Press, pp 148-80.

Boix, C. (1998) *Political parties, growth, and equality: Conservative and Social Democratic economic strategies in the world economy*, Cambridge: Cambridge University Press.

Brewer, M. and Gregg, P. (2001) *Eradicating child poverty in Britain: welfare reform and children since 1997*, Institute of Fiscal Studies Paper, 3 May.

Chote, R., Emmerson, C. and Simpson, H. (2003) 'The IFS green budget', Institute of Fiscal Studies Commentary 92, January.

Cloward, R. and Piven, F. (1971) *Regulating the poor: The functions of public welfare*, New York, NY: Vintage Books.

Deacon, A. (1996) *Stakeholder welfare*, London: Institute of Economic Affairs.

Deacon, A. (2002) *Perspectives on welfare: Ideas, ideologies, and policy debates*, Buckingham: Open University Press.

Ellwood, D. (1988) *Poor support: Poverty in the American family*, New York, NY: Basic Books.

Field, F. (1995) *Making welfare work*, London: Institute of Community Studies.

Field, F. (1997) *Reforming welfare*, London: Social Market Foundation.

Gais, T. and Weaver, R. (2002) 'State policy choices under welfare reform', in I. Sawhill, R. Weaver, R. Haskins and A. Kane (eds) *Welfare reform and beyond: The future of the safety net*, Washington DC: Brookings Institute, pp 33-40.

Garrett, G. (1998) *Partisan politics in the global economy*, New York, NY: Cambridge University Press.

Gilbert, N. and Voorhis, R. (eds) (2001) *Activating the unemployed: A comparative appraisal of work-oriented policies*, International Social Security Series Volume 3, New Brunswick, NJ: Transaction.

Gustafsson, S. (1995) 'Single mothers in Sweden: why is poverty, less severe?', in K. McFate, R. Lawson and W. Wilson (eds) *Poverty, inequality, and the future of social policy*, New York, NY: Russell Sage Foundation, pp 291-325.

Hall, P. and Soskice, D. (eds) (2001) *Varieties of capitalism: The institutional foundations of comparative advantage*, New York, NY: Oxford University Press.

Handler, J. (2003) 'Social citizenship and workfare in the US and western Europe: from status to contract', *Journal of European Social Policy*, vol 13, no 3, pp 229-43.

HM Treasury (2002) *The child and working tax credits*, Report Number Ten in Series on the Modernisation of Britain's Tax and Benefit System, April, 2002.

HM Treasury (2003a) *2003 Budget*.

HM Treasury (2003b) *Budget 2003* Press release, 9 April.

Hort, S. (2001) 'Sweden – still a civilized version of workfare?', in N. Gilbert and R. Voorhis (eds) *Activating the unemployed: A comparative appraisal of work-oriented policies*, New Brunswick, NJ: Transaction, pp 243-66.

Judge, K. (2001) 'Evaluating welfare to work in the United Kingdom', in N. Gilbert and R. Voorhis (eds) *Activating the unemployed: A comparative appraisal of work-oriented policies*, New Brunswick, NJ: Transaction, pp 243-66.

King, D. (1999) *In the name of liberalism: Illiberal social policy in the United States and Britain*, Oxford: Oxford University Press.

Levy, J. (1999) 'Vice into virtue? Progressive politics and welfare reform in continental Europe', *Politics & Society*, vol 27, no 2, pp 239-73.

Lødemel, I. and Trickey, H. (eds) (2000) *'An offer you can't refuse': Workfare in international perspective*, Bristol: The Policy Press.

Miliband, E. (1999) Presentation to the Institute for Fiscal Studies.

Ministry of Finance and Ministry of Industry, Employment and Communications, Swedish Government (2002) *Sweden's action plan for employment 2002* (http://europa.eu.int/comm/employment_social/employment_strategy/national_en.htm).

OECD (Organisation for Economic Co-operation and Development) (2001) *Sweden, 2000-2001*, Paris: OECD.

Orloff, A. (2001) 'Ending the entitlements of poor single mothers: changing social policies, women's employment, and caregiving', in N. Hirschmann and U. Liebert (eds) *Women and welfare: Theory and practice in the United States and Europe*, New Brunswick, NJ: Rutgers University Press, pp 133-59.

Piachaud, D. and Sutherland, H. (2002) *Changing poverty post-1997*, CASEPaper No 63, London: London School of Economics and Political Science, November.

Sawhill, I. and Haskins, R. (2002) 'Welfare reform and the work support system', in I. Sawhill, R. Weaver, and R. Haskins (eds) *Welfare reform and beyond: The future of the safety net*, Washington, DC: Brookings Institution Press, pp 107-19.

Sawhill I., Weather, R. and Haskins, R. (eds) (2002) *Welfare reform and beyond: The future of the safety net*, Washington, DC: Brookings Institution Press, pp 107-19.

Torfing, J. (1999) 'Workfare with welfare: recent reforms of the Danish welfare state', *Journal of European Social Policy*, vol 9, no 1, pp 5-28.

UK Government (2002) *UK employment action plan 2002* (http://europa.eu.int/comm/employment_social/employment_strategy/national_en.htm).

Visser, J. and Hemerijck, A. (1997) *A 'Dutch miracle': Job growth, welfare reform, and corporatism in the Netherlands*, Amsterdam: Amsterdam University Press.

Waller, M. (2003a) 'TANF reauthorization 2003: lessons from block grants', Presentation in New York City, 13 June.

Waller, M. (2003b) 'Welfare reform: building on success', Testimony to Senate Committee on Finance, 12 March.

Weaver, R. (1998) 'Ending welfare as we know it', in M. Weir (ed) *The social divide: Political parties and the future of active government*, Washington, DC: Brookings Institution Press, pp 361-416.

Weaver, R. (2000) *Ending welfare as we know it*, Washington, DC: Brookings Institution Press.

Weaver, R. (2002) 'The structure of the TANF block grant', in I. Sawhill, R. Weaver, and R. Haskins (eds) *Welfare reform and beyond: The future of the safety net*, Washington, DC: Brookings Institution Press, pp 89-96.

Weil, A. and Finegold, K. (eds) (2002) *Welfare reform: The next act*, Washington, DC: Urban Institute Press.

Weir, M. (ed) (1998) *The social divide: Political parties and the future of active government*, Washington, DC: Brookings.

Part Three:
Social policy since 1979 – the impact of Thatcherism

ELEVEN

Social policy since 1979: a view from the right

David Marsland

Introduction: left, right and straight ahead

If political orientations are to be divided into either 'left' or 'right', then I find the title of my paper – which was chosen for me by the editors – entirely acceptable. I should, however, start by reminding readers of the complexities underlying this simple classification. For both generically and in relation to welfare specifically, there are commonalities and overlaps between 'left' and 'right', ferocious factional divisions within both 'left' and 'right', and instances of important welfare analysts and welfare policy makers who belong to neither 'left' nor 'right' as conventionally understood.

For example, if the 'right' is presumed to be antithetical to state welfare, how is it that Bismarck – a nationalist conservative – is a key founding father of the modern welfare state? Again, if the 'left' is presumed to be broadly favourable to state welfare, why is it that in conditions of 'actually existing socialism' in the Soviet Union and the Soviet bloc, welfare provision was in general meagre, arbitrary and meanly administered? And again, if British Conservatism is assumed to be a part of the 'right', how are we to explain Conservative leaderships including strong supporters of state welfare (such as Neville Chamberlain, R.A. Butler and Kenneth Clarke), fundamental sceptics (such as Lord Salisbury and Margaret Thatcher), and ambivalent pragmatists (such as Stanley Baldwin, Harold Macmillan and John Major)?

These complexities given, this chapter is written from a perspective that I would prefer to call Thatcherite. From this perspective, I defend the welfare policy of Margaret Thatcher's administration (1979-90) as a fundamental and courageous break with past orthodoxy. I support, with some reservations, the record of John Major's (1990-97) as a brave attempt at implementing Thatcherite concepts. And I welcome the efforts of Tony Blair's governments since 1997 to slough off the cocoon of socialist ideology and collectivist vested interests that stand in the way of continuing welfare reform.

Overall I view the moves over the past 25 years away from the 'welfare state' and towards a 'welfare society' as beneficent and, bit by bit, at least partially successful. Like recent acceptance of profit and the markets in the industrial sphere by all except an eccentric and obscurantist minority, espousal of the radical new approach to welfare pioneered by Margaret Thatcher will come to be seen, I conclude, as neither 'left' nor 'right' – but simply as straight on towards realism, efficiency and justice properly construed.

Zenith of welfare and nadir of freedom: the welfare state before 1979

Analysis of developments in the recent history of welfare policy is crippled if it fails to take account of the longevity of the welfare state and of the extent to which, from the earliest period, a wide consensus of support for its operations was established. Like all the most powerful social institutions, the British welfare state developed gradually and over a long period of history. With important medieval origins (including our best hospitals, universities and schools), it developed rapidly in 19th-century conditions of population growth, industrialisation and urbanisation. Both major political parties – Whig/Liberal and Tory/Conservative – contributed significantly to expansion of the state's role in welfare provision. The extent of positive Conservative involvement is too often underestimated in modern analysis, as is the key role of the influential Radical faction in Parliament – a small vanguard group with immense influence in relation to child welfare, health, education and poverty – and located at a tangent to the 'left'–'right' vector.

By the start of the 20th century the welfare state agenda – or what Britain's greatest sociologist, Herbert Spencer, who opposed it, called "the policy of communism" (Duncan, 1908) – had already become an established, indeed conventional part of modernisation. With radical breakthroughs established by Lloyd George's 1906 budget, with Labour accepted as a governing party and the primary alternative to the Conservatives in the period after the First World War, and with the latter happy to make deals on welfare to preserve industrial peace and to secure competitive advantage over rival nations, the welfare state was already by

1939 extensive and powerful. Underpinned by the intellectual and moral authority of Keynes and Beveridge, it was soon largely taken for granted. Building on these foundations and armed with the centralising instruments and habits of War Coalition, the Attlee government of 1945-1951 rapidly built the general structure of the modern welfare state. The National Health Service was its ideological and symbolic heart but it covered the whole range of welfare, all of it brought under state ownership, control and regulation and all of it driven by a gradualist but unambiguous spirit of egalitarianism. The whole structure was underpinned by extensive nationalisation of industry and by economic policies directed primarily at maintaining full employment (Barnett, 1995).

Between 1951 and 1979 the Labour Party was in power for scarcely 10 years. The build-up of the welfare state continued, nonetheless, throughout this period. This was due in part to rapid expansion in welfare expenditure by the government of Harold Wilson and to extensive legislation introduced by his ministers that widened and deepened the concept of welfare. It was due at least as much, however, to active collusion by the Conservatives. During these years they seem to have traded acquiescence on welfare for whole-hearted struggle against industrial nationalisation. There were also electoral considerations, and many on the left of the party had become convinced that state welfare was inevitable and, within limits, desirable.

The welfare state, and the grip of its underlying ideology on the media and the population, inexorably grew to its most powerful point ever by the late 1970s. Extensive and expanding state welfare was by then viewed, except from the perspective of a minority on the Conservative right, as both necessary and desirable. This was common orthodoxy in Parliament, in the media and among intellectuals, social scientists especially but economists scarcely less (Marsland, 1988). A large and increasing proportion of the population received benefits and services from the welfare state. A huge and expanding workforce was employed in state welfare. A large and growing proportion of GNP was being expended on welfare. Taxation was high and steeply 'progressive' (Marsland, 1996). People of all ages and all social types had come to assume the welfare state entirely normal, and more than that – a mark of high civilisation.

Economic collapse and moral decay

Loss of faith in the welfare state was as quick and sudden as its institutional development had been slow and gradual. It was signalled by events occurring simultaneously in the economic and the moral spheres of social life – the former more obvious and unavoidable, the latter more subtle and more easily ignored in the short term.

The economic crisis of 1976 led rapidly to recognition of the near-bankrupt state of the British economy, to cruelly realistic and ruthless advice by the visiting IMF bailiffs, and to the most savage cuts in public expenditure – not least on welfare – in history. In the longer term these same events, and the 'winter of discontent' of 1978-79 which followed from them, led gradually to the Labour Party's reluctant conversion to monetarism, to the market and even, in the end, as we shall see, to welfare reform.

Moral decay attributable to the effects of state welfare was less immediately obvious and less widely acknowledged than the economic collapse which state welfare had so traumatically produced. But there had been signs of recognition of these more fundamental effects for some time.

The disincentive effects of welfare benefits on job seeking, work effort and enterprise had been accurately identified and courageously emphasised by Ralph Harris, Arthur Seldon and others working with them at the Institute of Economic Affairs for 20 lonely years (Blundell, 2003). Now their influence began to grow. The damaging effects of welfare ideology, with its almost orgiastic celebration of unqualified rights, on the now evidently collapsing family were honestly and thoroughly examined by Keith Joseph and by those few around him in the Conservative Party who were beginning to understand that the nation was at a crucial juncture in its development. Widespread concerns about rising levels of crime, particularly youth crime, began at this time to be interpreted in the media as attributable in significant part to the ideological and institutional impacts of state welfare – lack of discipline in fatherless families, shoddy state education, institutionalised envy, suppression of competitive and enterprising attitudes and engrained expectations of an easy life.

With economic collapse and moral decay coinciding in a society increasingly perceived as literally ungovernable, the scene was set for radical change in government and in welfare provision.

Rediscovering freedom: Keith Joseph and Margaret Thatcher

There were large-scale social forces at work in triggering the reform of state welfare which began in 1979 – particularly the impact of extreme economic stringency and of industrial disruption led by lawless trade unions. There was, in addition, a general change of mood among politicians and in the media, as a certain disenchantment with the overblown promises of the welfare state set in. Individual people, however, mattered crucially, especially Keith Joseph and Margaret Thatcher.

Unsurprisingly, Margaret Thatcher was a natural Thatcherite. Her long-established inclinations – deriving from her father's politics, her social background in the commercial petty bourgeoisie and her own adult life experiences – included key elements of what later came to be called Thatcherism: suspicion of the power of the state; commitment to hard work and self-reliance; antipathy to arbitrary and excessive government handouts; contempt for bureaucracy and a deep conviction that individuals, families and businesses are more likely to spend their own hard-earned income wisely and well than are central and local state institutions swollen by the same money confiscated as taxes.

However, if these Thatcherite inclinations were to be turned into a political agenda and social policies that could win electoral support and change Britain for the better, they had to be intellectually refined, supported by compelling arguments and grounded in convincing evidence. This was largely the work of Keith Joseph and a handful of intellectuals working with him – particularly Alfred Sherman, Head of the Centre for Policy Studies established in 1974 by Thatcher and Joseph (Denham and Garnett, 2002).

Joseph had researched and written on economic and social policy for many years, producing powerful books, articles and speeches. After the defeat of the Heath government in 1974 his influence grew considerably. He developed persuasive arguments against the extensive intervention by the state in the economy that Conservatives, under Ted Heath especially, had practised since the war almost as routinely and unthinkingly as had the Labour Party. To this economic analysis he now added, particularly in his remarkable Edgbaston speech of October 1976, a moral dimension. This was to play a key role in the Conservative leadership election, which – with Joseph himself deciding not to stand, Margaret Thatcher was shortly to win. The gist and significance of this speech are characterised by Thatcher herself in the following words (Thatcher, 1995, p 262):

> ... the speech sent out powerful messages about the decline of the family , the subversion of moral values and the dangers of the permissive society, connecting all these things with socialism and egalitarianism, and proposing the 'remoralization of Britain' as a long-term aim. It was an attempt to provide a backbone for Conservative social policy, just as Keith had started to do for economic policy.

Building on these intellectual foundations, and supported by Joseph, the CPS and a new team of shadow ministers, Thatcher established between 1976 and 1979 a fundamentally radical alternative to the collectivism of recent Conservative policies and to Labour economic and welfare orthodoxy. To the old commitment to full employment at any price, it offered the alternative of profitable enterprise. A free market was to replace state planning, controls and intervention. Instead of expanded state welfare, it promised freedom, lower taxes and self-reliance. On this platform the 1979 election was won by Thatcher and the Conservatives. The opportunity for radical reform of the welfare state had arrived.

The Thatcher governments: challenging the welfare state

Before the 1987 election the Thatcher government was largely preoccupied with salvaging and restructuring the economy, with dealing with the trade unions, with defending British interests, territory and people against invasion by armed force and with responding to the destructive challenge of the miners' strike. There was little enough time or energy left over for radical, large-scale reform of welfare (Thatcher, 1993).

However, even these early achievements made an indispensable contribution to that end. Without the active shakeout of the economy, without the liberalisation of capital markets, without sweeping tax-cuts, without wholesale privatisation and without the taming of the trade unions, the successful, modernised enterprise economy – on which the Blair government still relies today – would have been quite impossible. Without these economic achievements, radical reform of welfare would have been inconceivable. At best we would have had – as we did *not* have – merely savage cuts in public expenditure, social division, and no welfare reform at all. The triumph of Margaret Thatcher in transforming a near-bankrupt economy into a thriving enterprise culture should not – however much Labour spin-doctors may wish it – be underestimated.

But economic change is not in itself enough. As Margaret Thatcher herself put it in her 1974 speech to the Young Conservatives during the course of the leadership campaign (Thatcher, 1995, p 279):

> You can get your economic policies right, and still have the kind of society none of us would wish. I believe we should judge people on merit and not on background. I believe the person who is prepared to work hardest should get the greatest rewards and keep them after tax. That we should back the workers and not the shirkers. That it is

not only permissible but praiseworthy to want to benefit your own
family by your own efforts.

A powerful start on this mission of transforming the moral climate of
Britain was made with the introduction of the 'right to buy' council
properties, announced in the first Queen's Speech of Margaret Thatcher's
1979 government, introduced immediately and extended further over
the next 10 years. Long resisted by Labour on doctrinaire socialist grounds,
this move presented lower-income families with a unique opportunity
to acquire capital. It demonstrated the government's commitment to a
property-owning democracy. Not least it symbolised – along with the
privatisation of nationalised businesses – the ethos of the post-collectivist
society at which Margaret Thatcher was aiming.

Despite the temporary setback of negative equity in the 1990s and
complaints in recent years about rising house prices, it seems unlikely
that any government will dare to suppress this right, or to provide in any
significant amount subsidised state housing – a symbol of collectivist
state welfare more powerful perhaps than even the NHS.

On those twin pillars of the welfare state, the NHS and state education,
the government moved with caution. The Prime Minister realised only
too well how viciously the Opposition would attack any radical reform
that the media could be persuaded to interpret as an attack on the welfare
state. Nonetheless, careful analysis and thorough preparations were made
for reform on both fronts. Legislation and implementation came as late
as 1988 and 1989, stretching beyond the Thatcher government in both
cases (the 1988 Education Reform Act and the 1990 NHS and
Community Care Act).

In both cases the thrust of reform was similar – enhanced attention to
the consumer's role, introduction of competition, devolution of
management to local operating levels and tough central frameworking.
It has been argued that Mrs Thatcher was here too cautious and, even
worse, too centralising. I suspect her political judgement was sound – as
reactions even within the Cabinet to the radical proposals of the 1982
CPRS report, and the later debacle over the community charge,
demonstrated. Neither a voucher system for school education nor
privatised healthcare supplying free delivery was (or is even now) politically
feasible. And in the absence of real markets, central monitoring was
essential if the vested interests of teachers, doctors and nurses were to be
resisted successfully.

Moreover, these two great reforms – driven through against shrill
resistance in the late 1980s and the 1990s – have provided, despite cosmetic

changes under Labour since 1997, an essential basis for Tony Blair's attempts at modernisation since 2001. On education and healthcare it has to be concluded that Margaret Thatcher's achievements in challenging and permanently subverting the orthodoxy of welfare state thinking were considerable.

On the specifics of benefits and social security, unhitching pensions-uprating from wage increases and tying it instead to inflation, provided much-needed savings in public expenditure. It also saved Britain from the severe financial problems of our European competitors, where state pension payments are out of control. And it symbolised, along with legislative and financial encouragement of personal pensions, the government's commitment to self-reliance.

Otherwise – that is to say beyond housing, education, healthcare and pensions – less was achieved than might have been hoped, and certainly much less in the sense of either reduced expenditure or an increased role for the market than the Opposition and the media pretended. Even with strenuous wrestling by Norman Fowler in his years at the DHSS to hold down increases in benefits, welfare wage bills and other welfare expenditure, the welfare budget continued its inexorable expansion. It was not until health and social security were separated into two ministries in 1988 that radical measures, such as those recommended by Sir Roy Griffiths, on the administration of social services began to be implemented.

Even as Mrs Thatcher came towards the close of her tenure, it was obvious – as was shown by the hysterical reactions to John Moore's radical speech on poverty, so-called, of May 1989 – that wholeheartedly radical reform of the welfare state, reform which would reduce the state's role in welfare substantially, would be extremely difficult. On the other hand a basis was by then in place for a shift towards a quasi market and a mixed economy of welfare, and the culture of welfare had been transformed entirely. In 1979, the welfare state was taken for granted as a feature of British society: by 1990 it was widely recognised, even in the academic social policy community and among the leadership of the Labour Party, that fundamental change was unavoidable.

John Major: reforming the welfare state

To say that Margaret Thatcher was a hard act to follow would be an understatement indeed. The difference in strength of personality and leadership capacity compared with the Iron Lady has combined with the disastrous psychological impact of the ERM crisis to produce what seems to me an unfair underestimation of the achievements of John Major's administration. Given also constant split and struggle in the party and within the Cabinet on the crucial issue of Europe, 1990-1997 was a better period for British government since the war than many – not least in relation to welfare.

The nature of what was achieved by John Major by way of welfare reform parallels the nature of the man himself. His background and early life experience made him naturally sympathetic to the welfare state. He was politically closer to the centre or even centre left than Margaret Thatcher or most colleagues believed. He was much less than either Thatcher or Blair a political animal, much more of a business administrator (Major, 1999).

Hence his main achievements in the welfare sphere – beyond the increasing pressure applied to benefits claimants, including the powerfully symbolic transformation of Unemployment Benefit into the Jobseeker's Allowance – were consolidation of reforms initiated under Margaret Thatcher and importation into the welfare state of the criteria and methods of the business world. These may seem modest, but in the long run – as much after 1997 as before – they have proved significant.

In healthcare, education and social services, the quasi market, mixed economy model of 1987 – the year that David Willetts has called the '*annus mirabilis*' of Conservative social policy – was fully implemented in the face of powerful resistance by the welfare workforce and established social policy experts. On all three of these key fronts of the welfare state – with housing also added – a coherent national framework was established, incorporating both local competitive autonomy and central government frameworking, standard setting and regulation. Purchasing and providing partners were defined, where necessary created, and linked by competition and contract. The concept of quality was taken over from its industrial and business origins and implemented toughly with a view to consumer satisfaction.

Now, as Timmins (1996) says of the original 1987 proposals from which the reforms sprang, they could serve either of two contradictory purposes: as a springboard for radical de-nationalisation, or as a trigger for consumers to cling to state welfare and demand ever higher standards. While this is certainly true, it also has to be acknowledged that these reforms:

• Represent a fundamental challenge and a serious alternative to the pre-1979 paternalistic, monolithic welfare state.
• Are so patently an improvement on what went before that no government of whatever party would reverse them or change them more than partially.

- Keep alive the possibility of de-nationalisation, and provide a framework through which this could be accomplished.
- Take reform about as far as is, for the time being, feasible. Next steps will await economic stringency, popular dissatisfaction with poor state sector standards, or recognition of the positively damaging effects of state welfare.

These advantages, from the point of view of radical reformers of state welfare, are all the greater when they are seen in the context of the Major government's other key contribution – the invention of the Private Finance Initiative. This was kick-started and bullied into existence by Kenneth Clarke, John Major's redoubtable Chancellor of the Exchequer. Determined to hold down public expenditure within reasonable limits, Clarke saw in PFI a means of increasing public goods and services without resorting to public expenditure. It served the new, reformed structure effectively and powerfully – just as it has done ever since in modified form and on a larger scale for Tony Blair.

The danger as Timmins (1996) notes and as many on the right of the party recognised at the time, was that this new streamlined, modernised, business-friendly welfare state might actually succeed – as explicitly envisaged in Major's pet scheme, the Citizen's Charter – in persuading consumers to demand higher standards and increased public expenditure designed to secure them. Something very like this has happened since 1997 – and the Labour government has fallen into the trap. For, if increased spending does not bring significantly higher standards in the key public services – and the relevant benchmark is to be found in the population's daily experience of the market sector in general – the same framework provides an excellent basis for an opening to the market and for genuinely radical reform of welfare.

Between 1979 and 1990 Margaret Thatcher ruthlessly and against all expectations managed to secure the salvation of the ravaged economy she inherited from Labour. Between 1990 and 1997, John Major, with the indispensable assistance of Kenneth Clarke, successfully steered the economy through a recession into triumphant success. In his own accurate words: "... a sparkling economy with secure growth, high employment, low inflation, and low interest rates" (Timmins, 1996, p 459).

This was the economic legacy that fell to Tony Blair. In relation to real welfare needs, the period of Conservative government between 1979 and 1997 left everyone in the population with much higher standards of living, a hugely improved quality of life, significantly increased life expectancy and much, much more freedom. If the Conservatives had won the 1997 election, one would have expected in this context radical moves towards further serious reform of the welfare state. As it was, power was turned over to Tony Blair and with it a serious test of just how 'new' Labour was in the welfare sphere.

Tony Blair: to reform or not to reform?

The widely noted similarities between Tony Blair and Margaret Thatcher – their conviction, stubborn determination and single-mindedly iron wills – are real. There are also, however, not least in relation to welfare, intriguing similarities between Blair and John Major. Compared with Thatcher, they have both proved more pragmatic, more merely instrumental, and happier in particular to settle for whatever methods of administration and modes of organisation of the welfare state can be made to work effectively in practical terms. In Blair's case, pragmatism is allied to a remarkable rhetorical skill unequalled among post-war British Prime Ministers except by Harold Macmillan. Thus he has spoken regularly about the 'modernisation' of the welfare state, about its reform and – best of all in rhetorical terms – about its 'renewal'.

This welfare rhetoric is just one segment of the larger rhetorical device of the whole 'New Labour' concept. This provides a plausible facade for what one might call the end-crisis of democratic and revisionist socialism. Thus we have had:

- The independence of the Bank of England – long urged by Kenneth Clarke.
- The cosmetic, if in the longer term dangerous, minimum wage.
- The grand sham of the 'New Deal' – barely necessary in the economic conditions inherited from the Conservatives and unlikely to withstand a real recession such as it pretends to address.
- Maintenance in the early years of Conservative spending targets and income tax levels – accompanied and/or succeeded by longer-term promises of augmented public expenditure and by substantial increases in other taxes.
- Close alliance with big business – in ironical conjunction with concessions to the trade unions and tighter, more extensive business regulation.

The rhetoric of this overall 'Third Way' strategy is paralleled in the welfare sphere. This has so far seen:

- Maintenance of the general thrust of the Conservative reforms – with minor changes early, and these quickly reversed. Providers, purchasers, competition and contract still dominate healthcare, education and social services.
- An even tougher rhetoric of effort and responsibility in relation to benefits than Peter Lilley ever managed – combined unblushingly with politically correct chatter at every turn about 'rights', 'poverty', 'disadvantage' and 'social exclusion', and extravagant public expenditure in the name of all these dubious concepts (Dennis, 1997).
- Payments to disabled people, single mothers, pensioners and others as tax credits to disguise benefit increases and shift public expenditure off the spending bill.
- The appointment of Frank Field to Social Security to 'think the unthinkable' about welfare – and his early replacement as soon as the costs of his reforming ideas and the extent of opposition to them among Labour MPs and activists became apparent.
- The rhetoric of rights encouraged – while means-testing has been sustained and further extended.
- The presumptive service ethic of the public sector routinely emphasised and celebrated by contrast with the 'irresponsible greed' of the private sector – while the Conservatives' Private Finance Initiative, camouflaged as the Public Private Partnership, has been maintained and enormously extended.

What Labour's record on welfare reform since 1997 seems to suggest is this: the Prime Minister and the Blairite coterie around him do genuinely acknowledge the need for radical reform of the welfare state. On the other hand they have no clear idea about how to accomplish it. Moreover, at the slightest sign of difficulty or opposition they trim their reforming sails hard and either head for the safer waters of the status quo or settle for deals that blunt their radical cutting-edge. This was graphically demonstrated in the post-election increases in national insurance to pay for growth in public expenditure on healthcare, education and other aspects of welfare. It is quite clear that these steps were essentially designed to buy-off opponents of reform; that the modest reforms promised as a quid pro quo will not happen; that promised further investment in the public sector will require increases in taxation and borrowing; and that the underlying reform strategy – maintaining the public sector at its present scale and in its current organisational form, while 'modernising' its operations – will not work because it is not genuinely radical.

It seems the government is caught in a cleft stick between its commitment to reform welfare and a number of major structural impediments to reform which are inescapable by Labour, however 'new"(Marsland, 2002a). The first of these hurdles is the Labour Party's deep-seated antipathy to markets and inequality. The primary faults of the welfare state arise from its origins either in socialism, as in Britain and New Zealand, or in pseudo-socialist discourse intended to pre-empt the need for socialism, as in Germany and the United States. These socialist origins entail principled antipathy to free markets and unremitting antagonism to economic inequality. In consequence, post-socialist politicians of the left are caught in a contradiction. They can either yield on their opposition to markets and inequality in order to reform welfare or they can cling to the 'fundamental values' of the progressive movement and find their economic and moral concerns with welfare reform stymied. They cannot logically or in practice manage both.

The second impediment is Labour's ideological commitment to collectivist welfare. The Labour movement's obscurantist defence of the welfare status quo arises only in part out of antagonism to the market alternative. Socialists, and their modernising ideological inheritors, also love collectivist welfare for its own sake, because they believe that that is how welfare should be done by modern, enlightened societies. State welfare is an independent article of faith in the progressive canon, reaching well beyond Labour to the Liberal Democrats and into the left of the Conservative Party. The divisive effects of welfare reform will take New Labour not just beyond socialism but outside the parameters of the whole corrupted collectivist culture which has dominated the British mentality for more than 50 years.

The third impediment to welfare reform by Labour is the pernicious influence of the poverty lobby. Mr Blair may have kept the trade unions quiet in recent years, especially in the run-up to elections, but the poverty lobby has been given its head as a source of useful propaganda against the 'hard-hearted' Conservatives. Latterly, however, the Labour Party's debt to the poverty lobby is having to be honoured – in the breach at least and at the cost of postponing welfare reform indefinitely.

The fourth impediment to the success of the government's pretensions to reform the welfare state is provided by the power of vested interests. Here the key role among Labour supporters and activists of teachers, doctors, nurses, social workers and other 'new class' workers is crucial (Shughart and Razzolini, 2001). After 1997 it seemed, at first, that this resistance movement of latter-day Luddites would be, to some extent, moderated once welfare personnel had their own government in power, as it were. In short order, however, the reactions of teacher trade unions, some professional associations in healthcare and local authority public service workers to sensible proposals by the Labour government for raising the disgracefully low standards of welfare state services reopened the struggle, and it looks to be intensifying. If Mr Blair is serious about welfare reform, he can expect organised, militant resistance across the board.

Taken one by one, these four impediments to serious change in the welfare system is each a source of major difficulty for reformers in the Labour Party. In combination they seem to me to present an almost insuperable barrier to the Prime Minister's declared aims. If he fails, we must expect worsening inefficiency in the welfare state, escalating costs, growing public dissatisfaction, serious inflationary effects, savage and arbitrary expenditure cuts and industrial disputes, which could make the winter of discontent of 1979 seem like a long and merry Christmas.

On the other hand, if he can tough-out the resistance movement, Mr Blair's remarkable personal qualities might enable him somehow, with the luck that successful leaders need, to bring off radical reform triumphantly. If he is to do so he will have to persuade his colleagues and the public that choice, competition and high standards are as feasible in welfare services as in the modern economy as a whole. Harder still, he will have to persuade, cajole and bully the welfare workforce to accept that choice, competition and high standards presuppose at least significant components of privatised supply.

There have been modest efforts in this direction since 1997, for example private educational companies taking over failing schools and derelict LEAs, and the newly-initiated cataract clinics and other healthcare treatment centres. Indeed, in announcing the latter in January 2004, the Secretary of State for Health went so far as to refer boldly and positively to the 'mixed economy' of healthcare. In general, however, these experiments have so far been too scattered and small-scale. Too often – as with foundation hospitals and variable tuition fees – such radical proposals have been grossly diluted in the face of unrepresentative opposition.

If Mr Blair means what he says about radical reform of the welfare state along these lines, then I strongly support him in this bold venture. I would not, however, reckon his chances of success as better than modest – not a rank outsider perhaps, but certainly running with longish odds.

Conclusion: 25 wasted years?

The end of the 1970s found the social life of the British people enveloped in the spreading tentacles of the welfare state. Across a huge swathe of the social structure, state bureaucracy held unchallenged sway. Freedom and choice were absent. Condescending paternalism characterised the socialist state's relations with its dependent subjects – patients, pupils and their parents, tenants, clients and not least 'claimants'.

Stimulated to it by economic crisis and her deep-seated belief in the individual, the family and freedom, Margaret Thatcher challenged this everyday Leviathan. She set the process of radical reform on its way, reversing a hundred years of the long lurch towards British socialism. John Major consolidated her initiative and put it into practice – achieving a sort of halfway house on the road towards de-nationalisation and freedom. Tony Blair has not reversed what Conservative governments achieved in the way of welfare reform. Indeed, in the face of intransigent resistance from within his own party, he has pushed reform a little further and promised radical renewal of the welfare state to fit it for the 21st century. As of 2004, then, where have we got to in Britain with the modernisation of what we have been schooled to call the welfare state? Not terribly far yet, it has to be admitted. Certainly the basic attitudes of ministers and senior managers responsible for the welfare apparatus have been transformed – they know now that consumers and taxpayers have to be satisfied (Beresford and Croft, 1993). Public expectations have risen substantially. Competition and new forms of organisation have improved efficiency. The paternalistic culture of state monopoly has been shattered (Spiers, 2003).

In structural terms, however, little has changed. Education and healthcare remain, for no evident reason, predominantly state monopolies (Tooley and Stanfield, 2003). Social services, as inefficient as ever, are still largely in local state monopoly hands, with precious little scope allowed for charitable and private initiative. Even in pensions the rapid growth of occupational and personal schemes has failed to deliver its potential, dominated as it has been by the dead hand of state pensions assumptions and Inland Revenue thinking. Only in housing – the one field where significant privatisation has been pushed through – has there been a real and radical break away from the state socialism of postwar British welfare towards freedom.

This disappointing lack of fundamental structural change in the welfare state after so much effort is reflected and paralleled in the pattern of public expenditure on welfare during the same period. According to research reported by Myddelton (2003), expenditure on the welfare state as a percentage of national income has more than doubled since 1960. Welfare state expenditure (defined as 'health, education, pensions, and other social security', and expressed as a percentage of national income) was as follows at the start of recent decades: 1960 – 15.6%; 1970 – 22.2%; 1980 – 28.8%; 1990 – 27.9%; and 2000 – 32.8%.

These figures indicate some modest success in holding down extravagant expansion in the 1980s, but overall the trend is steeply and remorselessly upwards. Moreover, national income has expanded hugely over these four decades. The cost of state expenditure on welfare in absolute and real money terms has escalated grossly. Worst of all, the trend is currently increasing still further as the Blair government glibly compensates for what ministers inaccurately call 'under-investment'. It looks rather more like throwing good money after bad.

There is nothing necessary or inevitable about the condition of the welfare state. The reforms accomplished over the past 25 years could be carried on and carried further. The cost of welfare could be reduced enormously. State monopoly could be eliminated. It is a matter of political choice and political leadership. Vested interests, engrained habit, popular anxiety in the face of unaccustomed freedom, even the mysterious force of its magic spell – all these obstacles could be overcome (Anderson et al, 1981). What we lack, what we desperately need, is an analysis of the deficiencies of British state welfare as telling and as influential as Charles Murray's investigation of social policy in the USA (Murray, 1984). In my view, such an analysis needs to address five key questions: What is the welfare state for? Who really needs it? Why spend so much money on it? How can we tolerate its inefficiency? How can we ignore the harm it does?

- First, the whole concept of the welfare state is philosophically incoherent (Veit-Wilson, 2000). For some it remains, even as socialism withers and dies, a stepping-stone on the long road to paradise. Others view it as a new model society that transcends the contradictions of capitalism while somehow escaping the threat of domination by an autocratic state. Others support it more modestly, despite its persistent failures in this regard, as a method of helping the unfortunate. It means 'all things to all men', and nothing sensible to anyone.
- Second, the forward march of normal economic progress in a capitalist society and the massive generalised increase in living standards associated with it make the bloated system of universal state welfare entirely redundant. Temporary emergencies aside, poverty is a figment of poverty

lobbyists' fevered imaginations. Even the people at the bottom of the income distribution are substantially better off today than the average of the standard of living in the 1960s, let alone the 1930s. Who is this vast system for?

- Third, the costs of the welfare state have escalated to a pitch that threatens national bankruptcy (Tanzi and Schuknecht, 2001). Levels of state expenditure, taxation and public borrowing are grossly excessive. Money that should have been spent on investment for economic growth and future prosperity has been squandered for 50 years on extravagant welfare (Barnett, 1995). And so it continues, with salary increases for an arbitrarily expanding workforce of state employees fraudulently classified as investment – while actually comprising unnecessary and wasted costs. Why squander the nation's wealth?

- Fourth, the welfare state is largely ineffective. Quality of service in the education system, in the NHS, in state pensions provision and in income support is lamentable. The inevitable effect of its monopoly power, its irredeemably bureaucratic character and its structured inattention to the varied and changing needs of individual people is that it fails routinely to help those who genuinely need special support. It squanders billions of pounds every year on third-rate services delivered to the wrong people to little useful effect. Why not adopt more efficient institutions (Berger, 1987; Savas, 1987; Gilder, 1988)?

- Finally, and worst of all, state welfare wreaks enormously destructive harm on its supposed prime beneficiaries – the vulnerable, the disadvantaged and the unfortunate (Himmelfarb, 1995; Green, 1998; Marsland, 2001). It makes of perfectly normal, entirely capable people who happen to be in temporary difficulty a fractious, subjugated underclass of welfare dependents. It makes all of us more dependent and less enterprising. How can we continue to ignore the grave harm for which the welfare state is responsible?

We may have to wait some long time, perhaps another 25 years – until the costs of state welfare break the bank completely and its moral impact produces widespread social chaos – before we can expect Margaret Thatcher's initiative to be followed up. At least, in the meantime, we should be resisting the continuing flow of mischievous apologetics for state welfare (for example, Alcock et al, 1998; Gordon et al, 2000; Barr, 2001; George and Wilding, 1999; Manning and Shaw, 2001) and producing reform plans. The main lines – implicit in the reforms of the past 25 years – are evident (Marsland, 1996; Seldon, 1996; Green, 1999).

A small and changing minority of people need safety-net support from time to time. The vast majority do not. We should turn the whole machinery of state welfare over, gradually and by free choice, to the market and voluntary agencies. The state should play no part in the ownership, funding or delivery of welfare services for the prosperous 85%-plus majority in the mainstream of society. It makes no more sense for the state to supply education, pensions or healthcare in Britain than for the state to produce machine tools in China, food in Russia or cars in North Korea. The free, competitive market simply does it infinitely better.

As far as the bulk of the population is concerned, the state's role should be restricted to rational, light-touch regulation. Enormous reductions in taxation should be possible. Most people could look after themselves and their families, with prudent self-reliance, out of their own moral and economic resources, insuring against misfortune, planning for their future and choosing freely among competitive suppliers of real welfare.

For those – very few – people who are incapable from time to time of looking after themselves and their families from their own resources, the state should remain responsible. This does not, however, require the massive machinery of the welfare state or its extravagant costs. Modest, temporary, conditional help, organised through the tax system and by means of small-scale organisations at local level, making maximum use of voluntary charitable agencies, would be quite sufficient (Whelan, 2001).

In social policy terms, the past 25 years have been good. They have seen increasing recognition of the deficiencies of state welfare, the beginnings of radical reform and the establishment of an alternative vision of welfare freedom. If the incubus of continuing collectivist thinking in the universities can be lifted (Marsland, 2002b), de-nationalisation of the welfare state – too long postponed – may be achieved at last.

References

Alcock, P., May, M. and Erskine, A. (1998) *The student's companion to social policy*, Oxford: Blackwell.

Anderson, D.C., Lait, J. and Marsland, D. (1981) *Breaking the spell of the welfare state*, London: Social Affairs Unit.

Barnett, C. (1995) *The lost victory*, London: Pan Books.

Barr, N. (2001) *The welfare state as piggy bank: Information, risk, uncertainty, and the role of the state*, Oxford: Oxford University Press.

Beresford, P. and Croft, S. (1993) *Citizen involvement: A practical guide for change*, Basingstoke: Macmillan.

Berger, P. (1987) *The capitalist revolution*, London: Gower.

Blundell, J. (2003) *Waging the war of ideas*, London: Institute of Economic Affairs.

Denham, A. and Garnett, M. (2002) *Keith Joseph*, London: Acumen.

Dennis, N. (1997) *The invention of permanent poverty*, London: Institute of Economic Affairs.

Duncan, D. (1908) *The life and letters of Herbert Spencer*, London: Methuen.

George, V. and Wilding, P. (1999) *British society and social welfare*, Basingstoke: Palgrave.

Gilder, G. (1988) *The spirit of enterprise*, Harmondsworth: Penguin.

Gordon, D., Adelman, L. and Ashworth, K. (eds) (2000) *Poverty and social exclusion in Britain*, York: Joseph Rowntree Foundation.

Green, D.G. (1998) *Benefit dependency: How welfare undermines independence*, London: Institute of Economic Affairs.

Green, D.G. (1999) *An end to welfare rights: The rediscovery of independence*, London: Institute of Economic Affairs.

Himmelfarb, G. (1995) *The de-moralization of society*, New York, NY: Knopf.

Major, J. (1999) *John Major: The autobiography*, London: HarperCollins.

Manning, N. and Shaw I. (eds) (2001) *New risks, new welfare: Signposts for social policy*, Oxford: Blackwell.

Marsland, D. (1988) *Seeds of bankruptcy: Sociological bias against business and freedom*, London: Claridge Press.

Marsland, D. (1996) *Welfare or welfare state?*, Basingstoke: Macmillan.

Marsland, D. (2001) 'Markets and the social structure of morality', *Society*, vol 38, no 2, pp 33-8.

Marsland, D. (2002a) 'Renewing British welfare', *Journal of Economic Affairs*, vol 22, no 1, pp 5-11.

Marsland, D. (2002b) 'Progressing health and healthcare: a positive role for sociology?', in E. Krausz and G. Tulea (eds) *Starting the twenty-first century*, New Brunswick, NJ: Transaction Publishers, pp 79-100.

Murray, C. (1984) *Losing ground: American social policy 1950-1980*, New York, NY: Basic Books.

Myddelton, D.R. (2003) 'Tax reform and simplification', *Journal of Economic Affairs*, vol 23, no 1, pp 2-6.

Savas, E.S. (1987) *Privatisation: The key to better government*, London: Chatham House.

Seldon, A. (ed) (1996) *Re-privatising welfare after the lost century*, London: Institute of Economic Affairs.

Shughart, W.F. and Razzolini, L. (eds) (2001) *The Elgar companion to public choice*, Cheltenham: Edward Elgar.

Spiers, J. (2003) *Patients, power and responsibility*, Abingdon: Radcliffe Medical Press.

Tanzi, V. and Schuknecht, L. (2001) *Public spending in the twentieth century: A global perspective*, Cambridge: Cambridge University Press.

Thatcher, M. (1993) *The Downing Street years*, London: HarperCollins.

Thatcher, M. (1995) *The path to power*, London: HarperCollins.

Timmins, N. (1996) *The five giants: A biography of the welfare state*, London: HarperCollins.

Tooley, J. and Stanfield, J. (2003) *Government failure: E.G. West on education*, London: Institute of Economic Affairs.

Veit-Wilson, J. (2000) 'States of welfare: a conceptual challenge', *Social Policy and Administration*, vol 34, no 1, pp 1-25.

Whelan, R. (2001) *Helping the poor*, London: Civitas.

TWELVE

Mrs Thatcher's legacy: getting it in perspective

Howard Glennerster

Introduction

Even 25 years after her election as Prime Minister, Mrs Thatcher still arouses passions: fervent loyalty, nostalgia and hatred. There are at least four divergent accounts that have been developed over the years about her social policy legacy:

- She was a wicked neo-conservative witch who ushered in a new era of social and economic policy. Her reign marks a watershed in postwar history and her impact was malign. This could be called the strong agency view.

  Thatcherism, then, was able to 'seize the time' and place itself at the helm of a project of root-and-branch transformation of the existing consensus, commitments and understandings about the relationship between the state, the economy and the 'people'. (Hughes and Lewis, 1998, p 50)

This was an outlook shared not only by many on the left (Hay, 1996) but by moderate Conservatives such as Ian Gilmour (1992) and some political scientists (Bulpitt, 1986).

- Others see her as an actress destined to play a part written by history – the structural view. It is no accident that the big changes that we see in the 1980s followed the oil shocks of the 1970s and the combination of recessions and inflation of that time. They came on top of longer-run social changes like the ageing population and ideological shifts that went far beyond Mrs Thatcher's influence (Lowe, 1999). The fundamental shifts that were under way in the economic and social structures of the age were such that they would have produced such outcomes whoever was prime minister. The UK and the USA went furthest in dismantling welfare but other regimes faced difficulties and had to adapt (Esping-Andersen, 1996).

• A third view agrees that there have been big social and economic changes and that Thatcher and Reagan, with others, did try to seize the moment but, given the scale of these structural changes, it is the resilience of welfare regimes that is notable, even in the UK and the USA (Pierson, 1994, 1996).

> Over time, all institutions undergo change. This is especially so for very large ones, which cannot be isolated from broad social developments. The welfare state is no exception. But there is little sign that the last two decades have been a transformative period for systems of social provision. (Pierson, 1996, p 176)

To this kind of account can be added the view that there was more continuity in Conservative social policy than many realise. Many of the roots of 'Thatcherism' can be traced to policy preferences evident in the 1940s which the party decided quite explicitly to down peddle until the time was ripe to reassert them (Jones, 1992; Jones and Kandiah, 1996; Glennerster, 2000).

• A fourth view is that Mrs Thatcher initiated a necessary re-examination of some old established social welfare institutions. She did not get her way entirely, but the resulting reforms may have improved them from the point of view of their consumers and indeed may have saved them politically. The welfare state emerged stronger from the rethinking she initiated. This is argued by Nic Timmins, the public policy correspondent of the *Financial Times*, who wrote an account of postwar social policy informed by numerous interviews with participants (Timmins, 1995).

> At the end of the Thatcher era a remarkable paradox was apparent. A woman whose instincts were to unscramble the NHS and to increase charges, to roll back social security and the social services, and to return schools to selection and fee paying had instead headed a government which found itself promoting reforms that, however controversial, were plainly intended to improve existing health,

education and social services ... the middle classes, instead of being encouraged to abandon those key services, actually found their concerns being addressed. (Timmins, 1995, p 478)

To put Mrs Thatcher's contribution in perspective we need to weigh these versions of events.

The malign instigator

There are some powerful grounds on which such a case can be mounted. The first is the general conduct of economic policy. This tied macroeconomic policy to a strict money supply target, really for the first time since the 1930s. As it turned out there was no such thing as a clear money supply figure. Instead there were several, and they changed their significance as policy tried to centre on them. The single-minded attempt to target in this way led to a combination of high interest rates and a rising pound which was, in retrospect, unnecessarily harsh and destroyed a large part of manufacturing industry. More than this, it destroyed communities, which still have high levels of persistent unemployment. They form the hard core of the extremely deprived areas we have been studying in CASE over the past five years (Lupton, 2003). They have suffered the consequences of this harshness for a generation. Despite valiant efforts of many in these communities they will continue to do so for another generation or more.

One response is to say that this medicine was indeed necessary. Without it, rampant inflation would have destroyed the UK economy and these industries would have had to be replaced at some time anyway. Harsh medicine meant that the eventual recovery came quicker. There is certainly something in this defence. Sharp corrective action to reduce inflation, not continually to accommodate it, was necessary. The monetary and fiscal prudence of the Brown years reflects that scaring experience. Necessary too was some restructuring of the economy. However, the crudeness and severity of the monetary policy destroyed much economic capacity. It also led industrialists to be very wary of investing. So did the hyper boom of the late 1980s, which lead to a second sharp recession. Such sharp fluctuations in economic activity make investment risky and borrowing more costly.

The second devastating legacy has to do with her record on the distribution of income. As research for the Rowntree Inquiry into income and wealth (Hills, 1996) charted, the widening of inequality that occurred in the 1980s and early 1990s was unprecedented, certainly since 1949.

Since the 1880s the dispersion of male full-time earnings had changed very little. From 1949 through to 1975 there was a small reduction in overall inequality of incomes, mostly occurring after 1963. Around 1977, before Mrs Thatcher, the trend reverses. It then accelerates steeply after 1979 and goes on rising through to the mid-1990s. The scale of the changes in original market earnings reported in Table 1 is astonishing in historical terms. The Gini coefficient of inequality (described at the foot of Table 1) had moved only four points in the previous 30 years. And that was in favour of more equality. Then it was to move 10 points in 15 years. The result was to shift the UK from one of the more equal societies in the world to one of the most unequal of all advanced economies. The Gini index of inequality for the UK in 1995 nearly matched that of the USA (Gottschalk and Smeeding, 2000). Much the same remains true on the latest figures (Luxembourg Income Study, 2003). The overall Gini coefficient for the UK in the year 2000 remained at 0.345 while that for the USA was 0.368. No other country experienced that transformation except New Zealand, also a neo-conservative policy leader. Structural changes common to other countries certainly explain some of that change, but only part. On top of these were self-imposed benefit and tax changes that worsened the impact (Atkinson, 1996). Again Table 1 is instructive. Compare the first column with the post tax and benefit column showing the impact of cash benefits and taxes in combination. In 1979 taxes and benefit policy were reducing the inequalities of the market by 14.9 Gini points. In 1990, Mrs Thatcher's last year in power, the tax and benefit system was only reducing inequality by 11.2 points. (The final column shows the slightly more progressive impact of services in kind which we shall discuss below. But even taking them into account the total redistributive impact of social policy in mitigating original income distribution was attenuated during Mrs Thatcher's period.) In short, original incomes became much more unequal and social policy did less about it.

Nor should this have been any surprise. Before Mrs Thatcher became Prime Minister she delivered a lecture in America extolling the virtue of greater inequality, entitled 'Let them grow tall'. Without more rewards for those at the top and less cushioning for those at the bottom the signals a free market economy needs and the incentives it gives were simply not sharp and clear enough for the market to do its job. If we look for improvements in labour productivity that might have followed from such a policy they are difficult to find. The growth in output per person hour worked actually fell from 2.8% a year in the 1970s to just under 2% a year in the 1980s and 1990s. That is hardly evidence of fundamental change for the better.

It may be that the reduction in the very top rates of tax and the shift to indirect taxation reduced the scale of tax avoidance and did have some beneficial effects on efficiency but the evidence is far from clear. Moreover, it is wrong simply to blame impersonal international forces of trade competition from the third world. Atkinson (2002) argues that such explanations are only partly born out by the evidence and some are contradictory. In the USA and the UK something less 'economic' was going on. In the 1950s and 1960s rewards in big corporations were

Table 1: The distribution of income before and after taxes and benefits in cash and kind, 1977-1990. Household equivalised income[a] (Gini coefficients: per cent)[b]

	Original income[c]	Gross income[c]	Disposable Income[c]	Post all tax[c]	Final[c]
1977	42.8	29.5	26.7	28.9	23.1
1979	43.5	29.6	26.8	28.6	22.7
1980	44.4	30.7	28.0	30.4	23.8
1981	45.9	31.4	28.4	31.0	24.2
1982	47.1	31.1	28.1	30.9	24.7
1983	48.2	31.6	28.2	31.2	25.3
1984	48.6	31.2	27.7	30.3	24.5
1985	49.1	32.4	29.1	32.2	26.2
1986	50.4	33.9	31.0	34.8	28.2
1987	51.1	35.7	32.8	36.4	29.7
1988	50.9	36.6	34.6	38.4	31.4
1989	49.7	35.8	33.8	37.4	30.5
1990	51.5	38.3	36.5	40.3	33.3

Notes

[a] Equivalised: Households weighted to reflect the number in the household. The final column is not based on equivalised households. "The ONS do not think it is appropriate to equivalise the final income measure because this contains notional income from benefits in kind. The equivalence scales used in the original articles are based on household spending and do not therefore apply to such items as notional income for education."

[b] Gini: An index of inequality where 0 = perfect equality and 100 = maximum inequality (all income received by one person).

[c] Original income: Market incomes of households before tax or benefits.

Gross incomes: Incomes including state cash benefits.

Disposable incomes: Incomes after direct taxes.

Post all tax: Incomes net of indirect taxes paid like VAT.

Final incomes: Taking account of the value of public services in kind received by households like health and education.

Source: ONS special analysis, for the author, of the annual Economic Trends data derived from the old Family Expenditure Survey, a national sample of households in the UK, now the Expenditure and Food Survey

tempered by a notion of reasonable bounds and accepted norms (Reich, 1991). Those social norms seem to have broken in the 1980s. 'Get what the hell you can' seems to have replaced the institutional reticence that preceded it. Mrs Thatcher can be said to have helped promote that change.

The tide of history

Both the second and the third views of the period agree that there is more to history than powerful individuals but disagree on the scale of the changes the 1980s unleashed. The case here is not that there was no decisive break in the continuities of social policy in the 1980s but that this was the result of fundamental shifts in the world economy and modern capitalism. The UK was particularly susceptible because its international position was heavily dependent on imports and exports and its economy had been underperforming its rivals since the end of the 19th century. Given a sharp deterioration in the world economy it was in an exposed position. It is no accident that Mrs Thatcher's reign followed two oil shocks, the acceleration of inflation and the degeneration of public finances. The latter was a reflection not just of the new situation but of the systemic way public expenditure had been controlled since 1961. Over-optimistic assumptions had been made by all governments about the economy's capacity to grow and generate tax income. It was the economic crisis of 1976 that had brought this home and Mrs Thatcher continued, rather than instigated, the changes in public expenditure control that were maintained through her period until the present. It also produced changes in public opinion about taxation. The struggle to maintain public spending in the wake of the oil crisis had meant the UK public suffered a fall in real take-home pay over several years. After 1973 real consumer spending ceased to rise as it had done year on year for a generation. It fell in 1974 and again in 1975. It stabilised in 1976 and then fell again. It was soil waiting for neo-conservative planting. The UK was not alone in following that pattern. Even countries, like those we call Scandinavia, that held out for a time succumbed to the trend. The extreme examples were those countries in Eastern Europe whose economic collapse had been greater.

The opposing view is argued, as we saw, by Pierson (1996). The steady growth in social welfare, as a share of economic activity that had taken place in all advanced economies since the 1950s, checked in the 1980s. But it has not declined. We have not seen a rolling back of welfare states in terms of social spending. Far from it. Between 1980 and 2000 welfare spending has risen as a share of GDP in nine of the 17 largest OECD economies – in France and Germany from about 25% to 33 or 35%! In the UK it has fluctuated between 26 and 22%. At 25% in 2003 it is about the figure it was when Mrs Thatcher came to power. It has proved much more difficult to retrench than she thought. Popular attitudes that are favourable to a strong safety net and to state provision of health and education have remained unshaken by her period in office. Indeed, support for more taxation and state spending on these core services of the welfare state grew in her time, having waned before it (Glennerster, 2003).

Even so, there is something distinctive and long-lasting about the Thatcher revolution in terms of institutional change. A stable share of the GDP going to social welfare in the face of growing demands and expectations does not permit stability in institutional forms or social policy. Here I think Pierson underestimates the scale of those changes over the long haul. Few other countries continued to re-elect such neo-conservative governments as consistently as the UK or saw such a coherent programme of change. Many of its main elements were enshrined by the Blair government. So the bottom line has to be, were they all bad? Was she really so malign? I shall leave consideration of social security and family policy to Hilary Land (whose view may well be 'yes'!) and concentrate on health, schools and the personal social services where the story is more complex.

Possible lasting benefits of the Thatcher period

It is not Mrs Thatcher's original instincts or hopes for the future we must consider, but what her social policy reforms actually amounted to in the long run. Her initial ideas for the reforms to the NHS bear little relation to the 1989 White Paper, for example. She was headed off from an insurance-based system, leading to the extension of tax-subsidised private insurance. The most powerful opponents were in the Treasury, and her otherwise radical Chancellor. The Treasury argued that any such move would open a Pandora's Box of health services inflation that would force up public spending, not the reverse (Lawson, 1993). What happened was something quite different: the attempt to introduce a degree of competition and choice within a publicly funded 'free at the point of use' service. Mrs Thatcher and Sir Keith Joseph began by wanting to implement a version of school vouchers that would have been cashable at private schools and added to by rich parents (Blaug, 1984). What happened was a quasi-voucher-like system of state school funding. Mrs Thatcher wanted to abolish SERPS and began to phase out the basic state pension. She only got some way towards that goal. She wanted to give council tenants the right to buy their council houses and she succeeded. She wanted to widen the use of the private sector in the delivery of personal social services and she succeeded.

There is not space to consider in detail all these aspects of policy. Broadly speaking I think the trends in social security policy had malign consequences. So, too, did the sale of council houses, though the transfer of stock from local authorities to varied other social landlords is welcome. I do want to argue, that a clutch of important changes was begun in the delivery of public services and in benefit policy that have proved largely beneficial. These changes shared some common properties or theoretical starting points that were fundamentally different from those that had driven much of social policy since the Second World War.

The first was the unspoken assumption that public finance entailed service delivery by some agent of the state. Indirect methods of state support such as tax relief were hidden and largely captured by the middle class. Exceptions, like services provided by charities, were hangovers from the past and properly marginal to the core state activity.

This pattern had never held in the 19th century. State involvement in education began through funding church schools in England. Health insurance when it was introduced and extended after 1911 had been organised through approved societies. This was a pattern common in continental Europe. How and why the central state emerged as the legitimate agent of the common people, especially during and after the Second World War, is a topic for historians and another paper. I merely make the point that the dominant UK postwar pattern was somewhat new, unusual internationally and certainly not a logical or practical necessity. Nor should its extent be exaggerated. As Burchardt et al (1999) show, though this pure paradigm did dominate publicly-financed welfare it was by no means universal.

The second assumption was that universality and equality of access required uniformity of organisational form. Diversity might be beneficial in the early stages of developing a new service, like senior elementary schools in the prewar period or comprehensive schools after it, but common best-practice patterns would emerge and be required by the centre. This extended to the design of school and hospital buildings, the shape of urban renewal and much else. Indeed the proud independence local authorities enjoyed in the 1940s began to be eroded by governments of both parties and not least by Mrs Thatcher.

The third assumption was that professionals were the legitimate repository of authority, not just over matters of individual professional relationships, but also of resource allocation. Freed of the price barrier, they could be relied on to meet need, determine what need was and hence determine the priority use of public money. Users were, in Le Grand's term (2003), 'pawns'; 'voice', or consumer preferences, in so far as they were to be exercised, were to be communicated through the ballot box.

There were of course those who criticised these set paradigms, notably the Institute of Economic Affairs on the right and some on the left, but they were the central orthodoxy. Mrs Thatcher challenged and broke them, particularly in her third term.

A break from the uniform model

- Legislation allowed whole housing estates to be moved from public to private or not-for-profit ownership with tenants' approval.
- Parents were given free choice of state school even beyond their own local authority, limited by available places. The school was funded on the basis of the number of pupils it attracted.
- Social services departments were given incentives and were under pressure from the centre to cease to provide services themselves, and instead, to rely on contracting with not-for-profit and private-for-profit agencies.
- The National Health Service as an organisational entity was split into two kinds of organisation. Health authorities received public funds on a population needs basis, as did growing numbers of GPs. Hospitals and community services, organised as freestanding trusts, competed for these funds.

The political climate that produced this change was not, of course, Mrs Thatcher's doing alone. Julian Le Grand and I reviewed several explanations as to why quasi-markets came into vogue in the UK in the 1990s:

> We are not persuaded by either the 'heroic' or the 'villain' type of explanation. There is some merit in the deterministic and the have-to-do-something explanations. But, ultimately, we find most plausible the accounts grounded in the tension between more demanding consumers, especially middle-class ones, and limited resources. (Glennerster and Le Grand, 1995, p 216)

There had been some fundamental shifts in public attitudes since the Second World War. Gratitude for merely receiving free healthcare, even after waiting in a queue, had worn off. In the 1940s you queued for most things. Health was not that different. Expectations had steadily risen. Increasingly, educated consumers expected better. Voters' views of the acceptable began to be driven by comparisons with private sector services and the range of choice they seemed to offer. Yet, the Conservatives were also trying to stabilise and indeed reduce public spending. The idea that a way out of this maze lay in radical reforms was inevitably attractive. There, lying to hand, was the diagnosis of the public choice economists. Public services were monopolies. The profit, or rent, extracted from the users and the taxpayer was not drawn off by private owners but by those who worked in the services. There was convenient supporting mood music in the public sector strikes of the late 1970s. But there was also hard evidence on the ground for those who looked at the seamy side of public sector provision locally. Housing departments had steadily abandoned frontline offices, rent collecting and on-site maintenance of their estates (Power, 1987). The staff had migrated to more remote council offices in the city centre. There was no gain in efficiency. The reverse was true. Nor did the staff involved necessarily gain financially. But it was a quieter life. It was easier to survive and get through the day, as Lipsky (1980) put it. I remember a whole series of interviews and observations I made when I was out in local health services during the period I was studying GP Fundholding. I observed that local GPs in one area were unable to get their elderly patients' routine needs met by a hospital with outstanding facilities. "Why do you do so few standard hip operations?" they were asked. "They are a bore," the reply came eventually. "We do a few to keep the health authority happy but we did not come into medicine in this hospital to do boring things." This was not monetary gain but it was exploitation of a monopoly position. The monetary gain came at the weekend when patients, fed up with waiting and with cash in hand, could boost those consultants' incomes.

The neo-conservative diagnosis had some basis in reality. Yet it was not the solutions of pure privatisation that Mrs Thatcher instinctively favoured that won through, at least in the case of health and schools. It was the halfway measures outlined above that did. The pressure for change on the right met resistance from those in the services and from those still wedded to notions of equal access and social cohesion within the Conservative Party. The central bureaucracies, notably the Treasury and the education and health departments, also saw serious consequences of going down that route. The result was something midway – quasi-markets.

A balance sheet for quasi-markets

Looked on from this distance, these reforms were neither as successful nor as disastrous as the fevered debate of the time might have led us to believe.

Care

The earliest of the moves affected the personal social services. Local authority social services departments were to become purchasers and market makers, not primary providers. To a significant extent that has happened. In the Thatcher and Major periods local authorities were given incentives and indeed instructions to use private providers. The Labour government merely required them to choose the most efficient and appropriate providers. But a big shift has occurred that spans both governments. In 1979 there were more than twice as many residential care places for old people in local authority ownership as in private profit and not-for-profit hands. Now there is more than four times the number provided by the private sector than the public (Glennerster, 2003, using LSE/PSSRU figures). Private domiciliary care has also grown, as has the scale of domiciliary care compared to residential care.

Making an overall judgement about the quality and responsiveness of social services before Mrs Thatcher and now is difficult. Perhaps the most comprehensive review that tried to do this was the paper by Knapp et al (2001). They conclude that the bureaucratic, take it or leave it packages of services that characterised social services have become more flexible and user-friendly. Services are less thinly spread and more intensively provided for those with high need. There are more out of hours, dependency contingent packages of care. There is a broader range of residential care, more intermediate care. The range of providers has grown. More not-for-profit specialised agencies are involved. Yet it is difficult to judge how the quality of care has changed over time in residential care homes. Levels of pay and quality of staff may have fallen. Larger companies have moved in and are providing larger homes that some believe provide less humane environments. Because local authorities do not face direct criticism for standards in the private homes where they place people, they may be tempted to strike too harsh a priced contract and to load private homes with unreasonable regulations. There is room for very different judgements here but my reading of the evidence is that, on balance, the introduction of a mixed market, or more accurately the extension of mixed markets, has brought advantages. Care is more matched to need than it was in the 1970s. One reason we shall discuss later is that there is a real opportunity for new entrants in the market. Enterprises are small enough and the voluntary sector is heavily involved.

Schools

The second major reform, chronologically, was to schools. Keith Joseph, as Secretary of State for Education in the early 1980s, had been keen to move to a full voucher scheme. All parents would have had a voucher worth the average spending on state schooling and they would have been able to spend it in any school, public or private. The killer problem was that all those already sending their children to private schools would have had to receive a voucher. This would have increased public spending by 7% at a stroke. At a time when the government's prime objective was to reduce spending, this problem was fatal. For an insight into the internal debate and the dilemma see Blaug (1984).

What happened was a 'second best' model in the eyes of the reformers. It built on changes pioneered in the old ILEA and Cambridgeshire where budgets had been devolved down to school governing bodies with freedom to spend and appoint teachers within a budget. Parents were given an in-principle right to choose their school. Priority for an actual place went to those who lived nearest the school or had siblings there. These enhanced rights were legislated in a way that enabled parents to choose schools from other local authorities. A pupil signing on at a school triggered a formula-based sum that the local authority would give the school. No pupils, no cash. The budget was held and managed by the school and its governing body. That was representative of staff, parents and the local community, in theory. The schools had to deliver a nationally defined product – the National Curriculum – and schools' success in achieving defined standards was published and parents told of their children's progress as measured by national tests administered to all children at ages 7, 11, and 14.

All of these changes came in Mrs Thatcher's second term in the 1988 Education Reform Act. It was the biggest change to the finance and administration of education in England since the 1944 Education Act. Initially there was considerable opposition to all of these changes, especially from the teachers' unions. Some of the fears have proved justified, as we shall see. But, here again, the Blair government continued with the thrust of this policy. Indeed, it introduced tougher targets and expectations. Overall, I think it is difficult to deny that a really striking change has occurred for the better. Between 1964 and 1990 very little improvement could be discerned in the mathematical achievements of British school children aged 13 or so. In 1995 less than half of children aged 11 were reaching a kind of educational subsistence level in maths or reading. That had been true for the previous 30 years. By 2001 the proportion achieving the set expected levels in maths had reached nearly three quarters, and four fifths in reading. In the same period, English schoolchildren moved from being average in the international league tables of performance, to near the top, higher than all the major European countries and the USA.

There are all kinds of caveats one should enter about the figures. Some schools may have cheated, taught to the tests. But when you consider them all it is very difficult to avoid the conclusion that something rather remarkable has happened (Glennerster, 2002). It is more difficult to apportion credit. Was it the National Curriculum? That is difficult to credit. Important as it is, there had been curricula of all kinds operating in schools for many years. The fact that this was one agreed nationally was unlikely to have had a decisive effect. What really made the difference, I think, from interviews with head teachers, were the tests. They gave teachers a clear signal about how their classes were doing compared to an agreed national measure. If you had been teaching in a tough school and you had kept the children in the class reasonably quiet and active you could go home satisfied. If you were scared of teaching maths and found it difficult there were other things you could do with the class – all entirely worthy, but not maths. Then the tests showed, in an irrefutable way, that only one in five of your pupils, say, was achieving what was expected nationally. "The parents knew, you knew, your governors knew and the local press knew", as one head put it to me. "You knew you were failing those children and you had to do something about it." However much the original league tables might have been misleading in not taking account of the children's background, the realisation that most of your pupils were not up to the national expected levels was difficult to accept professionally. (There are now results for each school that take the children's starting points into account.) This professional knowledge was reinforced by the fact that parents had the power to remove your funding which meant that doing nothing was for most heads not an option. The statistics show that those schools with the worst results in 1995 improved most. Schools with the most pupils on free school meals improved more than the schools with the fewest on free meals, in terms of reaching these targets. Those schools facing most competition from neighbouring schools improved most (Glennerster, 2002). Most middle class parents always had a good idea about their children's progress. These tests put knowledge and power in the hands of a wider group. Despite the objections that have been raised about testing seven-year-olds, that early diagnosis is crucial. By the time a child is 11 it is almost too late to remedy the lack of basic skills in school. By 14 it is pretty much too late.

But if this policy was, in my view, a success it also had major limitations. The rate of improvement is not continuing. The main 'culprits' are some schools in the poorest areas. Their results have hardly improved at all. The gap has grown, leaving these bottom schools behind (Lupton, 2004). The targets here are counterproductive, as such schools seem to have given up. Again the quasi-market measures have probably worked for the majority but it is not working for those at the very bottom. Many less-educated parents are not acting like informed purchasers. Middle class parents take this to extraordinary lengths (Ball, 2002). Ordinary average parents do to some extent. But parents who hope for little from the system or know little about it have little leverage. Schools that have a captive pool of children have little financial incentives and are demoralised. Quasi-markets may reach some important parts of the system but not all. That does not mean giving up the tools that have worked. It means concentrating more resources and recognition on success with the poor performing students.

Health

The NHS was the third major area of reform. As we saw, contrary to Mrs Thatcher's own instincts it did not end up privatising the funding of healthcare. The one move in that direction, tax relief on private health insurance for those over 65, failed to attract more than a few thousand new entrants. Private insurance companies are not that keen to have expensive old people on their books. The premiums were too high. This experience was just more evidence of the market failures on the funding side of healthcare that economists know a lot about.

What the reforms did do was to open up the delivery side to experiment. It showed that it was possible to introduce some diversity and competition into the forms of health delivery that could be combined with a tax funded scheme, free at the point of use. This was a revelation to many politicians and politically-aware people. It shows how homespun are many of our national myths. Countries like the Netherlands, Germany and France had had mixed forms of ownership and choice from their inception. What was innovative about the English reforms was that they kept the predominance of public provision but tried to introduce competition between public hospitals and other providers like community services. Most innovatively of all, they devolved funds and the right to purchase services for their patients to general practitioners. These ideas had a significant influence worldwide, particularly in countries with tax funded systems of healthcare – New Zealand, Sweden, Finland, parts of Canada and Italy. Even in countries with insurance-based mixed provision the GP Fundholding experiment attracted unusual interest. When I researched and published on the topic I remember receiving invitations to speak from every region of the world.

Whatever the rights and wrongs of these reforms, they put England at the forefront of health service innovation in a way it had not been since 1948. (I keep saying England since the Scots showed deep reservations from the start. They largely kept clear of GP Fundholding and since devolution have returned to a largely pre-Thatcher form of organisation).

There is still no consensus about the outcome of these controversial reforms, though in my view one is beginning to mount. For a start, they made much less difference than many expected. Institutional habits and medical power structures are not that easily shifted. The number of patients treated per pound spent was increasing by about 0.5% a year in the late 1980s (1.6% over the decade). This rose to about 2% between 1991 and 1995 (Le Grand and Vizard, 1998). The health authorities had been freed from the day-to-day management issues that kept bubbling for district managers under the old system. They were now free to think about strategic issues of health priorities for their area. But they felt they had relatively little leverage or knowledge to affect the big hospitals in their area. Fear of undermining them meant they dared not threaten to move contracts to get a better deal. There was little in it for a manager except hassle. For the most part things went on as before. Money was transferred to the hospitals with little knowledge about what happened to it, or recourse to sanctions if budgets were overrun and treatment underperformed. Later research by Propper et al (2003) suggested that the prime emphasis placed on low prices might have had some deleterious results. Those hospitals facing the most competition had higher death rates in their accident and emergency departments. This is a bit odd because these departments were excluded from the internal market and faced no competition. The authors speculate that with other departments under pressure, hospitals may have skimmed funds from the A&E departments.

It was the relatively small GP fundholders, sometimes combining in larger consortia, who did begin to make an impression by being more prepared to move contracts and demand quality improvements. It was not in their interests to press hospitals to reduce quality for price. That could mean getting a bad reputation and attracting fewer patients and hence less income. Unlike districts they had the capacity to monitor quality outcomes as far as their own patients were concerned. For Fundholders with identical budgets to their health authority counterparts, waiting times were reduced. Since pharmaceutical-prescribing costs came in their budget too, they showed they could reduce the costs of treatment. There were some significant innovations that began to challenge the accepted boundary lines between primary and hospital care. (The research on this is summarised in Glennerster, 2003.) But these were small actors working on only a small part of the budget – 20% of hospital and community costs in areas where everyone was a Fundholder. Moreover, the fact that only part of the population could benefit from such advantages proved a killer politically.

In Sweden some county councils decided to go down the new English route of purchaser–provider splits and some choice and competition. The result here to seems to have been that productivity rose faster than in more traditionally run public hospitals.

In 1998 the Fundholding scheme in England was abolished and districts were told to collaborate with local trusts and not to seek to pursue a competitive approach. The result was almost immediate. The small productivity gains seen in the 1990s disappeared and became increasingly negative (Le Grand, 2002). It was this that convinced the then Secretary of State for Health, Alan Milburn, to return to the kinds of incentives that had been seen to work in the post-Thatcher period and in the countries that had modified but continued that road, notably Sweden and Denmark. Patients were to be given freedom to choose their hospitals with payment of a set fee following the patient. Hospitals were to be given greater freedoms to act as independent units. In many ways the model resembled that for schools. Again these are exclusively English changes, they are not yet in place and, as in Mrs Thatcher's time, they are highly controversial. The intention is to keep tax funding and free access but give patients exit power and choice within the public sector and allow private providers to challenge the public providers.

Comparisons north of the border, and with our Scandinavian and Dutch neighbours in particular, are going to be very interesting in the next 10 years. Cross-system learning is now beginning to take place. That was never possible before the 1980s when the British were so convinced they had the world's best healthcare system.

So Mrs Thatcher lives on. And no bad thing. If these services are to retain voter support for higher taxes they have got to perform in ways demanded by modern consumers. They may be more secure as a result. Not a result Mrs T would have expected or wanted.

Overall

Mrs Thatcher's reign was malign in important ways, notably the manner in which her economic policies and social philosophy sharpened the already serious trends to inequality in the UK. Scars of her reign remain in many poor communities. Her undermining of the institutions of local government may prove a lasting loss to the British polity and one that her Victorian forebears would have been shocked to observe. She forcefully promoted and celebrated the virtues of consumer choice and more flexible labour markets. This may well have enhanced the productivity of the UK economy. She was also right to see the evils of monopoly and producer power when they operate in the delivery of social policy. The changes she set in train in this last respect, even if not the ones she ideally favoured, have had lasting effects. Not all were good and many still need to be debated. The relatively recent presumption that state funding of services must entail monopoly state provision was challenged. In my view the balance sheet here is positive and not what I would have predicted, or did indeed, predict in the late 1980s.

References

Atkinson, A.B. (1996) 'Seeking to explain the distribution of income', in J. Hills (ed) *New inequalities: The changing distribution of income and wealth in the United Kingdom*, Cambridge: Cambridge University Press.

Atkinson, A.B. (2002) 'Is rising income inequality inevitable? A critique of the "transatlantic consensus"', in P. Townsend and D. Gordon (eds) *World poverty: New policies to defeat an old enemy*, Bristol: The Policy Press.

Ball, S.J. (2002) *Class strategies and the education market: The middle classes and social advantage*, London: Routledge Falmer.

Blaug, M. (1984) 'Education vouchers – it all depends on what you mean', in J. Le Grand and R. Robinson (eds) *Privatisation and the welfare state*, London: Allen and Unwin.

Bulpitt, J. (1986) 'The discipline of the new democracy: Mrs Thatcher's domestic statecraft', *Political Studies*, vol 31, no 1, pp 10-39.

Burchardt, T., Hills, J. and Propper, C. (1999) *Private welfare and public policy*, York: Joseph Rowntree Foundation.

Esping-Andersen, G. (1996) *Welfare states in transition*, London: Sage Publications.

Gilmour, I. (1992) *Dancing with dogma: Britain under Thatcherism*, Hemel Hempstead: Simon and Schuster.

Glennerster, H. (2000) *British social policy since 1945*, Oxford: Basil Blackwell.

Glennerster, H. (2002) 'United Kingdom education 1997-2001', *Oxford Review of Economic Policy*, vol 18, no 2, pp 120-36.

Glennerster, H. (2003) *Understanding the finance of welfare: What welfare costs and how to pay for it*, Bristol: The Policy Press.

Glennerster, H. and Le Grand, J. (1995) 'The development of quasi-markets in welfare provision in the United Kingdom', *International Journal of Health Services*, vol 25, no 2, pp 203-18.

Gottschalk, P. and Smeeding, T.M. (2000) 'Empirical evidence of income inequality in industrialised countries', in A.B. Atkinson and F. Bourguinon (eds) *The handbook of income distribution*, vol 1, Amsterdam and New York: Elsevier.

Hay, C. (1996) *Re-stating social and political change*, Milton Keynes: Open University Press.

Hills, J. (ed) (1996) *New inequalities: The changing distribution of income and wealth in the United Kingdom*, Cambridge: Cambridge University Press.

Hughes, G. and Lewis, G. (1998) *Unsettling welfare: The reconstruction of social policy*, London: Routledge and Open University Press.

Jones, H. (1992) 'The Conservative Party and the welfare state 1942-1955', thesis, University of London.

Jones, H. and Kandiah, K. (1996) *The myth of consensus: New views on British history*, London: Macmillan.

Knapp, M., Hardy, B. and Forder, J. (2001) 'Commissioning for quality: ten years of social care markets in England', *Journal of Social Policy*, vol 30, part 2, pp 283-306.

Lawson, N. (1993) *The view from No 11: Memoirs of a Tory radical*, London: Corgi.

Le Grand, J. (2002) 'The Labour government and the National Health Service', *Oxford Review of Economic Policy*, vol 18, no 2, pp 137-53.

Le Grand, J. (2003) *Motivation, agency, and public policy*, Oxford: Oxford University Press.

Le Grand, J. and Vizard, P. (1998) 'The National Health Service: crisis change, or continuity?', in H. Glennerster and J. Hills (eds) *The state of welfare, the economics of social spending*, Oxford: Oxford University Press.

Lipsky, M. (1980) *Street-level bureaucracy: Dilemmas of the individual in public services*, New York, NY: Russell Sage Foundation.

Lowe, R. (1999) *The welfare state in Britain since 1945* (2nd edn), London: Macmillan.

Lupton, R. (2003) *Poverty Street: The dynamics of neighbourhood decline and renewal*, Bristol: The Policy Press.

Lupton, R. (2004) *Schools in disadvantaged areas: Recognising context and raising quality*, CASEPaper No 76, London: London School of Economics and Political Science.

Luxembourg Income Study (2003) 'Income inequality measures' (www.lisproject.org)

Pierson, P. (1994) *Dismantling the welfare state? Reagan, Thatcher and the politics of retrenchment*, Cambridge: Cambridge University Press.

Pierson, P. (1996) 'The new politics of the welfare state', *World Politics*, vol 48, pp 143-79.

Power, A. (1987) *Property before people*, London: Allen and Unwin.

Propper, C., Burgess, S. and Abraham, D. (2003) *Competition and quality: Evidence from the NHS internal market 1991-1999*, Bristol: Centre for Market and Public Organisation.

Reich, R. (1991) *The work of nations: Preparing ourselves for 21st century capitalism*, New York, NY: Simon and Schuster.

Timmins, N. (1995) *The five giants: A biography of the welfare state*, London: HarperCollins.

THIRTEEN

Privatisation, privatisation, privatisation: the British welfare state since 1979

Hilary Land

Introduction

> Privatisation, no less than the tax structure, was fundamental to improving Britain's performance. But for me it was also more than that: It was one of the central means of reversing the corrosive and corrupting effects of socialism ... privatisation is at the centre of any programme of reclaiming territory for freedom. (Thatcher, 1995, p 676)

The Conservative government elected in the summer of 1979 openly challenged the fundamental assumptions upon which the British postwar welfare state had been founded. The relationship between social and economic policies changed, calling into question the commitment to full employment that both Keynes and Beveridge believed was an essential underpinning of a social democratic welfare state. As Jessop (2002, p 61) much later wrote, reflecting on what he called the "Keynesian national welfare state":

> To the extent that markets failed to deliver the expected value of economic growth, balanced regional development inside national borders, full employment, low inflation, a sustainable trade balance and a socially just distribution of wealth and income, the state was called upon to compensate for these failures and to generalise prosperity to all its citizens.

In this model, public expenditure and the growth of the public sector is desirable because the 'social wage', funded by progressive taxation, guaranteed all citizens access to the health, education and welfare services when needed, irrespective of their capacity to pay at the time of their use. Thus inequalities in money income are less important, money wage increases can be restrained and inflation kept within bounds. The risks that individuals face over their lifetime, such as unemployment, sickness and old age are collectivised.

This chapter will follow the transformation over the past quarter of a century from a 'Keynesian national welfare state' to one based on supply side economics and a fundamental distrust of public and collective provision, that is, a residual liberal welfare model in Esping-Andersen's typology (Esping-Andersen, 1990) or a Schumpeterian competitive welfare model in Jessop's terms. I will look, in particular, at how privatisation shaped not only the development of social policies but also their very function and meaning. Privatisation can mean returning collective responsibilities to the family – 're-commodification' (O'Connor et al, 1999; Jessop, 2002) as well as moving activities from the public sector to the market – 'marketisation' (see, for example, Ungerson, 1997; Knijn, 2000).

In the space of one short chapter it is not possible to provide a comprehensive coverage of the British welfare state as it developed in the last quarter of the 20th century. I will therefore focus on changes that illustrate both meanings of privatisation, drawing examples from social security policies and social care services. Unlike health and education services, neither social care nor childcare were part of Britain's postwar universal welfare state. Changes in the extent and form of state involvement in their provision therefore exposes the boundaries between the state and the private sector both when private means 'family' and private means 'market'. These can in turn be used to clarify the meaning and relevance of privatisation to our understanding of welfare states in the 21st century.

The legacy of the 1970s

Events in the 1970s had shaken some of the foundations of the British postwar welfare state before the Conservative government was elected in 1979. The sharp rise in world oil prices in 1973 and the ending of the Bretton Woods agreement, freeing finance capital to go where it could get the highest return, exposed and exacerbated the problems of low productivity and declining industrial investment and profitability, which the possession of empire had masked until the 1960s. Unemployment in Britain rose in the 1970s, slowly at first. In 1976, when the inflation rate was running at 26%, there was an alarming run on sterling and unemployment exceeded 1 million for the first time since the 1930s. Britain sought a loan from the International Monetary Fund (IMF), which required a cut in public spending of £1 billion. The Labour government abandoned its commitment to full employment. Unemployment fell slightly in late 1978 but by the end of 1979 it had reached 2 million. Inflation continued in double figures.

The trade unions, whose membership then totalled over 13 million (over half the working population), were struggling to maintain the real value of their members' wages. The Social Contract, negotiated between the Labour Party and the trade unions between 1970 and 1974, in which the unions accepted wage restraint in return for increases in the social wage, was far too fragile (with the exception of protecting the basic state pension) to survive the economic turbulence of the latter half of the 1970s. Unionisation in the 1970s had grown most rapidly in the public sector, which by 1979 accounted for 30% of all employees. It was essential for the government after 1976 to resist significant wage increases in the public sector if it was to succeed in cutting public expenditure. During the winter of 1978-79 (the 'winter of discontent') large numbers of public sector workers went on strike to prevent the further erosion of the real value of their pay and to protect their jobs and the services in which they worked. Such disruptive action fed a growing perception that those who worked in the welfare services were more concerned with protecting their own interests than the interests of those who relied on their services.

Criticism of state provision came from the left of the political spectrum as well as from the right. The big public sector strikes exposed the contradictions inherent in the strikers' situation as workers providing essential social services:

> Militant workers in the state, and their unions, partly because of limited
> vision blinkered by the way union struggle has developed historically,
> have difficulty finding forms of action that do not damage the working
> class as much or more than they damage the state. (LEWRG, 1980, p
> 46)

This group of socialists and feminists, all of whom worked within the welfare state, recognised that "many people, from hard experience, have come to identify official services with being put down, with lack of care, and on the contrary to value help voluntarily given as being somehow more humane" (LEWRG, 1980, p 139). They therefore argued that "we have to fight for what we need of the state. But at the same time we can develop strategies which become seen to be struggle, not charity". Many in the women's movement, which had re-emerged at the end of the 1960s, challenged the patriarchal nature of the state and demanded more – but different – state benefits and services, which were more responsive and accountable to those who used them (see, for example, Rowbotham et al, 1979).

While these features of the British welfare state at the end of the 1970s provided fertile ground for those wanting to challenge the basis and form of public welfare provision, there were other policy developments signifying trends that successive governments would have to accommodate. Benefits for children were finally rationalised in the 1976 Child Benefit Act, when child tax allowances (reducing the tax fathers paid) and cash family allowances (paid to mothers) were combined into a tax free child benefit paid in cash to mothers for every child. This recognised the equivalence of a tax relief to a direct cash transfer as well as a defeat for those who wanted to strengthen the male breadwinner model (Land, 1977). The 1970 Equal Pay Act, the 1975 Sex Discrimination Act, the introduction of maternity pay and maternity leave all recognised, however imperfectly, that the inequalities faced by girls and women in education, training and employment were unacceptable. By the end of the 1970s there were over 9 million women employees, over a million more than at the beginning of the decade, but this increase was in part-time employment and masked the loss of women's full-time jobs which had started in the early 1950s and was not reversed until the 1990s. Childcare services were not taken seriously and most mothers in employment continued to work part-time, adjusting their hours of work around their children's needs and relying on informal care. Not surprisingly, only 6% of married mothers and 11% of lone mothers with pre-school children were in full-time paid employment in 1979. These figures remained low until the early 1990s when rising housing costs meant more families needed two earners. The introduction of independent taxation in 1990 facilitated this trend. By 1975 when the 1970 Equal Pay Act was fully phased in women's average hourly earnings had increased from 63% to 75% of men's. More girls were staying on in full-time education and going to university where, by the end of the 1970s, they represented 40% of all undergraduates, compared with a third a decade earlier.

Changes in the divorce laws at the beginning of the 1970s had made it easier for women to leave unsatisfactory marriages. By 1979 there were over 700,000 divorced women who had not remarried – double the number at the beginning of the 1970s. Over the same period the proportion of births outside of marriage had increased from 8% to 12% of all births. Feminism, together with the growing welfare rights movement, supported lone mothers in resisting the stigma associated with their circumstances and with claiming means-tested benefits. Feminism also played a significant part in putting domestic violence and the physical and sexual abuse of children on the political agenda in the 1970s. The question of men's responsibilities for maintaining their children and the mothers of their children at the end or outside of marriage had become a contentious issue. By 1979 there were over 300,000 lone parents receiving supplementary benefit. However, they were then outnumbered by unemployed claimants (over half a million). The unemployed attracted much of the attention in the press as scroungers and undeserving of help. The distribution of income had narrowed in the decades following the Second World War. "The living standards of all income groups were rising most of the time, with those of the bottom groups generally rising fastest" (Hills, 1995, p 27). At the end of the 1970s, 10% of children in the UK were living in poverty (measured as less than half the average household income).

Britain had joined the European Economic Community (EEC) in 1972 and its membership meant that some key aspects of employment, education and social security legislation had to conform to EEC directives. The 1978 Equal Treatment Directive was of particular importance in the UK because social security, tax and family law were not covered by the 1975 Sex Discrimination Act. What many of us did not foresee was that in the new welfare regime of the early 1980s, equal treatment would be achieved by levelling benefits *down*, not up. The Conservative governments of the 1980s and 1990s did not sign up to some subsequent key directives (for example those affecting the rights of part-time workers). They opted out of the Social Chapter. However, as Leibfreid and Pierson (2000) argue, although *direct* efforts to develop what they call "an activist European social policy" have been modest, the creation of a Single Market meant that by the 1990s "market compatibility requirements have resulted in legal challenges to those aspects of national welfare states that conflict with the single market's call for unhindered labour mobility and open competition for services" (Leibfreid and Pierson, 2000, p 269). European competition law has become an important influence in the determination of the boundary between economic and social policy across the EU, as will be illustrated later in the chapter.

Public expenditure and the retrenchment of social security

> Extra public spending – whatever it was spent on – had to come from
> somewhere. And 'somewhere' meant either taxes levied on private
> individuals and industry; or borrowing, pushing up interest rates; or
> printing money, setting off inflation. (Thatcher, 1995, p 124)

When the Conservative government came into office, the world economy
was moving still further into recession, inflation in the major Western
economies was increasing sharply and oil prices had doubled following
the revolution in Iran. In the UK, the social security system was
immediately the object of the search for cuts – it accounted for a quarter
of all public expenditure. These cuts had to be significant both in the
short *and* longer term for there were demographic trends fuelling higher
expenditure as well as high current and rising levels of unemployment.
By the autumn of 1980 unemployment was 2 million, rising to over 3
million in 1983. In 1980 flat-rate contributory unemployment benefit
was cut by 5% and in 1982 the earnings-related supplements and additions
for children in all contributory short-term benefits were abolished. Short-
term benefits became taxable for the first time. However, pensions were
the largest single item in the social security budget, so attention was
immediately paid to ways of curbing their cost.

Pensions

Between the mid-1970s and mid-1980s the number of pensioners
increased by 1 million. Thereafter the increase was slower – a further
increase of 600,000 by 2000. Within a month of the Conservatives
winning their second term, the 1975 Pension Act's commitment to
indexing the basic state pension to the higher of average male earnings
or prices, was ended. This, together with the downgrading of the state
earnings-related second pension (SERPS) in 1986, for lower earners and
for carers, meant increasing dependence on means-tested benefits and
pensions in old age. This is the opposite of Barbara Castle's objective in
framing the 1975 Pension Act. Had the link been maintained, the basic
pension would have been £30 a week more in 2003, making the means-
tested Minimum Income Guarantee and the Pension Credit introduced
that year largely unnecessary. For women it has meant increasing
dependence on their husbands in old age because credits use the couple
as the basis of assessment.

Higher earners were encouraged to join the private pension sector. First, the change in indexation affected the range of earnings over which employees paid national insurance contributions, as the higher earnings limit was set at seven times the basic pension. At the beginning of the 1980s the higher limit was 1.5 times average male earnings. By the early 1990s it was closer to average male earnings. There were generous rebates for those who opted out of SERPS, costing annually no less than £7 billion in foregone revenue throughout the 1990s (*Hansard*, 1999, col 397WH). Moreover, unlike national insurance contributions, the contributions made into a private pension scheme attract tax relief. This was costing over £5 billion a year by the end of the 1990s. Adrian Sinfield has calculated that the current annual cost in forgone revenue of these regressive tax reliefs is more than the cost of *all* selective or means-tested benefits paid to the poorest old people (Sinfield, 2002). The increased involvement of the private pension sector has changed the form but *not* the magnitude of state support for pensions. This restructuring has been done in a way that increases inequalities between high and low earners as well as between pensioners (Hills, 1995, p 62). Nearly 50 years ago, Richard Titmuss warned against creating two nations in old age by failing to curb the growth and greed of the financial services sector (Titmuss, 1958). He also criticised the accounting conventions that kept this kind of tax subsidy off the public expenditure balance sheet.

At the end of the 1980s the Chancellor of the Exchequer quietly dropped the state contribution to the national insurance 'fund', which had been 18% following the 1975 Pension Act. As a result, the scope for redistribution between higher and lower income groups has been diminished. It has also reduced the revenue of the national insurance 'fund' thus making it *appear* that higher state pensions were not affordable under a Pay As You Go scheme. (In fact for most of its existence the 'fund' has been in surplus. See Davies et al, 2003, p 48.) The myth that Pay as You Go schemes are no better at delivering adequate pensions than funded-defined contribution schemes has been perpetuated. However, in the wake of the recent scandals, widespread fraud and poor performance of the latter and the breaking of commitments in the former, no one in the UK trusts *any* method of saving for old age. Moreover, unlike means-tested pensions, which act as a ceiling, the basic state pension acts as a floor on which to build additional pensions. The current 'crisis' in pensions has as much to do with this growing penalty on saving, together with lack of trust in any savings vehicle, as with demographic trends. In any case, dependency ratios should take account of the number of economically active within the population of working age, not just its overall size. When this is done the projected dependency ratios look far less alarming (Huber and Stephens, 2001, p 137).

Young people

In 1964 the number of births in the UK had peaked at nearly 1 million. In 1980, 600,000 of this large cohort of young people were entering the labour market for the first time (Government Statistical Office, 1983, p 48). Those with no qualifications were black or from some minority ethnic groups; those from regions with a declining manufacturing base were particularly disadvantaged in the labour market. In the past, 'surplus' young people, in particular young men, were helped to emigrate to parts of the empire short of labour, by the state and voluntary organisations. Alternatively, the boys joined the army or navy. The ending of the British empire was accompanied by a reduced standing army and navy and national service ceased in 1960. Unemployed young men were therefore more visible in the figures – and on the streets – when unemployment rates rose. David Donnison, reflecting on his time as chairman of the Supplementary Benefit Commission (which was abolished by the government in 1980) at a time when there had already been the first inner city riots of disaffected youth, wrote

> with the spread of nuclear weapons and the ending of conscription sheer cannon fodder has been devalued, and one more motive for building a healthy and united nation has been lost. More recently, the rejection of Keynesian economic policies has had a rather similar influence. (Donnison, 1982, p 24)

The subsequent erosion of young people's entitlement to benefit, their increased dependence on their parents, and their growing homelessness support this view. Since 1948, unemployed teenagers, including students in their vacations, were eligible to claim means-tested benefits in their own right when they left school, either as non-householders if they lived with their parents or as boarders or lodgers if they moved away from home in search of work. In the early 1980s there were stories in the press of such unemployed young people enjoying holidays at the seaside while living on benefits which, it was alleged, were too high compared with the wages on offer (see Allbeson, 1985, p 88). Eligibility conditions and level of benefits were cut for 16- and 17-year-olds. Unemployed teenagers were channelled into special training and work experience programmes which had expanded greatly since the mid-1970s. There were tough benefit penalties for those who failed to participate. At the same time the protection of pay and working conditions, which Wage Councils since the beginning of the century had offered workers in certain trades, was withdrawn from those under 21. Young people's wages relative to adults fell throughout the 1980s. Greater dependence on their parents was therefore presumed whether they were in or out of employment. This has continued. The minimum wage introduced at the end of the 1990s was lower for those under 22 years of age. Following the recommendation of the 1986 Social Security Review, the under-25s would in future receive lower benefits than the over-25s. This practice has continued and eligibility for the new Working Tax Credit is restricted to those aged 25 years and over. Meanwhile, changes in housing benefit rules mean young people *in* employment and living at home were, and still are, expected to make a large contribution to their parents' rent, thus reducing the parents' housing benefit. These changes created an incentive for young employed adults to *leave* the home of poor parents. Thus the traditional method poorer families used to keep a roof over their heads, namely by sharing housing costs, has been made more difficult since the early 1980s (over 850,000 families were affected by these reductions in the first instance). As Paul Lewis, then Youth Aid director, wrote in the mid-1980s: "We do not just have the unemployment of the 1930s, we are getting the hated family means test too" (cited in Allbeson, 1985, p 97). The government, however, insisted on seeing growing homelessness as due to the "younger age at which people *choose* to leave home" (DoE, 1991, p 93).

The reduction early in the 1980s in young people's eligibility for benefits also established an important precedent undermining the concept of basic social rights for *all* citizens. As *The Times* pointed out in 1986, these cuts were " more important for the long run, to establish the violability of basic social benefits and do it for a group over which the political screams will not be too loud". Overall, despite the cuts in unemployment benefit and the redefinition of 'unemployed' to exclude young people on special schemes, benefits to the unemployed cost twice as much in real terms in 1982 and three times as much in 1985 as they had in 1979 (Ward, 1985, p 23). At the end of the 1980s lone mothers were made scapegoats in a similar way. This coincided with the beginning of another recession in the UK.

Lone mothers

Lone mothers attracted very little attention until the end of the 1980s when, rather suddenly, it was noticed that their numbers were growing.

(The 1986 Review had hardly mentioned them, for their numbers and the proportion dependent on benefits were expected to remain the same or even fall, depending on overall unemployment.) What was really worrying was that the growth was fuelled by the numbers of *never married* mothers who accounted for 40% of all lone mothers compared with 20% a decade earlier. Worse, the majority had become dependent on means-tested benefits. By 1989 1.3 million children, 60% of all children receiving Income Support, were living in a lone parent family. This was a threefold increase since 1979. Altogether the proportion of children living in poverty in the UK had increased to over a third (Hills, 1995). Economic activity rates among lone mothers, in contrast to married mothers, had fallen in the 1980s, partly because they were no longer living with or near a relative who could provide childcare, and partly because most of them had few if any qualifications (Kiernan et al, 1998). Moreover, only a minority were receiving any maintenance from the children's fathers. Reluctant to abandon the male breadwinner model, the government attempted first to push these mothers back into dependence on the fathers of their children, irrespective of their marital status. Hurriedly, the 1991 Child Support Act was passed, containing punitive cuts of 40% in the mother's benefit if she refused 'without good cause' to name the father(s). The formula for calculating the maintenance to be paid was complex and opaque and took precedence over any previous court settlement. Worse, any maintenance paid was offset *in full* against the benefit being paid to the mothers, so they and their children were no better off if the father did pay. Increasing the welfare of children was *not* the priority. Indeed, the minister responsible for social security later described this as an attempt to "reverse the inadvertent nationalisation of fatherhood" (Peter Lilley, BBC Radio 4, World at One, 6 March, 1993). Fathers organised to reject the adjective 'feckless' and lone mothers were publicly pilloried by ministers and by the press. Only when it became clear that the ill-fated Child Support Agency had failed spectacularly did the government turn its attention to getting lone mothers into employment (Kiernan et al, 1998). The government did nothing to increase childcare provision apart from increasing the childcare disregard in the Family Credit scheme. However, they planned to cut lone parents' benefits on the grounds that these had become too generous compared with those of two-parent families, thus devaluing marriage. The New Labour government in 1997 made these planned cuts in benefit shortly after they had been elected. They also launched a New Deal for Lone Parents alongside the New Deal for Young People as part of their overall welfare-to-work strategy. Unlike their predecessors, they *did* take the need to develop childcare services seriously. They relied heavily on the private sector to create more places because they were committed *not* to increase taxes. When Labour had left office in 1979, the basic tax rate was 34% and the top rate was 83%. Under the Conservatives these had been reduced to 22% and 40% respectively. They also included a childcare tax credit in the Working Families Tax Credit that replaced the Family Credit in 2000, to help with the costs of formal childcare.

Social security – an easy target?

The government was able to make significant cuts in the coverage and level of benefits in the social security system because the UK has one of the most centralised systems in the world. Administered entirely by civil servants who are employed directly by central government, there is no local government involvement except in the payment of housing benefit, which in any case was made subject to Compulsory Competitive Tendering in the late 1980s. There are no professionals involved comparable to teachers, doctors and nurses in resisting cuts in education and health. Trade unions had not been involved in the administration and provision of unemployment and sick pay since the interwar years. The attempt in 1986 to pay family benefits to fathers in the wage packet instead of directly to mothers was successfully resisted by the rather unlikely combination of the National Farmers Union, the Federation of Small Businesses and the poverty lobby supported by trade unions. The private insurance sector did intervene successfully when *its* interests were threatened by the total abolition of SERPS but they were hardly champions of the lower paid. Indeed they mis-sold personal pensions to tens of thousands of workers who would have been better off staying either in their occupational scheme or in SERPS – as was subsequently admitted, allowing many to successfully sue the companies concerned.

Taking a comparative perspective on the restructuring of welfare states in Western industrial societies over the past 25 years, Huber and Stephens (2001, p 106) concluded that:

> ... only in Great Britain and New Zealand could one speak of an actual system shift from welfare state regimes that used to provide basic income security to welfare state regimes that are eventually residualist, relying heavily on means-testing. We argue that the exceptional nature of these two cases can be traced to their political systems which concentrate power ... and make it possible to rule without a majority of popular support.... Thus in both cases, the

Conservative governments were able to pass legislation which was deeply unpopular.

Further retrenchment

Margaret Thatcher waited until her third term of office in 1987 to tackle other parts of the welfare state, pushing her privatisation programme further. By then she had curbed the power of trade unions, which had been weakened by prolonged unemployment, the defeat of the miners and the further decline of the traditional manufacturing sector. Their membership was falling and by the end of the 1990s would be halved. The professions involved in the welfare state had been sidelined and tenure in universities was about to end. Local government had been reorganised. The Greater London Council and the other big metropolitan authorities had been abolished and all faced tighter financial controls. Mrs Thatcher was planning to replace rates with the community charge (the poll-tax) "which by bringing home to people the true cost of local government, would maximise the pressure for efficiency and low spending" (Thatcher, 1995, p 651).

The privatisation agenda was broadening. The first stage had been to sell off state-owned industries, having first made sure they were in a profitable state. By 1987 the public utilities of gas, electricity and water and British Telecom were in the frame. At the same time there were plans for requiring local authorities under a compulsory competitive tendering scheme to put out many of their services such as school meals, cleaning, refuse collection and the maintenance of parks and public buildings. By the time Mrs Thatcher left office in 1990 – the timing of which was hastened by the unpopularity of the poll tax – she later boasted that "the state owned sector of industry had been reduced by some 60%. Around one in four of the population owned shares. Over six hundred thousand jobs had passed from the public to the private sector" (Thatcher, 1995, p 687). These developments were in tune with developments elsewhere in Europe. EU competition law from the mid-1980s became increasingly involved in areas "which were hitherto not only shielded from competition, but also widely perceived to be best organised as monopolies. Key examples are the public utilities of energy, communication and transport, as well as other sectors such as insurance, banking, sport and media" (McGowan, 2000, p 132).

The next stage moved closer to the heart of the welfare state as local authorities' role as the *providers* of social services changed to that of managers and regulators. This is an illustration of how the scope of economic policy has been widened and deepened because of the increased importance for capital accumulation of what was previously regarded as 'extra-economic'. Thus while the Keynesian national welfare state tried to extend the social rights of its citizens, the Schumpetarian competitive welfare state is now concerned to provide services that benefit business and thereby demote individual needs to second place. (Jessop, 2002, p 51)

Developments in the residential care sector in the UK provide a clear example of how this shift occurred. In particular they show how, in the 1980s, a private market was first developed, heavily subsidised by the state, so that by the 1990s the big transnational corporations could move in and use the competition legislation to further undermine local authority provision.

Residential care

By the 1970s the objective of policies for elderly people was to keep them in their own homes as long as possible, cared for *in* and *by* the community. There were, however, some for whom this was not possible because they were too old and frail. Their numbers were growing. In 1974 there were just under 2.5 million people aged 75 years and over in England and Wales; by 1984 there were nearly 3.2 million. By the end of that year there were over 190,000 elderly people in residential homes compared with just over 140,000, 10 years earlier (Audit Commission, 1986). Despite anxiety that these figures included growing numbers who did not *need* to be there, detailed research failed to find them. "As few as 6.6% if account is taken of existing services, about 10% if ordinary domiciliary services or sheltered housing *had been* available and no more than 17.5% if alternative and more intensive relevant services had been available" (Bradshaw and Gibbs, 1988, p 80). Significantly, nearly all the increased provision was in the private sector but the social security system was picking up the bill, which was growing at an alarming rate. The explanation for this can be found in the way both the social security system and local authority budgets were being used.

Board and lodging allowances had been paid to a small number of elderly people in private or voluntary homes since 1948. However, prior to 1980, the level of the allowance was set with reference to the prevailing local charges that an *independent adult* would have to pay for board and lodging. Board and lodging payments were an insignificant part of the Supplementary Benefit budget, costing, in 1978-79, £6 million (£12 million in 1986 prices). By 1987 they cost £489 million and, by May 1989, £1 billion (including nursing homecare). There were a number of reasons for this alarming escalation.

The increased pressure on the social security budget first arose from the impact of the cuts in local authority spending which had started in 1976. Capital programmes are easier to cut in the first instance than revenue-costly programmes, hence local authority provision of new residential places slowed down. If necessary, old people were sponsored in the voluntary or private sectors. However, after the 1980 changes in the regulations described below, local authorities began encouraging the *direct* use of the private sector because the social security system would then meet the old person's bill. They were thus able to shift the cost of residential care for elderly people from their budgets to the DHSS. Between 1980 and 1984 the number of local authority *sponsored* residents in private homes fell by 57% and the numbers sponsored in voluntary homes by 30% at the same time as the overall numbers in these homes was increasing (Audit Commission, 1986).

After 1980 it was made clear that the level of the board and lodging allowance was to be set by reference to charges in an 'equivalent establishment' and that 'the needs of residents' could be taken into account. This meant that local board and lodging charges could be set on a par with charges for elderly people in the private and voluntary residential sectors. Ministers became alarmed as costs escalated. New regulations were introduced in 1983, removing local discretion in setting the charges. These only made matters worse because the allowances were higher, being set with reference to the *highest* reasonable charge in the area. Consequently the cost of board and lodging payments in 1983 escalated from £205 to £380 million while the proportion of Supplementary Benefit claimants among residents in the private sector increased from 20% to 30%. There was continuing pressure to make the allowances more sensitive to local variations and the national limits were increased again and again.

This increased growth in the use of residential care occurred without any professional assessment of the old person's need for it because, unlike social service departments when admitting old people to one of their *own* homes, the social security system was not required to limit support only to those who had been *assessed* to *need* it. There was no upper limit of capital that disqualified an old person from entering a local authority home or being sponsored in a voluntary home but it was assumed that any capital over a minimum amount earned a weekly tariff income.

The major social security review, resulting in the 1986 Social Security

Act implemented in 1988, contained strategies for curbing the cost – to the public purse – of residential care. The most important were that an assessment of the old person's *need* for residential care was required and the budget was no longer open-ended. Moreover, following local authority practice, under the rules of Income Support, which was replacing Supplementary Benefit, old people needing to move into residential care had to sell their house as quickly as possible, unless a member of the family aged 60 or more was living there. By this time, the government's policy of selling council houses to local authority tenants at large discounts had succeeded in extending owner occupation to many more working class families. Between 1979 and 1987 more than one sixth of the total stock of council houses had been sold. Many tenants had bought their homes thinking they would have something to pass on to their children. They had not realised that they had acquired an asset which would then be used to pay for the residential care they needed *and* would support the private-for-profit residential care sector whose expansion had been so generously funded by the taxpayer in the 1980s.

At the beginning of the 1990s as part of the reform of community care, the whole budget for residential care *and* homecare was moved to social service departments. The government ensured that the private-for-profit and the voluntary sectors would grow because from 1993 local authorities were *required* to spend at least 85% of their social care budget in these sectors. "The government wishes to ensure that Local Authorities have every incentive to make use of the independent sector when placing people in residential settings" (DHSS et al, 1989 para 3.7.10). The decline of residential homes run directly by the state was inevitable. In the early 1970s over 90% of elderly people in residential care had been living in local authority homes. By 1994, 52% of elderly residents were in homes in the independent sector and by the end of the decade this had increased to 88%. The majority were and still are sponsored by the local authority. At the same time, the private market for homecare had been given a kick-start (Laing and Buisson, 1999). In 1993 only 3% of homecare contact hours were provided by the private sector. By 2001 this had risen to 60% and is still rising. By this time only a third of all social care staff were employed directly by a local authority.

Conclusion

Although European competition law started from the early 1960s with Regulation 17/1962, it was not until the mid-1980s that its impact on social policies became significant. Leibfried and Pierson (2000, p 270) argue that EU legislative activity by 1995 had become "at least as extensive as, for example, federal social policy activity was in the US in the era of the New Deal". They also conclude that the EU's social dimension has developed "as much as part of a market building process than as a corrective or counter to market building"(Leibfried and Pierson, 2000, p 277). In other words the Keynesian national welfare state has been replaced by one subordinate to the supranational marketplace. It is still possible to argue for social policies that are in the interests of sustaining 'economic and social cohesion' and therefore should not be subject to competition law. The distinction between a commercial activity and a social service has become very important and in the UK was tested as soon as the 1998 Competition Law came into effect.

In 2000, the BetterCare Group Limited, which has residential and nursing homes in the UK and in Canada, complained to the Office of Fair Trading that the North and West Belfast Health and Social Services Trust was abusing its dominant position as purchaser of residential places in the private sector, by offering unfairly low prices and unfair terms, compared with what they were spending on their own homes. In effect the trust was accused of subsidising poor elderly people in its own homes and of paying its own staff higher wages. Although the Office of Fair Trading first rejected the complaint BetterCare won when it appealed to the Competition Commission Appeals Tribunal. Unable to afford to pay higher fees to Bettercare, the trust transferred its homes to the private sector knowing that the pay and conditions of the staff and possibly the quality of the care would fall. However, the law has not been settled because the European Court of First Instance subsequently ruled in the spring 2003 that the Spanish national public health body was *not* engaged in a commercial activity when purchasing supplies and services because the use to which they were subsequently put was "one of a purely social nature" (Case T-319/99).

One of the most important changes over the past 25 years, crucial to the future of welfare states, has been the growing role of competition law in determining what is 'economic' and what is 'social'. As the World Trade Organisation's General Agreement in Trade in Services (GATS) takes effect it will be even harder to sustain a broad definition of 'social'. The narrower the definition of 'social' the bigger the market for the large transnational corporations and the more public social services will be provided on the basis of poverty rather than citizenship, that is, as part of a residual welfare state. When the provision of social services is regarded as a commercial activity then education, health and social care are treated as commodities whose consumption is largely a private matter. This is very far from seeing these services as public goods that are part of the social wage to which all citizens are entitled. This is a clear example of what Zsuzsa Ferge has described as "the individualisation of the social" (Ferge, 1997). While the New Labour government is committed to ending child poverty and has quietly redistributed benefits to poorer families, it, as much as Conservative governments since 1979, is in danger of forgetting what Tawney wrote over 50 years ago:

> No individual can create by his isolated action a healthy environment, or establish an educational system with a wide range of facilities, or organise an industry in such a manner as to diminish economic insecurity, or eliminate the causes of accidents in factories or streets. Yet these are the conditions which value the difference between happiness and misery, and sometimes, indeed, between life and death. In so far as they exist they are the source of a social income, received not in the form of money but of increased well-being. (Tawney, 1964, p 127)

References

Allbeson, J. (1985) 'Seen but not heard: young people', in S. Ward (ed) *DHSS in crisis*, London: Child Poverty Action Group, pp 81-102.

Audit Commission (1986) *Making a reality of community care*, London: HMSO.

Bradshaw, J. and Gibbs, I. (1988) *Public support for private residential care*, Aldershot: Gower.

Davies, B., Land, H., Lynes, T., MacIntyre, K. and Townsend, P. (2003) *Better pensions: The state's responsibility*, London: Catalyst.

DHSS (Department of Health and Social Security), DSS (Department of Social Security) Wales and Scotland (1989) 'Caring for people – community care in the next decade and beyond', Cm 849, London: HMSO.

DoE (Department of the Environment) (1991) Annual Report 1991, *The government's expenditure plans 1991 to 1993*, Cm 1508, London: HMSO.

Donnison, D. (1982) *The politics of poverty*, Oxford: Martin Robertson.

Esping-Anderson, G. (1990) *Three worlds of welfare capitalism*, Princeton, NJ: Princeton University Press.

Ferge, Z. (1997) 'The changed welfare paradigm: the individualisation of the social', *Social Policy and Administration*, vol 31, no 1, pp 20-44.

Government Statistical Office (1983) *Social trends 14*, London: HMSO.

Griffiths, R. (1988) 'Community care: agenda for action', London: HMSO.

Hansard (House of Commons) (1999) Written answers, col 1397, London: The Stationery Office.

Hills, J. (1995) *Inquiry into income and wealth, vol 2*, York: Joseph Rowntree Foundation.

Huber, E. and Stephens, J. (2001) 'Welfare state and production regimes in the era of retrenchment', in P. Pierson (ed) *The new politics of the welfare state*, Oxford: Oxford University Press, pp 107-45.

Jessop, B. (2002) *The future of the capitalist state*, Cambridge: Polity.

Kiernan, K., Land, H. and Lewis, J. (1998) *Lone motherhood in twentieth century Britain*, Oxford: Oxford University Press.

Knijn, T. (2000) 'Marketisation and the struggling logics of (home) care in the Netherlands', in M. Harrington Meyer (ed) *Care work, gender, labor and the welfare state*, London and New York, NY: Routledge, pp 232-48.

Laing, W. and Buisson, C. (1999) 'Promoting the development of a flourishing independent sector alongside good quality public services', in *With respect to old age*, Royal Commission on Long Term Care, Cm 4192, vol 3, pp 87-102.

Land, H. (1977) 'The child benefit fiasco', in K. Jones (ed) *Yearbook of social policy in Britain 1976*, London: Routledge and Kegan Paul, pp 116-31.

Leibfried, S. and Pierson, P. (2000) 'Social policy: left to courts and markets', in H. Wallace and W. Wallace (eds) *Policy-making in the European Union* (4th edn), Oxford: Oxford University Press, pp 267-92.

LEWRG (London Edinburgh Weekend Return Group) (1980) *In and against the state*, London: Pluto.

McGowan, F. (2000) 'Competition policy: the limits of the European regulatory state', in H. Wallace and W. Wallace (eds) *Policy-making in the European Union* (4th edn), Oxford: Oxford University Press, pp 122-40.

O'Connor, J., Orloff, A. and Shaver, S. (1999) *States, markets, families*, Cambridge: Cambridge University Press.

Rowbotham, S., Segal, L. and Wainwright, H. (1979) *Beyond the fragments*, London: Merlin.

Sinfield, A. (2002) 'The cost and unfairness of pension tax incentives', in *The future of UK pensions*, House of Commons Work and Pensions Committee, First Report 2002-03, HC 92-III, pp 300-05.

Tawney, R. (1964) *Equality* (5th edn), London: Allen and Unwin.

Thatcher, M. (1995) *The Downing Street years*, London: HarperCollins.

The Court of First Instance of the EC, Case T-319/99, Federaccion Nacional de Europresas de Instrumentacion Cientifica, Medica, Tecnica y Dental (FENIN) v Commission of the European Communities, 4 March 2003.

Titmuss, R. (1958) *Essays on the welfare state*, London: Allen and Unwin.

Ungerson, C. (1997) 'Social politics and the commodification of care', *Social Politics*, vol 4, no 3, pp 362-81.

Ward, S. (1985) 'Introduction: the political background', in S. Ward (ed) *DHSS in crisis*, London: Child Poverty Action Group, pp 1-14.

FOURTEEN

Social policy since 1979: a view from the USA

Joseph White

Introduction

I keep in my desk drawer the National Health Service cards issued in 1967 to me, my wife and our son, who was one-and-a-half years old during the time we were living in Britain. I keep them in full knowledge of the fact that for years they have been completely useless. As to why they are useless and why they cannot be turned in for a new set of cards – which I am guessing are now made out of plastic – I strongly suspect that many readers have already figured out the answer, which is that, because I am an American citizen, my family and I are no longer eligible for NHS services.

What does this foible of mine have to do with the subject of this chapter? The answer is that this little anecdote illustrates an almost chemically pure instance of the 'sea change' brought about by the Thatcher government and its successors. That is, one did not always have to be a citizen of Britain in order to receive some of the services of the welfare state – and in the case of the NHS, the crown jewel of the welfare state to boot. Nor was this generous coverage some kind of policy oversight or unanticipated consequence. Aneurin Bevan had it put in intentionally. This in turn is of more than merely antiquarian interest, since it has become a virtual axiom in recent scholarly writing on the subject that the extension of citizenship and the creation of the welfare state everywhere meant – and had to mean – the *inclusion* of some people and the *exclusion* of many others. As a broad generalisation, this is perhaps sustainable. But Bevan's intentional extension of NHS coverage to non-citizens of Britain stands on the face of it as an unambiguous counter example, unless one wishes to make the logically costly gambit of arguing that it is an 'exception that proves the rule' – costly because it is by no means clear that the exception ever proves the rule.

So why do I still keep the cards? My tendencies toward 'packratism' and common-garden-variety nostalgia – which no doubt are real enough – take us only so far. More helpful is the fact that in 1967 the NHS already epitomised, for me, the British welfare state at its best, and as it turned out, in my experience the system worked better than even its staunchest defenders said it did. The process of getting our cards and choosing our general practitioner was simple and elegant. Dr Adler of Finchley Road, Golders Green, London, provided us with superb medical care, though the fact that all three of us were in fine health obviously did no harm either. He even made house calls, which were unheard of in America in 1967.

To attempt to write about Thatcherism's first 25 years from an American perspective raises the uncomfortable question of what that would consist. Is there a distinctly American perspective and am I myself capable of accurately and adequately expressing it? I am by no means sure that a distinctly American perspective exists. As an historian whose speciality is modern Britain, I have never tried to develop an American 'angle' in my writings on Britain. (It may be a peculiarity or professional deformation of academic historians of all nationalities to suppose that they are uniquely able to adopt a standpoint of cosmopolitan objectivity.) And I absolutely reject the notion that just because I am American, my writing will somehow spontaneously capture the essence of my putative 'Americanness' any more than I believe that there is such a thing as German or Jewish physics. I therefore leave it to the reader to judge for himself or herself the Americanness of what follows. What I do subscribe to is the idea that, with some luck, a modicum of talent and a lot of hard work and thinking, an outsider can occasionally see things about another country's history, politics and culture that might not seem all that distinctive, important or even visible to the locals.

In any case, I never asked for my Americanness – whatever it might consist of and amount to. My socialism is another matter altogether. Without a doubt I am one of the 'latter day Old Believers' to whom Professor Tony Judt referred in a recent – and highly critical – review of Eric Hobsbawm's memoirs, *Interesting Times*, in the *New York Review of Books*[1] (Judt, 2003). I intend neither to expound nor defend my 'correct views on socialism' as such. But they might well buttress, shape and otherwise influence much of what follows.

A quarter century of 'Thatcherism'. Historians are always on the lookout for continuities and throughout the 1980s and 1990s some made out the case that Thatcherism did not go 'all the way down'. I do not wish to continue that debate here and will instead take a Thatcherite sea change as given. Relatedly, I endorse the notion of a Labour sea change as well in the form of New Labour. This plainly implies that before Thatcherism things were substantially different. I believe that to be so, and accordingly, will first describe at some length aspects of that difference, with major emphasis on the influence and the British welfare state upon American thinking and practice in the realm of social policy before 1979. I then turn to the period of the almost 18 years of unbroken Tory rule between 1979 and 1997, with a view primarily to examining the attempts to explain Thatcherism's many victories and its influence on American developments. Third, I shall look at New Labour from the standpoint of its representing the continuation of Thatcherism as well as a sea change in the Labour Party itself. I conclude with a (necessarily speculative) discussion of future prospects for the welfare state in both Britain and America and a statement, as best as I am able, of how 25 years of Thatcherism have influenced my own thinking.

Influencing the USA? The postwar British welfare state

I first heard the following joke as a child some time between 1952 and 1954. An American and an Englishman were having an amiable chat. "Tell me about your country's political system," asked the American. "We have two major political parties," replied the Englishman. "One is the Labour Party. You Americans would call them socialists. The other is the Conservative Party. You Americans would call them socialists".[2] I suppose that the response today by academics who know their British history would be to observe that it is a mistake to exaggerate the degree of policy and ideological consensus – Butskellism, for short – that obtained in Britain in the 1950s. But I am less concerned with the joke's strict historical accuracy than with its political point, which of course is that Britain was far ahead and to the left of America. As has often been observed, most jokes do not age well but I still find this one funny.

Half a century on, the joke's underlying assumption still seems right. Britain was a real welfare state whereas in America the New Deal was at best what I shall call a minimalist welfare state. Moreover, Americans back then – both on the left and right of the political spectrum – watched closely and commented at length on British developments. To cite two examples from the right, unless I am mistaken the origin of the term, socialised medicine, is American, and it was not used as a term of endearment. In addition, around 1949-50, conservative political commentators on the radio and in print began to attack Harold Laski as if he was the devil incarnate for reasons that I once knew but have since forgotten. Of equal or greater import, progressives and leftists derived great hope and inspiration from Britain. Helen M. Lynd's *Britain in the 1880s: Toward a social basis for freedom* (1945) was clearly a tract for the times. Karl De Schweinitz, *England's road to social security* (1943, p v) begins with the words,

> those who are interested in the development of social security in the United States are turning today, as they have for many years, to Great Britain.... No better evidence of this could be had than the attention we have given to the recent report upon social insurance and allied services presented to Parliament by Sir William H. Beveridge.

Well into the 1960s, this book was assigned reading for American university undergraduates majoring in social welfare. *Midcentury journey* (1952) by the journalist and historian William L. Shirer contained a long and ardent description and defence of the British Labour Party and welfare state and why both would be very good things for Americans to emulate.

But America got eight years of the Republican Eisenhower administration instead, just as Britain got 13 years of the Tories. Taking the last 50 years as a whole, it is fascinating and important to note how electoral outcomes in Britain and America have been similar but never quite in perfect synchronisation. It is therefore apposite to ask why the social policy status quo survived essentially unchanged in both countries. As regards Britain, the standard accounts (Morgan, 1992; Gladstone, 1995) with their emphasis on one-nation Toryism and outright opposition to the welfare state as a vote-loser on election day seem right to me as a first approximation. But with regard to America, if, *ex hypotheo*, the New Deal was such a lighter and weaker version of the welfare state, then why didn't its enemies get rid of it altogether? For in fact the New Deal was not rolled back. It wasn't even touched. One reason was that, just as in Britain, it was very poor practical electoral politics to launch frontal attacks on the New Deal and, more generally, on the 'American standard of living'. Senator Robert A. Taft (Republican, Ohio), whose nickname was Mr Republican, and whom Dwight Eisenhower defeated in order to gain the presidential nomination in 1952, found this out to his cost when, in response to a reporter's question, "Senator Taft, what should the American housewife be doing about the high cost of beef?" answered, "Eat less." There were other reasons as well. In 1954 the Democrats regained the majority in both Houses of Congress and kept their majorities until the 1990s. Despite the anti-union 1947 Taft-Hartley Act, which among its other provisions outlawed secondary boycotts, the trade unions more than held their own. In the 1950s about five eighths of all 'blue collar' industrial workers were unionised and the union penetration ratio as a whole, which stood in the neighbourhood of 35% of the entire labour force, represented what has turned out to be its all-time high. Finally, I think that the Cold War and the very existence of Soviet Russia need to be considered. To be sure, the Russian factor probably cut both ways. On the one hand, many American politicians of both parties took it as axiomatic that there was virtue and electoral mileage to be had from tarring any and all policies that they did not like with the brush of communism. They certainly did plenty of Red baiting – of persons and policies – even after the fall of Senator Joseph R. McCarthy. On the other hand, policy measures in the interest of the common people (a term which pretty much disappeared in both Britain and America in the 1950s) were occasionally justified in terms of how deprivation and oppression of all sorts, starting with racial oppression, provided grist for the communist propaganda mill. Also, some American leftists argued that the shrewder thinkers in ruling circles had come to the conclusion that, in the absence of government intervention in the economy and social welfare programmes, the country would be torn to shreds by economic class struggle. They accordingly deemed the New Deal to be a wholly acceptable price to pay, all the more so as it was the working class and the middle strata who were doing the lion's share of the paying to begin with. The subject of social welfare in the countries of Western capitalism in relation to the Cold War is an under-researched one that in my view could use more work.

For these reasons and others, social policy in both countries did not 'go backwards' in the 1950s and indeed advanced in the 1960s. In Britain, however, there was one exception. In November, 1967, following the devaluation of the pound from $2.80 to $2.40, Harold Wilson reimposed drug charges: five shillings (25 pence) per prescription and nothing for refills, if memory serves. In the United States liberals and leftists welcomed the passage of Medicare (medical insurance for everyone over 65) and Medicaid (access to medical services for poor people) and the other 'Great Society' programmes as major breakthroughs and regarded the attainment of socialised medicine for all as 'only a matter of time'. They were wrong. The Vietnam war, which killed the Civil Rights Movement and brought to a screeching halt progressive social policy initiatives, was for me, looking back at it, the beginning of 35 years of continuous political defeats. A case can be made out that the long winter of reaction commenced not with Reagan/Thatcher but in the 1960s.

But while in retrospect one can see clearly that in both countries the welfare state rested on shakier foundations – if not outright feet of clay – that is not the way it appeared at the time. The welfare state did not seem to be in any immediate peril. For me, Britain was still a powerful ideas-generating station – Edward Thompson, Raymond Williams and R.M. Titmuss to name but a few. When it first appeared in 1970 – and again on re-reading it for this chapter – I felt that Titmuss's *The gift relationship* was an absolute masterpiece by virtue of its powerful restatement of a view of society in which market forces and self-interest did not reign supreme.[3]

To repeat: one would have had to be either paranoid or clairvoyant at the start of the 1970s to predict that either Britain's or America's version of the welfare state was in serious trouble. To say this might sound one-sided: those who remained unalterably opposed to the welfare state and everything that it represented were still to be seen and heard. But consider the conservative American political writer Kevin Phillips, who in *The emerging Republican majority* (1969) urged the Republicans to adopt a 'Southern Strategy' – that is, play the race card – which indeed they did with devastatingly successful effects that have lasted to this day, tempered only by the fact that, thank goodness, black people in the South also have the vote. (The dismantling of apartheid in the 1960s is America's most significant achievement in advancing human rights in the entire 20th century.) Phillips did not utter so much as a whisper of advice to the Republicans that they should oppose social welfare programmes as such and in fact President Richard Nixon, like Eisenhower before him, did not touch them with so much as a 10-foot bargepole. He had other things on his mind.[4]

I come now to the ambiguous 1970s – and will be brief. Many people on the left, including myself, thought that the 'system' in both Britain and America had entered a period of continuous – and maybe even terminal – crisis and was discrediting itself beneath everyone's nose. Watergate and America's impending defeat in Vietnam were two big markers. In Britain, the 1970-74 Tory government of Edward Heath proved to be no more successful at taming the trade unions than Harold Wilson and Barbara Castle had been. For all one knew, Northern Ireland might become Britain's Vietnam and was in any case the only instance at the time in all of Western capitalism of a state having to deploy the military *within its own territory* to impose law and order, and not particularly successfully either. When Thatcher succeeded Heath as Tory leader in 1975 who could (and did) say for certain that she would be any worse than any other Tory then on offer? In short, she was not yet the Iron Lady.

Thatcherism and welfare

With this long 'overture' now in place we can commence the second theme of this chapter, the Thatcher years and its coda of John Major. My thesis is: *for the first time since the end of the Second World War, Britain was no longer, for Americans – and I should have thought everyone else who looked towards Britain – a source of ideas and actual policies whose aim was to improve and extend the welfare state.* Unfortunately this has not changed. One aspect of the Thatcherite sea change is that it has altered Britain's place in the world.

I can't speak for anyone else, but from 1979 to 1983 'sea change' was not yet in my vocabulary. There seemed no way of telling how long Thatcher would last, what with severe inflation, skyrocketing unemployment, and monetarism being denounced as snake oil and voodoo economics by hundreds of economists in full-page advertisements. Then there was the turmoil in the Labour Party. The one thing that could be definitely ruled out was that no change at all would result. Either the SDP split would severely weaken the Labour Party or the result would be a meaner, leaner and socialist Labour Party. *Tertium non datur.*

But with the election of 1983 things became much clearer indeed. It was now crystal clear that the parliamentary opposition to Thatcherite Toryism was hopelessly split and crippled, that she had her own 'Wets' pretty firmly under control and would now stop at nothing. The miners' strike, privatisation, deindustrialisation, means-testing, welfare cuts and much else were the results. The outcome of the 1987 general election was pretty much a foregone conclusion, as I recall. Not until the poll tax, the demonstrations against it, and Thatcher's fall were there anything but straws to grasp at and even they were in short supply by the start of the 1990s. The only important ones that stuck in my mind then and now was the Tory percentage of the vote, which remained stuck at around 45%, and the demonstrations against the poll tax.

But one's memories of the Thatcher years really must take a back seat to attempts to explain why it happened. First off the mark – and still the best starting point – was Eric Hobsbawm's *The forward march of Labour halted?* (first edition 1979, question mark dropped from the second edition of 1981). The fact that he propounded his thesis that Labour was in serious trouble a few months *before* Thatcher's first victory, while not perhaps up there with Karl Marx and Frederick Engels predicting the

Revolution of 1848 in the *Communist Manifesto* six weeks before its outbreak, is still impressive. There is thus an irreducible sense in which Hobsbawm was right, however much one might disagree with his political recommendations.[5] It turned out – as the 1981 edition showed – to be a powerful catalyst for debate and discussion and in this way performed a real public service.

Hobsbawm might be a Marxist but he is also an empiricist. One gets the sense that he never met a fact he did not like. For him the key facts were that the Labour vote had gone into the tank and so had Labour party individual membership figures. The numbers for trade union membership were not much better. Sectional differences – the term as used by historians of trade unionism and others is a protean one that refers to many sorts of divisions within occupational groups, unions and the working class at large – were becoming sharper and deeper. Unless something was done – and soon – much harm would result. Hobsbawm brought in his own answer of what had to be done in 1981 with his insistence that only a popular front strategy could save the day. Bluntly – but I think accurately – he was arguing for a coalition led by the Labour Party of anyone and everyone who opposed Thatcher. Now, I did not agree with what he was saying at the time and I'm not sure that I do today. But that is not the point. Rather, the point is that given his premises, Hobsbawm's logic was close to irrefutable. If one thinks that the Labour movement has gone to the dogs and that the working class (for whatever reasons) is in no condition to do its historic thing (if you are not a Marxist, all this may well sound like metaphysical gibberish) then the best one can do is to come up with a new minimal programme to rally around. Nor is it any good arguing that Hobsbawm's popular frontism was some kind of Stalinism, post-Stalinism or abandonment of Marxism altogether. According to Isaac Deutscher, Leon Trotsky himself, with the horrors of Nazi Germany and Stalin's Russia before him in the late 1930s, seriously considered a new minimum programme, though in the end he rejected the idea.

In the 1981 edition of *The forward march of Labour halted?* most of the contributors – some more grudgingly than others – had come round to the conclusion that Hobsbawm had got the key facts right. Particularly helpful in my opinion was Raymond Williams's contribution. He made the crucial point that the Labour Party and the working class had suffered a significant *defeat*. This might sound unexceptional enough in this or any other context except that, oddly, Hobsbawm himself did not use the word, though of course the whole metaphor of an army being halted is perfectly compatible with defeat being the reason why it was halted.

Equally helpful was Williams's argument about the loss of any live notion of what constituted the common good. This part of his argument was to sound even more impressive when Thatcher herself announced soon afterwards that there is no such thing as society.

The 'Hobsbawm debate' was hardly the last word. There has been enough written on the causes of Thatcherism's victories and Old Labour's defeats to fill a small reference library. My sense is that a consensus has not emerged, save to note that Hobsbawm's own worst-case scenario is now a definite part of the canon, centring on deindustrialisation, de-alignment and apathy. Except for Labour's traditional strongholds in what was once 'smokestack' Britain, poor people (and not all of them), and a minority of middle class people who, for mainly ideological reasons, remain committed to Labour, are Labour's core voters? The difficulty of even describing the contemporary British working class is nicely epitomised by Philip Gould's statement (in Lilleker, 2002, p 70) that a majority of British workers are "not disadvantaged, not privileged, not quite working-class, not really middle class – they don't even have a name". This lack of precision is more than understandable. My own view is that the working class in both Britain and America has for decades been going through a process of making and remaking that has arguably not been seen since the origins of the Industrial Revolution.

Gloomy as things were – the outcome of the election of 1992 only added to it – it was nevertheless clear by about 1995 that the Tories were probably going to lose the next election. What predictions were made for Tony Blair and New Labour, and, seven years on, what predictions does one dare make for the near future? (Virtually everyone agrees that diminished expectations and Thatcherism go together and this might just include diminished expectations for the ability of the social and historical sciences to make accurate predictions.)

One of the most interesting predictions was advanced by David Coates in 1996. Assuming a Labour victory (that, after all, was the easy part), Coates argued that Labour's self-defined historical mission consisted of essentially two projects: a social reform project and a modernising project. Not that previous Labour governments had been all that effective in realising either one, though when the matter is put this way, Labour's social reform legislation of 1945-48 would get the nod. In addition, Labour had never succeeded in constructing a 'hegemonic bloc,' in Gramscian terms, or in becoming the 'natural party of government,' to use the more widespread term. Coates further claimed to have detected a qualitative change in New Labour inasmuch as Old Labour at least tried to be close to the unions when it could and recognised the need for a class base. But New Labour is currently having none of that. Notwithstanding Blair's attempts to distance New Labour from Labour's past, Coates wrote that "previous Labour Governments have been clawed to death by the opposition of organized capital; and all the indications are that a Blair government will experience a similar fate" (Coates, 1996, pp 71-2). A Tory government following on – led by Portillo, Redwood and the like – would be unremittingly reactionary.

One would have to have a heart of stone to criticise Coates for not getting it quite right. The subsequent record has shown that he was on the right track in arguing that a qualitative change had occurred. His mistake was that he did not perhaps go far enough. It strongly appears that Blair and New Labour shared Coates's prediction about fierce opposition and thus did everything in their power to placate Rupert Murdoch. (Compare Bill Clinton's determination not to be 'Willie Hortoned'. While Governor of Arkansas, Clinton inflicted the death penalty upon an Afro-American man who was plainly mentally retarded because he did not wish to be hounded by the Republicans, in the way that they attacked Michael Dukakis in 1988, for releasing a convicted murderer named Willie Horton from prison – whereupon Horton started murdering again.) Nor perhaps should Coates be criticised unduly for failing to predict that, for once, a Labour government would not have an economic crisis on its hands immediately on taking office.

The 1997 election introduced a new cliché into the discourse of British electoral politics – there might only be a razor thin difference between New Labour and the Tories but that margin makes all the difference in the world. (Actually it's a new way of advocating the old idea of supporting the lesser evil.) My own reaction to Blair, 1997-2001, was conventional enough. I read Nick Cohen's pieces in the *Observer* with great enjoyment (Cohen, 1999). As promised, Blair repealed no Thatcherite legislation, and this was in stark contrast to the Attlee government's 1946 repeal of the punitive 1927 Trade Union Act – "simply, briskly, triumphantly", in the words of the historian C.L. Mowat. Like millions of London citizens, I found his attempt to withhold the official Labour endorsement for mayor of London from Ken Livingstone quite appalling and was able to follow it closely, as I was living in London during the autumn of 1999. There was a major social policy dimension as well. The London Underground was falling apart. Livingstone proposed that it remain in public ownership and that financing of the rebuilding of the infrastructure should take the form of a public–private venture. This was evidently too collectivistic for Blair, though not the only or even the most important reason he opposed Livingstone. I thought then – and still do – that

Blair's other reason was that Livingstone's popularity gave the lie to New Labour's claim that Old Labour was an electoral albatross. I found the episode all the more bizarre because this sort of thing does not happen in the United States – at least not in the same way. The primary system of selecting candidates – for all its numerous faults – at least ensures elections in which the principle of 'one person, one vote' prevails. Party structure is also very different. The Democratic and Republican parties are essentially providers of metaphorical space for political entrepreneurs – in the person of the politicians themselves – and organised interests to go about their business.

Just when it looked as if things were not going to get any worse, 11 September, 2001, happened and unleashed in America and – so far to a lesser extent – in Britain a veritable carnival of reaction. In the larger context of this chapter, Blair's unwavering support of George W. Bush demonstrates clearly my argument that in the USA–UK equation, the USA is now more than ever the larger and more important player. The history of Britain's 'special relationship' with the United States has always been one of diminished sovereignty for Britain. But Blair has taken Britain's diminished sovereignty to depths previously unplumbed. His support of Bush has been incomparably more supine than the stance of Harold Wilson on the Vietnam war, whose mantra was that if he thought it would do a scintilla of good to oppose Lyndon Johnson publicly he would be the first to do so. That was mealy-mouthed and hypocritical, no doubt, but Wilson fell short of being Johnson's poodle.

In short, the immediate prospects for any measures to undo Thatcherism in Britain seem to me to be very bleak. The only silver lining that I see in an otherwise very dark cloud is that Labour and the Liberal Democrats have between them won a large majority of the votes in the last two elections. But against this, the prospects for proportional representation being adopted look asymptotic to nil, while the Socialist Alliance did very poorly in the last election and its immediate prospects look no better. The claim that New Labour has become the 'natural party of government' strikes me as fatuous. The percentage of people who turn out on election day continues to fall, though it is still higher than in America. Perhaps most distressing to an Old Believer and labour historian like myself is the news coming out of northern towns like Burnley, where a half dozen out-and-out racists recently won seats in the 2003 local council elections. As the *Guardian* (2003) reported, "Labour has been in office in Burnley since the Plantagenets". This is a lovely turn of phrase, but the even more interesting electoral history of Burnley is that in 1906, H.M. Hyndman came within 350 votes of being elected the town's MP, standing not as the endorsed Labour candidate but in the Social Democratic Federation interest, as they said in those days. In 1914 the Burnley Power Loom Weavers were the largest single trade union branch – they had 18,000 members – in the *world*. I do not see a quarter century of Thatcherism in Britain coming to an end any time soon.

The impact of Thatcherism on the USA

It is now time to attempt to evaluate the impact of Thatcherism on American politics. My starting point is the election of Ronald Reagan in 1980, which came as more of a surprise to Europeans than to Americans, as seen by the hilarious song by *Not the Nine O'Clock News* that ends with the lines, "I believe that the Devil is ready to repent/but I can't believe Ronald Reagan is President". From the outset Reagan and Thatcher proclaimed loudly that they were ideological soul mates, the evidence for which is indeed compelling. The amount of adulatory coverage that Thatcher received in the American media was awesome. If for no other reason, I think it would be naive to argue that Thatcherism played no part in shifting American public opinion to the right during her years in office.

In broad terms there certainly were similarities. Thatcher took on the miners and won. Practically the first thing Reagan did on taking office was to break the strike and union of the air traffic controllers – despite the fact that their union had endorsed Reagan in 1980! Thatcher's tax policies favoured the wealthy. So did Reagan's, and once again he was first off the mark with major tax cuts in 1981, in which endeavour he was aided by the bemused and disoriented Democrats, who still controlled both Houses of Congress but who nonetheless voted for the tax cuts. But it is harder to say with assurance that anything Thatcher said or did had any *direct* influence on specific social policy measures of the Reagan administration. Whatever one thinks about convergence and globalisation, Britain and America in the 1980s were still separate countries with distinct political structures and issues, rhetorics and economic problems. One example is legalised abortion. Thatcher refused to make a political issue of abortion. In America it already was. After his re-election in 1984 Reagan made available office space in the White House for the right-to-lifers to carry on their campaign to overthrow the US Supreme Court's decision, Roe v Wade, and add an anti-abortion amendment to the US Constitution. But in fact the administration dragged its feet and Mrs Reagan was heard to burst out, "Who gives a damn about the right-to-lifers?"

A second and final example comes from the fact that the macroeconomic circumstances of the two countries were significantly different. By most criteria the British economy really was in worse shape when Thatcher came to power than was the American economy when Reagan took office, and Thatcher's attempt to actually apply monetarist doctrines only made matters worse. That is why monetarism was abandoned. Under Reagan, on the other hand, annual budget deficits and the national debt were allowed to take off into the stratosphere. As his budget director, David Stockman, cynically explained, more pressure on the public finances meant less political space and credibility for welfare state liberals. My tentative conclusion is that, in the end, Thatcher's contribution to the Reagan administration was more spiritual than practical. For what it is worth, the (admittedly quirky) neo-conservative journal, *The Public Interest*, carried no articles on Thatcher and what she was accomplishing until after she left office, when one panegyric to her was published. Conversely, the American neo-conservative social policy writer Charles Murray was invited to Britain in 1989 and 1994 to produce two reports on the 'underclass' (Murray, 1996). His arguments were embraced by both the Major administration and New Labour.

The election of Bill Clinton in 1992 did not change the basic policy orientation of the past 12 years and was in any event something of a fluke. Clinton won with just over 43% of the votes because the multi-millionaire businessman, H. Ross Perot, running for president as an independent, took 19% of the votes, of which the large majority would have otherwise been cast for George Bush. Clinton's social policy record consists of two major initiatives. The first was a national health insurance scheme of baroque complexity. President Clinton and his wife, Hillary Clinton, who was put in charge of the process to draft the legislation and steer it through Congress, made no attempt whatsoever to construct a movement of popular support. The scheme was attacked vehemently by the Republicans and the insurance industry and failed utterly. The second, in the form of the 1996 Personal Responsibility and Work Reconciliation Act, which succeeded, removed millions of women and dependent children from the welfare rolls. The only positive things that can be said about the Clinton years is that because of the economic boom the number of Americans living in poverty did not increase, according to official statistics, and that Republican calls for the partial privatisation of social security (old age pensions, essentially) were opposed by the Democrats.

Space does not permit a full treatment of how George W. Bush came to be elected in the nightmarish presidential election of 2000. Suffice it to say that although Al Gore received more than 400,000 votes more than Bush, in a first-past-the post system, pluralities are not always decisive. It's where you get your votes that counts. In 1951, Labour received a little over 100,000 more votes than the Tories but still lost – for the same reason that Gore lost.

Whether September 11 would have happened if Gore had been elected president is, of course, unanswerable. But it is conceivable that, even if he had, a Gore administration might not have invaded and occupied Afghanistan and Iraq. Turning to social policy, one can say with considerable assurance that a much more generous version of Medicare reform would have been enacted in 2003 than the one which was actually passed. The main issue was drugs, the costs of which have been rising rapidly. Medicare, enacted back in the 1960s, did not provide for drugs. Many elderly Americans cannot afford to take their medicine. Some buy their drugs from Canada, where prices are lower because Canada has real health insurance. The provinces can use their market power vis-à-vis the drug companies to get better deals. The Bill just passed forces people to sign up with a private insurance scheme in order to be eligible for the drug benefit. Senator Ted Kennedy angered many of his fellow liberals in Congress by voting for this provision. His rationale was that a fraction of the loaf is better than nothing at all.

Is this legislation the proverbial camel's nose under the tent to prepare the way for the full privatisation of Medicare and much else besides? Quite possibly. In a recent *Nation* article the financial writer William Greider argued that an attempt is already under way to "roll back the 20th century – quite literally" (Greider, 2003, pp 11-18) by such measures as the repeal of the estate tax (already accomplished despite an advertisement by economists in the *New York Times* reminiscent of the advert against monetarism in 1981); elimination of federal taxation of private capital; the elimination of the graduated income tax and its replacement with a stiff value added tax (which does not yet exist in America); withdrawal of the federal government from a direct role in housing, healthcare, assistance to the poor and other social priorities; and public funding of private and religious schools by means of vouchers. Not that these measures will be enacted all at once or that the Bush administration has woven them into a coherent programme. Nor are the right-wing think tanks and their paymasters in any great hurry. They see time and history as being on their side. And they may be right. We may be on the eve of a gradual instalment of super-Thatcherism.

Can one imagine counter scenarios? One is that the Democratic Party might make a spectacular recovery and that the Bush administration might commit outsized blunders, possibly starting with their failure to resolve the mess they created in Iraq. The historical precedent for this line of speculation would be along the lines of what happened to the Tories 100 years ago that led to the Liberal–Labour landslide of 1906. The Tories had got themselves into all sorts of hot water with the Taff Vale decision, the 1902 Education Act, Tariff Reform and indentured labour in South Africa. The Liberals were shrewd enough to do a backroom deal with the Labour Representation Committee and were lucky enough to have a leader like Campbell-Bannerman. The prospects of a latter-day Democratic landslide in 2004 or 2008 along similar lines should be obvious. It is not going to happen.

A second counter scenario is that the right will be defeated because of a severe recession. That is certainly possible. The Keynesians have been predicting one for several years (Godley, 2000). But will the Democrats be the beneficiaries? If the experience of both Britain and America in the 1980s and 90s has taught us anything, the answer must be, not necessarily. Accordingly the most sober and plausible prediction is that the right will be in power in America for some time to come and will continue to cast its shadow over Britain. I am not predicting fascism or anything resembling it. For the time being, America seems quite immune. Consider the real, homegrown terrorism perpetrated by Timothy McVeigh in Oklahoma City. Many people predicted that his execution would make a martyr out of him. Nothing of the sort has happened. Rather, the historical precedent I have in mind is more along the lines of Imperial Germany before 1914 – with entrenched reaction to be found everywhere in the state and civil society; an opposition which, while numerous, could not construct an electoral majority; ever decreasing competence on the part of the political elite; and finally and most worrisome of all, an increasingly reckless foreign policy. The only good news is that, as a general proposition, history does not repeat itself.

Conclusion

I come finally to address a topic specifically asked of me for this chapter: how has a quarter century of Thatcherism changed my thinking? I have already let most of my cat out of the bag by admitting that I am an Old Believer. I believe that state-of-the-art health, education and welfare services should be made universally available to all people who find themselves residing in Britain and America, which are, after all, two of the wealthiest countries in the history of the world, though this is hardly ever mentioned nowadays. I am for 'work or maintenance' – as the hunger marchers of the 1930s demanded, which is to say that I am also in favour of full employment. A steeply graduated income tax is a good way to start paying for these services, to say nothing of deep cutbacks in defence spending, space programmes and the like. To this extent my thinking has not changed at all.

My views on how to define and think about the welfare state have undergone some change. I used to think that, far from being my kind of socialism, the welfare state was essentially a consolation prize to the working classes in Western capitalist countries in lieu of the 'real thing'. I do, however, disagree with one variety of Marxist thinking that sees the welfare state as a means of social control of workers in general and women in particular, constructed and maintained in a diabolically clever way to produce a more productive working population of what C. Wright Mills long ago called cheerful robots. Instead, I now see the welfare state as part of the social wage earned by working people and a very important part at that. This makes the welfare state itself something like trade unions. They are not perfect but they are absolutely needed. Not only will things not get better by themselves, but without unions and the welfare state, things would be much worse. Of course, unions and welfare states can, as a matter of the historical record, be strong or weak and do their jobs well or poorly from the standpoint of those being served. Yet another implication of looking at matters in this way is that, even if unions and the welfare state should continue to falter or even disappear outright, the determination of wages, hours and working conditions, and state policy and provision in the areas of unemployment insurance, old age pensions, health education and welfare would still have to be addressed in one way or another. If I were forced to predict the limits of further decline, I would rule out such things as a return of the workhouse for 'able-bodied paupers', but would also note that a return to orphanages was seriously proposed in the 1990s by the right-wing American politician and lumpen-intellectual, Newt Gingrich.

A quarter century of Thatcherism has seen de-industrialisation and the demise of the 'classical' working class carried to a much greater extent than I once thought likely. I now see the working class in both Britain and America in the first 80 years of the 20th century as a historical formation and not its final shape, so to speak. I see no way around the proposition that the classical working class had a capacity for collective action and for being a presence in civil society that today's working class seems to lack or has not yet attained. To that extent its disappearance is to be regretted. But as Sidney Silverman – who for many years was the Labour MP for Nelson and Colne, right next to Burnley in Lancashire, and whose campaign against capital punishment finally won through in the 1960s – once said, the good old days were not so hot to begin with. Second-wave feminism and the New Social Movements are crucially important and welcome developments. That said, a new working class presence is definitely still needed – for despite its surface plausibility, I do not subscribe to the notion that the welfare state is an essentially middle class development. Even if one grants, as a matter of fact, that the middle class has benefited mightily from the welfare state, I do not see how the welfare state can be maintained – much less extended – without solid working class support and a renaissance of the labour movement.

But perhaps the working class itself is on the way out? I doubt it. I will adduce only two considerations. Recent data on the net worth of American households show that in 1998 the median was $55,000. Now this might sound like a lot of money, but the average price of a dwelling house in America is well over $100,000. In other words, a typical American family does not possess assets that come close to equalling the cost of the roof over their heads. For my British example, I note that the consumer debt in Britain is at an all-time high and cite the study showing that the casualisation of post-secondary teaching work in contemporary Britain *exceeds* the casualisation of the dock labour force in the 19th century.

My thinking about socialism has also changed. Is Marxism irreducibly teleological? If it is and if one rejects teleological thinking, then what should be put in its place? A profession of hope in something you really do not think is going to happen is unlikely to persuade many people. Perhaps Christian Socialists do not have a problem here, but secular socialists plainly do. The secular varieties of socialism – Marxism, Fabianism, though not anarchism, which seems to me more timeless than Whiggish – are unambiguous examples. To put it the other way around, doesn't there have to be something in the shape and structure of things as they already exist and in people as they go about their business that connects with socialism's critique of society as usual? I am not asking for a guarantee of inevitability. I'm just asking for decent odds. I do not know whether other people also worry about this, or whether I am well and truly speaking for myself.

I would like nothing better than to conclude this chapter with the watchword *la lutte continue* – and am sure that working people's resistance to attacks on their material standard of living and the quality of their lives will continue, whatever forms resistance takes. But to end on that note really would dilute the pessimism which I have been expounding and which I do not wish to jettison just to make us feel better. A quarter century of Thatcherism *has* been damaging and has degraded practically everything it has touched. *There is no such thing as society* (Margaret Thatcher herself). *Price rises* reduce *inflationary pressures* (her American economics advisor, Alan Walters). *A new era of imperialism is good for America and the world* (the British celebrity historian, Niall Ferguson, now teaching in America). *Those less well off than oneself are responsible for all or most of society's economic and social woes* (anonymous, but a very widespread, very illogical and largely unremarked notion held by who knows how many millions of people, including Thatcherite and neo-conservative social policy makers).

Finally, *there is no alternative* (Thatcher again), which is all the more mind-boggling, coming from somebody who presumably thinks that rigid determinism is a defining characteristic of Marxism. One can think of several rejoinders. My preferred one is, "there must be a better way". When that idea becomes comprehensible and credible to the majority of people it won't be a moment too soon and will signal the beginning of the end of Thatcherism.

Notes

[1] Judt (2003). In his view Believers, latter-day and before, include the Socialist Party of Great Britain, the Independent Labour Party, Fabians, assorted Social Democratic and anarchists federations, not to speak of Trotskyites – in other words just about all democratic and libertarian socialists in 20th-century Britain.

[2] I have never seen this joke in print; my only source is my memory. If anyone has seen it in print, I would greatly appreciate the reference.

[3] A few years ago I underwent hip replacement surgery. My doctor told me that I would need two pints of blood. Would I be donating my own blood, my wife's or whose? I replied, none of the above, and began to quote Titmuss. Dr Susan Hunt, who is well read and progressive, listened with rapt attention and allowed as to how she had never heard such a thing about blood but that it sounded very interesting. The blood I used came from the Central Blood Bank of Pittsburgh.

[4] Which the Watergate scandal revealed in stark clarity, leading as it did to Nixon's undoing and resignation in August, 1974.

[5] There is a curious but I think real parallel in the crisis of American psychoanalysis as brilliantly chronicled by Janet Malcolm's *In the Freud archives*, first edn, New York, 1984.

References

Coates, D. (1996) 'Labour governments: old constraints and new parameters', *New Left Review*, vol 219, pp 62-77.

Cohen, N. (1999) 'Cruel Britannia: reports on the sinister and preposterous', *The Observer*, 16 May.

De Schweinitz, K. (1943) *England's road to social security*, Philadelphia, PA: University of Pennsylvania Press.

Gladstone, D. (1995) *British social welfare*, London: UCL Press.

Godley, W. (2000) 'What if they start saving again?', *London Review of Books*, 6 July.

Greider, W. (2003) 'The Right's grand ambition: rolling back the 20th century', *The Nation*, 12 May.

Guardian (2003) 'Back to Burnley', 16 October.

Hobsbawm, E. (1979) *The forward march of Labour halted?*, London: Verso.

Hobsbawm, E. (1981) *The forward march of Labour halted?* (2nd edn), London: Verso.

Judt, T. (2003) 'The last romantic', *New York Review of Books*, 20 November.

Lilleker, D. (2002) 'Whose left: working-class political allegiances in post-industrial Britain', *International Review of Social History*, vol 47, supplement 10.

Morgan, K.O. (1992) *The people's peace: British history 1945-1990*, Oxford: Oxford University Press.

Murray, C. (1996) 'Charles Murray and the underclass', in R. Lister (ed) *Charles Murray and the underclass*, London: IEA.

Phillips, K. (1969) *The emerging Republican majority*, New Rochelle, NY: Arlington House.

Shirer, W.L. (1952) *Midcentury journey*, New York, NY: Ferrar, Strauss and Young.

Index

Page references for notes are followed by n